AFRICAN LITERATURE AND
SOCIAL CHANGE

AFRICAN LITERATURE AND SOCIAL CHANGE
Tribe, Nation, Race

Olakunle George

Indiana University Press

This book is a publication of

Indiana University Press
Office of Scholarly Publishing
Herman B Wells Library 350
1320 East 10th Street
Bloomington, Indiana 47405 USA

iupress.indiana.edu

© 2017 by Olakunle George

All rights reserved

No part of this book may be reproduced or utilized in any form or by any means, electronic or mechanical, including photocopying and recording, or by any information storage and retrieval system, without permission in writing from the publisher. The Association of American University Presses' Resolution on Permissions constitutes the only exception to this prohibition.

The paper used in this publication meets the minimum requirements of the American National Standard for Information Sciences—Permanence of Paper for Printed Library Materials, ANSI Z39.48-1992.

Manufactured in the United States of America

Library of Congress Cataloging-in-Publication Data

Names: George, Olakunle, author.
Title: African literature and social change : tribe, nation, race / Olakunle George.
Description: Bloomington, Indiana : Indiana University Press, 2017. | Includes bibliographical references and index.
Identifiers: LCCN 2017032853 (print) | LCCN 2017024198 (ebook) | ISBN 9780253029324 (e-book) | ISBN 9780253025463 (cloth : alk. paper) | ISBN 9780253025807 (pbk. : alk. paper)
Subjects: LCSH: African literature (English)—19th century—History and criticism. | African literature (English)—20th century—History and criticism. | Literature and society—Africa—History—19th century. | Literature and society—Africa—History—20th century. | Social change in literature. | Ethnicity in literature.
Classification: LCC PR9340.5 (print) | LCC PR9340.5 .G44 2017 (ebook) | DDC 820.996—dc23
LC record available at https://lccn.loc.gov/2017032853

1 2 3 4 5 22 21 20 19 18 17

Dedicated to Isidore Okpewho, 1941–2016
Rest in peace, Prof.

Contents

	Acknowledgments	ix
	Introduction: Missionary Moments	1
1	Crossing Currents: Postcoloniality, Globalism, Diaspora	23
2	Mission Tide: Bishop S. A. Crowther and the "Black Whitemen"	62
3	Decolonization Time: Abrahams, James, Wright	106
4	Globalization Time: Achebe, Soyinka, and Beyond	143
	Epilogue: Gaps	183
	Bibliography	197
	Index	209

Acknowledgments

This book has taken longer than I envisaged when I fitfully started working on it. Along the way, I have benefited from the assistance of many institutions, colleagues, and friends. I thank the staff of the following libraries for their help while I tried to find my way around the materials in their possession: Cadbury Research Library Special Collections, University of Birmingham, Edgbaston; Special Collections, School of Oriental and African Studies, London; Public Records and Archives Administration Department of Ghana (PRAAD), Accra; and the Divinity Library, Yale University. For permission to reproduce images for which they hold copyright, I am grateful to the Church Missionary Society, the Wesley Historical Society library, Oxford Brookes University, and Stuart Franklin/Magnum Photos. In particular, thanks to Peter S. Forsaith, Ian Killeen, Liz Millard, Ken Osborne, and Michael Shulman for responding expeditiously to my inquiries.

Over the years, the following colleagues invited me to present talks or conference papers that pushed me to impose a semblance of coherence on my arguments: Susan Andrade, Yogita Goyal, Jeanne-Marie Jackson, Arlene Keizer, Luís Madureira, Piret Peiker, Bonnie Roos, and Nathan Suhr-Sytsma. I thank Susan Andrade also for recommending Magnum Photos. I owe a debt of gratitude to colleagues and countless conference interlocutors who posed questions or offered comments on portions of the book in its long road up to this point. You will know who you are; please know as well that I am profoundly grateful. I feel privileged to be able to salute Kofi Agawu for being a tireless interlocutor-in-chief, Patrick Mensah for conversations that reenergize, Conrad James for helping to make my Edgbaston visits enjoyable, and Harry Garuba for the gift of our marathon phone conversations. Many thanks as well to Mark Seltzer for providing his distinctive critical eye at a crucial stage of my revisions, and to Rey Chow for her collegiality and the lunches on Thayer Street.

The following friends, compatriots, and senior colleagues contributed in many different ways, often without knowing it, to enriching and moving this work along: Leke Adeeko, Moradewun Adejunmobi, Remi Raji-Oyelade, Sina Gbadamosi, Kunle Akinsipe, Akin Adesokan, Kunle Ajibade, Simon Gikandi, Abiola Irele, Biodun Jeyifo, Eileen Julien, Neil ten Kortenaar, Loka Losambe, Moji Olaniyan, Teju Olaniyan, and Femi Taiwo. Thanks, all, for your support and for being there. Another round of thanks are due to my undergraduate teachers at the University of Ibadan, most especially Dan S. Izevbaye, Molara Ogundipe,

Chikwenye Ogunyemi, and Niyi Osundare. Isidore Okpewho left us too soon, yet I will forever think of him each time I teach the epic of *Sundiata* in any version. To echo the language of the griots you studied, Prof: this tune is calling you!

I am grateful to my colleagues at Brown, and the wonderful staff of the English department office: Marianne Costa; Jane Donnelly, Lorraine Mazza, Suzie Nacar, Marilyn Netter, and Ellen Viola. I am grateful, too, to graduate students who took my seminars over the years and had to tolerate my half-baked ideas. In particular, I thank these fellows for putting up with me: Weihsin Gui, David Babcock, Adrian Genette, Chris Holmes, Derek Ettensohn, David Liao, Sachelle Ford, Minta Zlomke, Swetha Regunathan, Jenny Snow, and Anna Thomas. My undergraduate students deserve a special word of appreciation: they continue to teach me that the classroom is one place where literary studies can come into its own in concrete social articulation. I count myself lucky that Dee Mortensen was my editor on this project. Dee's great e-mail "reminders" seemed always to arrive when I most needed them, and I sincerely thank her and her staff. Her professionalism and critical advice contributed in a big way to making this book possible. Finally, hearty thanks to Evelyn Oby, in everything my coconspirator, and to our children, Ayo and Tosin, for giving us so much joy.

Portions of this book appeared earlier as journal articles and are used here in revised form: "The Narrative of Conversion in Chinua Achebe's *Arrow of God*," *Comparative Literature Studies* 42, no. 4 (2005): 344–62, copyright (c) 2005, The Pennsylvania State University, by permission of The Pennsylvania State University Press; "The Native Missionary, the African Novel, and In-Between," *Novel: A Forum on Fiction* 26, no. 1 (2002): 5–25, (c) Novel Corp., 2003; and "The National and the Transnational: Soyinka's *The Interpreters* and *Aké: The Years of Childhood*," *Novel: A Forum on Fiction* 41, no. 2/3 (2008): 279–97, (c) Novel Corp., 2008.

Introduction: Missionary Moments

THIS BOOK IS about iterations of what I call missionary moments in the representation of Africa by selected African and black diasporic intellectuals. By the term *missionary moments*, I refer to three historical junctures and the writers' varied responses to them. First is the mid-nineteenth century, marked by abolitionism, Christian evangelism, and the tainted productivities of mercantile capitalism. Roughly, this would span the years 1834–84—that is, from the British abolition of slavery to the era of the Scramble and the Berlin Conference. The second moment is the first half of the twentieth century, marked by black internationalism, anticolonialism, and discourses of development and modernization. This we can date from the turn of the century to the decolonization era of the 1950s and 1960s. The third is our contemporary context, marked by globalization in political economy and paradigms of globalism in literary studies. I focus specifically on three kinds of texts about Africa: writings by black missionaries and converts—the so-called black whitemen, who worked in West Africa in the nineteenth century; nonfictional texts by intellectuals associated with the Pan-African internationalism of the 1950s; and imaginative literature by the Nigerian writers Chinua Achebe and Wole Soyinka, both of them central to the discursive field of African Literature as it is read and taught today.[1]

My purpose in the chapters that follow is to accomplish three things. I aim, first, to demonstrate ways in which the texts expose the contradictory interplay between notions of tribe, nation, and race in modern Africa. Second, I argue that the texts often deploy a familiar rhetoric of sacrifice, even as they invite us to question its universal seductiveness. Following this, I suggest that in our moment of globalization and so-called failed states, African writing is best approached under the sign of social change, not cultural or identitarian retrieval. In unveiling the interplay of tribe-nation-race, and in grappling with sacrifice as trope and trauma, the writers position "Africa" differently, such that the continent is not merely an object of quantitative social-scientific knowledge or—as is often the case in popular media—static signifier of crisis. Instead, Africa emerges as a testament to the challenge and promise of social change, a site for the specific kind of knowledge that imaginative literature, and acts of language more broadly, can yield.

We don't need to look far to identify the intellectual and political background to my concerns. Since the public self-immolation of Mohammed Bouazizi, the

Tunisian young man who set himself on fire in December 2010 and thereby ignited protest movements of various stripes across the Middle East and the rest of the world, the term *Arab Spring* has entered the lexicon of popular and academic discourses. The uprising demonstrates the possibility and precarity of collective struggle, the power and unpredictability of mass movements, one through which we are still living. On January 4, 2012, about a year after the onset of the protests in the Arab world, a series of nonviolent demonstrations erupted in Nigeria. Combining the language of the Arab Spring with that of the Occupy Movement in Europe and the United States, the demonstrations quickly came to be called the Occupy Nigeria Movement. The protesters were reacting to a sharp increase in the price of gasoline that resulted from the Nigerian government's withdrawal of oil subsidies. The demonstrators emphasized that their ad hoc struggle is nonviolent and should not be associated with the Boko Haram insurgency in northern Nigeria. Boko Haram is a Hausa phrase that translates into "Western education is sinful." It refers to a militant Islamist group, The Congregation of the People of Tradition for Proselytism and Jihad, which has been operating in the northeastern part of Nigeria, costing much in loss of lives and security. Boko Haram draws on the language of international jihadism, opposes Western education, and seeks to establish shari'a across the country's thirty-six states. In contrast to this militant organization, the Occupy Nigeria protesters specifically identify their struggle as secular and economic; in their spontaneous self-representation, they affiliated themselves with a global Occupy Movement. In interview after interview, men and women of varying social classes and ethnicities referred to the uprising as "our own Arab Spring." In halting English language, a middle-aged woman who is unlikely to have had college-level education tells her interviewer in a YouTube clip, "This will be the Nigerian Spring."

The public demonstrations and strikes were resolved—one is tempted to say "pacified" and wince at the irony—when the central government reinstated the oil subsidies after negotiations with labor organizations and other representatives of the movement. But its underlying political causes remain with us, and the epistemic implications should not be taken as self-evident. In the brief series of demonstrations of January 2012, the global scope of the signifiers Arab Spring and Occupy Movement took on a distinct singularity in Nigeria, where frustration over state action had to negotiate its way around antecedent anxieties about Boko Haram, itself a local transposition of so-called global jihad. The Occupy Nigeria example should serve as reminder of the persistent excess of events on the ground, as opposed to the knowledge that academics work to generate. Here, then, is the context for the series of readings undertaken in this book. For what it offers us is one evidence of *postcoloniality* as concrete, ongoing singularity—at once cultural and political—that cannot be grasped through the language of either crisis or revolution. As the Cold War era ended with the twentieth century—the century Eric Hobsbawm christens the "age of extremes" and Alain Badiou boldly labels "the century"—the first two decades of the twenty-first century continue to stupefy everyone, grand philosophers and policy analysts alike, with the proliferation of suicide bombings and systematic mass shootings.[2] In light of ongoing upheavals having to do with religion, immigration, and so forth, might it be productive to suggest that the old civilizational dichotomies are today quite limited as sources of knowledge? We often hear of the West spoken of as a Christian civilization, code for "white civilization." Yet, the ubiquity of Pentecostal groups in many parts of Africa is clear evidence that if Europe is Christian, much of contemporary Africa has become equally so. Likewise, the translation of antistate militancy using the language of jihad to the Nigerian setting indicates that modern Africa speaks in the antinomial lexicon of religious faith and profane frustrations, just like the rest of the world in the globalized age. Understood this way, the continent is on the move as the world moves; modern Africa is mutilated by wars in part because it partakes of the Eurocentric modernity that continues to be sullied by righteous violence. Where Africa is concerned, then, something is in the process of changing. The problem is that as things currently stand in the humanities disciplines, we have neither the robust theory nor the disciplinary wherewithal to illuminate Africa's unfolding changes in fine specificity.

This book is not devoted to developing such a theory, but it probes the issue of disciplinary wherewithal. My interest is in how imaginative literature and related writings can illuminate social processes in rewarding ways. I began with two simple observations. First, after the era of high theory in Anglo-American literary and cultural criticism, not much has changed in the way African cultures enter the discussion in humanities disciplines. Second, with the exception of Africanist subspecialties in the social sciences, the signifier Africa is rarely thought of in relation to the category of diaspora, understood here as cultural uprootedness and the creole newness it elicits. Scholarship on modern Africa tends to treat diaspora mainly in the context of the Atlantic slave trade and only as a dimension of Africa's recent past: recent, to be sure, but nonetheless *past*. By extension, Africa's present is identified with contemporary horrors of despotic leaders, bad governance, and unrelenting violence. Pushed by these observations, I wanted to explore how the arts of writing and close reading can equip us to approach Africa's present from a fresh perspective. My concerns therefore became at once Africanist and methodological. To what extent does the African experience of literature as self-negotiation equip us to challenge glibly universalizing tendencies in literary globalism? How might a transgressive reading of African literature intervene productively in conversations about globalism in literary and cultural criticism?

That the study of things African has generally been slanted toward the social sciences should be obvious to anyone who cares to look. The disciplines of anthropology, history, and political science have in recent years risen to the challenge of interdisciplinary dialogue by taking on questions of expressive creativity, social marginality, and identity—qualitative issues of life and self-negotiation that are the bread and butter of the humanities.[3] My purpose in these pages is to explore the ways in which literary representations about Africa yield knowledge about such themes as change, intercultural encounter, and language itself as human resource. In this direction, it is helpful to begin by restating a profound double bind: the terms *Africa* and *African* are neither prediscursive nor ontologically empty. That one feels the need to begin with the reiteration is perhaps the strongest argument for posing the issue of "African identity" as a representational question, open to resignification.

Let me press this last point in specific relation to literary and cultural criticism. Methodologically and in terms of its archive, African literary studies has become more richly variegated in the last three decades or so. A range of recent works have been moving the field away from cultural-nationalist preoccupation with linguistic adequation and cultural authenticity. Others have redrawn the boundaries of African literature by attending to the underexplored nexus of South Asia and the Indian Ocean in Africa's modernity, or looking at popular and subaltern avenues of expression and self-making.[4] These developments mark for us the ongoing realignment of the scope and definition of African literature as an institutional category. This book advances the defamiliarizing potential of African literary and cultural criticism by positioning black Africa as center of action, where the action is a ferment of change in social alignments and structures of feeling. An important aspect of my argument is thus that as a term of identity, *African*, like *black*, is neither given nor illusory. Precisely as datable signs of social positioning, identity categories like African and black can be meaningful and agential when—and only when—they are immanently complicated, ruptured by and interlayered with, other identity categories. But for the interlayering to be pedagogically and politically enabling, it is helpful to set out how we got here. Understood this way, the present book is about how we got here with regard to notions of the black and the African.

In what follows, I depart from the common tendency to frame African literature primarily as cultural self-retrievals or disillusioned critiques of dictators. I also challenge the tendency to reduce all instances of nationalism to pathological self-enclosure away from transnational flows and cosmopolitan identities. I argue instead that African writing contributes to literary globalism precisely because of the slippages of cultural-nationalism to be found in it. The story I tell is not one of beginnings and arrivals, neither is it the Eurocentric literary-historical emplotment that moves from realism to modernism, postmodernism, and whatever else is supposed to come after the postmodern. Each of the figures and moments I analyze should be understood as provocation to thought: in my reading, each moves on its own steam and arrives at universality by virtue of particularity. My aim is to go beyond narrow aestheticism in order to position the texts as language at work in the world: that is to say, the world of civil wars and failing states.

Chapter 1 begins in the present of Anglo-American literary and cultural criticism, so to speak. Critically engaging discursive trends in postcoloniality and literary globalism, I demonstrate the sense in which the theory debates of the 1980s have taken on new intonations even as the issues remain fundamentally the same. As in the 1980s, the idea of crisis operates as a leitmotif in literary studies, on the one hand, and international affairs, on the other. This situation is especially meaningful if looked at from the vantage point of African studies because the continent is almost always talked about in terms of crisis: the crisis of heathenism to the Christian sensibility in the nineteenth century, the crisis of underdevelopment and fratricidal wars in the twentieth. Lost in the midst of the metaphorics of crisis is the sense in which Africa's experiences in modernity are at once particular and universal. Chapter 2 goes back to the nineteenth and early twentieth century. Setting aside the problematic of "Victorianism" as a periodizing category of traditional English studies, I focus instead on the lifework of Bishop Samuel Ajayi Crowther, perhaps the most celebrated native African of the nineteenth century. My concern is to elaborate what we might learn from taking Crowther's writings seriously as instance of black-Atlantic self-construction in language. Along the way, I touch on other African missionaries and educationists such as Rev. Thomas Birch Freeman, Philip Quaque, and Kwegyir Aggrey.

Chapter 3 moves closer to our own moment and turns to the work of three intellectuals associated with Pan-Africanism: C. L. R. James, Richard Wright, and South African émigré Peter Abrahams. For these black internationalists, decolonization and modernization demanded that tribe be sacrificed. Tribe signified a traditional order that can fulfill its mandate of collective preservation only by submitting to immolation by modernity. From our vantage point it is easy to identify the problems in this Eurocentric dialectic. However, my claim is that the best of what we now know as postindependence African writing retains a version of this thinking. And so, chapter 4 returns to the contemporary moment in order to read selected works by Chinua Achebe and Wole Soyinka. Rather than read them as purveyors of an African worldview, or heroic critics of corrupt rulers, the chapter suggests that the most durable value of their work lies elsewhere. I tease out the ways in which, implicitly and often against the grain of authorial intention, their texts share the hierarchical valuation of tradition and modernity that lies at the heart of early twentieth-century internationalism. What to do with this modernity therefore becomes the most enduring provocation of their works. Two key issues around which my analyses in the chapters to follow will devolve are (1) the problem of change, understood as implosion and reconstitution of subjectivities amid social turbulence and (2) the role that imaginative writing, fictional and nonfictional, might play in the midst of social change and realignments.

Taken together, the writers and texts I examine invite us to imagine a future subject that can neither be guaranteed nor foreclosed. The texts thereby equip us to reposition Africa within ongoing discussions of globalization and intercultural understanding. They challenge the reader, African and non-African, to contemplate the possibility of subjectivities and identifications that are yet to emerge, throbbing with the spasms of unpredictability. Here, Africa is not just an object of social-scientific knowledge or a signifier of lack and unrelenting crises. The focus turns to the continent as site of human yearning and the possibility of change. For literary criticism, the challenge is to seek to influence that future—through our intellectual work as critics, teachers, and citizens—so that its unfolding can serve intercultural understanding and a truly collective good.

Contending with Tribe

Because of the colonialist implications that the term carries in African studies, it is helpful at this point to explain my reason for using the word *tribe*. In an important essay from 1990 titled "Social Anthropology and Two Contrasting Uses of Tribalism in Africa," the Nigerian sociologist Peter E. Ekeh has argued that although Africanist anthropologists and historians rejected the term as relic of colonial anthropology, popular and official discourses in Nigeria use it—most often in its accusatory form "tribalism." Ekeh undertakes to explain why scholars have rejected *tribe* and opted instead for *ethnicity*, even as popular and official discourse in Africa continue to use the former with little interest in its entanglement with the colonial discursive capture of African populations. As is well known, the notion of tribe suggests simple collectivities as opposed to modern states that are seen as more advanced and governed by articulated rationality, not kinship. Ekeh accounts for the social and existential role that kinship systems play in Africa in terms of the slave trade and the weakness or absence of precolonial state structures. For him, the slave trade and the complicity of chieftains led to a splintering of "state" from "society," the consequence being than kin groups served to protect individuals from their own rulers—chiefs, warlords, and other profiteers of the slave trade. As he puts it, "in the extended centuries of the slave trade in Africa . . . the most enduring social structure within which Africans could be assured some measure of protection was provided by the kinship system, not the capricious state institutions that rose and died with the turbulence of the slave trade" (682).

It is these kinship systems that were later consolidated into tribes under the biopolitical regime of colonial and postcolonial bureaucracy. After juridical independence, the African state "continued . . . to be plagued by the divisiveness of kinship loyalties implanted during the slave-trade era and emboldened during colonialism" (686). By arguing that attachments to tribe arose because of weak precolonial African state formations, Ekeh does not so much demystify the category of tribe, as explain why kinship systems became central in the lives of people that anthropologists call tribal groups and postcolonial bureaucracies document as such in demographic statistics. In their succinct entry on "Ethnicity" in *New South African Keywords*, John L. Comaroff and Jean Comaroff (2008) offer an opening toward the desedimentation and critique that I consider necessary. Building their argument on the corporatization of the Bafokeng and the San as ethnicities in South Africa, the Comaroffs account for these ethnicities as "a process of becoming rather than a finished phenomenon" (88). Such an approach allows cultural criticism to avoid a reification that "has the effect of *ex*tinguishing a class of producers" in order to incorporate them as statistical ethnicities "in a neoliberal sense of the natural, the inevitable, the given" (88, emphasis in original).

In this book, I purposefully use *tribe* and *ethnic group* interchangeably. Beyond the opprobrium attached to the label in African studies, merely getting rid of it does not get us any closer to the truth of the people whose lives are impacted by it. In my usage, the term *tribe* is as catachrestical as nation and race. It served to define groups in Africa as part of an apparatus of knowledge in which the colonizer sought to render and master the realities of the colonized for the latter's putative "good." It testifies, therefore, to the moment of the West in contact with itself and its abjected others. As such, it is neither transcendental nor objective in the positivist's sense; however, it is not thereby rendered inconsequential. My usage signals this irresolvable tension to mark the historicity of names but also to desediment this particular name so it does not constrict and debase reality. In different ways, Ekeh and the Comaroffs dramatize why issues of tribe/ethnicity are inseparable from the upheavals of economics and politics—the very stuff of history. Whether one calls them intelligible history in the Hegelian sense or reduces them to opaque chaos, it has implications for the way we approach Africa on the global stage. I argue that we call them events, testaments to social change, rather than mere repetitions of inherited clichés.

Impatience with the stereotype of Africa as a perennial basket case informs Achille Mbembe's "African Modes of Self-Writing." According to Mbembe, dominant tendencies in African humanities and social sciences are hobbled by a sense of historical victimhood and polemical relationship to something called modernity; worse, modernity is perfunctorily attributed to Western Europe construed as solitary agent of history—even if the agency is that of bad guy. This is not the place for extended critique of Mbembe's characterization of the presuppositions of African studies, but we can touch upon some salient problems.[5] In a measured retort aptly titled "Keeping Africanity Open," Souleymane Bachir

Diagne suggests that Mbembe is too quick to dismiss the intellectual traditions and modes of thought he claims to be engaging. Likewise, he conflates fairly distinct—and not nearly compatible or coextensive—strains of thought together, doing so without much argument. The consequence is that the modes of thought he is arguing against become metaphorical signs—vacant poetries of origins and victimhood—rather than intelligible philosophical or methodological positions.[6] Notwithstanding these limitations, Mbembe's intervention demands to be taken seriously precisely because of its polemical tone. If we set aside its arguable generalizations, the essay releases two core payoffs for its unapologetic ardor. One is his rejection of liberal-humanist lament for problems that may otherwise be read under the sign of change. Another is his claim that the event of the Atlantic slave trade has been badly undertheorized in African letters.

For Mbembe, Atlantic slavery has been the major unthought, the repressed element, of African self-writing. African studies and continental Africans have a peculiar difficulty, in his words, "with the project of recuperating the memory of slavery." Mbembe outlines two reasons for this difficulty:

> First, between African Americans' memory of slavery and that of continental Africans, there is a shadowy zone that conceals a deep silence—the silence of guilt and the refusal of Africans to face up to the troubling aspect of the crime that directly engages their own responsibility. For the fate of black slaves in modernity is not solely the result of the tyrannical will and cruelty of the Other, however well established the latter's culpability may be. The other primitive signifier is the murder of brother by brother, "the elision of the first syllable of the family name," in Jacques Lacan's phrase—in short, the divided polis. Along the trajectory of the events that led to slavery, this is the trail that dominant African discourses of the self try to erase. . . . As long as continental Africans neglect to rethink slavery—not merely as a catastrophe of which they were but the victims, but as the product of a history that they have played an active part in shaping—the appeal to race as the moral and political basis of solidarity will depend, to some extent, on a mirage of consciousness. (260)

The cost of the repression is a lacuna in the way African historicity is either grasped on its own terms or mobilized in relation to present challenges. We may disagree with the nonspecific, allusive shade of Mbembe's characterization, especially because we are expected to accept them as stringent methodological and ethical lapses. Yet, Mbembe has alighted on a promising provocation. Before him, the work of V. Y. Mudimbe (*The Invention of Africa*, 34) had followed the path of Michel Foucault's archaeology in an attempt to "rewrite" the "ambiguous passion" of African letters. In his discussion of Edward Wilmot Blyden in *The Invention of Africa*, Mudimbe addresses the epistemic infrastructure of Blyden's representation of Africa as civilizational other of Christian Europe. Elaborating an ethic of critical cosmopolitanism, Kwame Anthony Appiah had rejected the essentialization of race and African identity that runs from the thought of Crummell to the Pan-Africanists of the twentieth century. For Appiah, these figures bought into nineteenth-century pseudoscience of race. Mbembe, Mudimbe, and Appiah are wary of various forms of nativism and divisive identitarian claims. It comes from their concern that essentialist self-affirmations often feed a logic of sacrifice that can easily be conscripted by power. I am fully persuaded by their vision but will add that one can complicate the rhetoricization of sacrifice without bracketing history—that is, without leaving brute reality altogether for the realm of philosophical abstraction. For on the grounds of daily life and away from the towers of theory, these categories continue to interpellate individuals in paroxysms of violence—either of the self or the other. My approach is to elicit the ways in which African writing can equip us to desediment and rehistoricize the categories of race, nation, and tribe as they pertain to the continent.

Mbembe concludes his reflections on African self-writing by arguing that easy celebrations of instability, indeterminacy, and so forth, would not constitute a worthwhile alternative. "It is no longer enough," he writes,

> to assert that only an African self endowed with a capacity for narrative synthesis—that is, a capacity to generate as many stories as possible in as many voices as possible—can sustain the discrepancy and interlacing multiplicity of norms and rules characteristic of our epoch. . . . Perhaps one step out of this quandary would be to reconceptualize the notion of time in its relation to memory and subjectivity. Because the time we live in is fundamentally fractured, the very project of an essentialist or sacrificial recovery of the self is, by definition, doomed. Only the disparate, and often intersecting, practices through which Africans *stylize* their conduct and life can account for the thickness of which the African present is made. (272–73)

For me, the crucial issue might be formulated as follows: to what extent are writings from the three missionary moments potential sites for eliciting the "thickness" on which Mbembe insists here? Though he recognizes the role that imaginative literature might play in the epistemic structure he is diagnosing, Mbembe's interdisciplinary range is weighted toward critical theory and the humanistic social sciences. My concern in the pages to follow is to consider the ways in which the specifically rhetorical dimension of African self-writing might be probed, beyond the circumscriptions of authorial intentionality, to yield the "open-Africanity"—to borrow Diagne's phrase—that animates Mbembe's critique of nativist instrumentalism.

It is commonplace to say that a major source of Africa's difficulties is the transition from tribe to nation—that is to say, transition from governance founded on inherited kinship systems to one founded on the Western experiment with democracy. And yet, as Reinhart Koselleck has shown, Western intellectual history can itself be organized according to an archive of debates and complaints about one crisis or another. His review of the concept of crisis in Western discourses, from antiquity on to the present, leads him to a deeply resonant conclusion: "In our century, there is virtually no area of life that has not been examined and interpreted through this concept with its inherent demand for decisions and choices" (358). Koselleck's account of the historicity of crisis as concept and signifier shows its malleability. As he puts it,

> "Crisis" is often used interchangeably with "unrest," conflict," "revolution," and to describe vaguely disturbing moods or situations. Every one of such uses is ambivalent. . . . The concept of crisis, which once had the power to pose unavoidable, harsh and non-negotiable alternatives, has been transformed to fit the uncertainties of whatever might be favored at a given moment. Such a tendency towards imprecision and vagueness, however, may itself be viewed as the symptom of a historical crisis that cannot as yet be fully gauged. This makes it all the more important for scholars to weigh the concept carefully before adopting it in their own terminology. (399–400)

Koselleck's immediate subject is the intellectual history of the West, but his insight is relevant to literary globalism and African studies. It implies that any claim that Africa's crises are somehow unintelligible or radically unprecedented is ahistorical and precritical. In other words, recognizing Africa's many crises should be the threshold of analysis, not its point.[7] An instructive illustration of the ways in which the study of Africa is too readily elided with the good faith commitment to maximizing the continent's human and material resources is the little controversy that emerged in 2000. The controversy was sparked by the publication of an essay by Gavin Kitching, a scholar who began his career in the 1960s and, by his account, abandoned African Studies because the ruling elite failed to deliver the promise of independence to the millions who continue to suffer from the continent's economic backwardness. For Kitching, the hopes of development and decolonization were dashed by the failures of the continent's political and professional elite, and scholars are being dishonest if they shy away from facing this grim reality. In this way, Kitching becomes the disillusioned hero of a story of quest and altruistic hope that were dashed in the aftermath of decolonization. A set of basic questions that should be pertinent here are as follows: for whom is it really new to learn that the nominal independence of African states is a sham? Might the declamations about Africa's woes be differently pitched, and more refreshingly historicized, if we focus on how modern Africa came to be rather than what it fails to be—in other words, in terms of change rather than crisis? In engaging this sort of question from the direction of political economy and public policy, scholars have their work cut out for them as the twenty-first century lumbers on. My own approach to the question is from the perspective of stories and self-accountings made available by African and black-Atlantic intellectuals from the mid-nineteenth century on.

However we come down regarding the question of its applicability (or otherwise) in specific areas of African life, the notion of crisis is overused in reference to the continent on the global stage. The discourse of crisis that readily makes itself available in our experience of the world often confuses the indeterminacies of change for mere pathology. Truly grasping Africa's universality requires fresh perspectives on the continent's intrusion into the Eurocentric archive, as well as its challenges in the postcolonial present. The stock motif of crisis renders as pure negativity a social ferment that should more appropriately be posed as unpredictable. In this sense, Africa's difficulties could well be threshold of a newness that, although not guaranteed, remains thinkable because imaginable.

Of Borders and Selves

Let me return to Mbembe, who pursues the specific issue of violence and how to think it in his oft-cited essay, "Necropolitics." In that essay, he argues that Foucault's concept of biopower is inadequate as a way of grasping contemporary forms of sanctioned violence across the globe because these forms subjugate "life to the power of death" and thereby "profoundly reconfigure the relations among resistance, sacrifice, and terror" (39). Mbembe positions Western philosophy, from Hegel to Bataille, Arendt and Agamben, on the side of biopower as a politics committed to life in deathly preservation. In opposition to this, Mbembe "put forward the notion of necropolitics and necropower to account for the ways in which, in our contemporary world, weapons are deployed in the interest of maximum destruction of persons and the creation of death-worlds" (40). In my view, the biopolitical and the necropolitical need not be so rigidly separated conceptually or historically. I agree that the theory of biopower does not in itself—as Foucault inherits it from Arendt and Agamben replenishes it for our age of "global jihad" and "war on terror"—account for chattel slavery or all contemporary forms of warfare. But to this I add that many African writers expose the interlinkage between the biopolitical and the necropolitical. The writers show the ways in which metaphorics of sacrifice carry an intrinsic ambivalence, whereby life and death, the socially generative as much as the destructive, carry indissociable hermeneutic and existential force.

This appropriately brings us to one of the biggest challenges facing the continent in our time: the vibrant profusion of ethnonationalisms of various stripes. As we approach this subject, we need to note in passing that (1) ethnonationalisms are proliferating globally, not just in Africa, and (2) the proliferation is occurring even as the world becomes ever more connected through immigration (voluntary and otherwise) and digital technology. To speak of nationalism is of course to step onto the explosive domain of political identities. In the media as well as in academic scholarship, much has been written about the problem of identity, ontological or political, as it pertains to sub-Saharan Africa. In this area, the humanities in general are well behind the social sciences. Beyond self-righteous humanism or abstract deconstruction, Anglo-American literary studies cannot as yet apprehend self-other eruptions in non-Western settings that exceed the familiar "West and the rest" paradigm. And yet, nuanced attention to the complex interplay of identity categories in the African context is necessary if the continent is to be brought into the conversation about literary globalism in meaningful ways. I will be considering the interplay of notions of race, nation, and tribe with particular attention to the theme of sacrifice. The philosophical indices and ramifications of sacrifice have been explored at length in twentieth-century critical thought. From Marcel Mauss, Walter Benjamin, and Georges Bataille to Hannah Arendt, René Girard, and Giorgio Agamben, the dynamic of sacrificial violence is unveiled as modern civilization's disguise for what used to be thought of as primitive ritual.[8] My recourse to the motif of sacrifice is not meant to offer a new approach to this dynamic. Rather, I seek to show how it allows us to reframe modern African letters. In this way, my readings consider the varied ways in which categories of race, nation, and tribe come into contact in modern Africa.

As I approach it, the concept of sacrifice is to be understood on two levels: that of politics and, of course, culture or literature. As is well known, the term carries a number of meanings in academic and popular usage. We might think of the notion of sacrifice as it gets deployed in statist rhetoric where, for instance, soldiers lost in a war are eulogized as patriots who made the "ultimate sacrifice" for their country. There is also the sense it carries in Christian religious discourse, where Jesus submits to self-sacrifice to make possible humankind's salvation. In this understanding, the inaugural violence of Christ's crucifixion is an occasion of sacrifice that makes possible, through the triumph of resurrection, the sovereignty of peace. Finally, we might think of sacrifice in the discourse of cultural anthropology. At one level, the texts I study in the chapters to follow enact or relay the topos of sacrifice. For example, the black missionaries I examine in chapter 2 draw on a notion of Christian sacrifice to understand the world and their role in it. The black Atlanticists and Pan-Africanists of chapter 3 see African traditions as vestiges of a past that needs to be superseded—sacrificed—so that formerly tribal communities can ascend to secular-scientific modernity. In other words, tradition needs to be sacrificed for modernity. The contemporary writers of chapter 4 inherit this commonplace of the decolonization era and see their role as working toward modernization and prosperous nationhood.

It would be easy to show that many African writers depict African realities in terms of the costs and ambivalences of sacrifice. Communal rituals of sacrifice abound in Achebe's novels, and as we shall see in chapter 4, Soyinka in particular figures sacrifice as the very engine of sociality—for example, in the scapegoat mechanism at work in *The Bacchae of Euripides*, *The Strong Breed*, or *Death and the King's Horseman*. Some memorable protagonists in African literature emerge as differing instances of the logic of sacrifice: to take a couple of examples, Cheikh Hamidou Kane's depiction of Samba Diallo (*Ambiguous Adventure*), Ahmadou Kourouma's portrait of Fama, "the last Dumbuya," in *Suns of Independence*, or Yvonne Vera's Phephelaphi (*Butterfly Burning*). Ngugi's rewritings of biblical motifs from his youthful *The River Between* all the way to *Devil on the Cross*, or his figuration of the mugumo tree in *Matigari* can also be seen in this light.

We may illustrate the simultaneous recurrence and ambivalence of the sacrifice motif in African literature by briefly considering key moments from Achebe's *Things Fall Apart*, Ngugi's *A Grain of Wheat*, and Farah's *Maps*. The centrality of Ikemefuna's execution to Okonkwo's tragic narrative is obvious. What has not been as closely examined is Achebe's evocation of the moments leading up to the socially sanctioned murder. The elders of Umuofia are taking Ikemefuna to the outskirts of the village to be executed, and the journey is described in Achebe's characteristic simple sentences:

> At the beginning of their journey the men of Umuofia talked and laughed about the locusts, about their women, and about some effeminate men who had refused to come with them. But as they drew near to the outskirts of Umuofia silence fell upon them too.
> The sun rose slowly to the center of the sky, and the dry, sandy footway began to throw up the heat that lay buried in it. Some birds chirruped in the forests around. The men trod dry leaves on the sand. All else was silent. Then from the distance came the faint beating of the *ekwe*. It rose and faded with the wind—a peaceful dance from a distant clan.
> "It is an *ozo* dance," the men said among themselves. But no one was sure where it was coming from. Some said Ezimili, others Abame or Aninta. They argued for a short while and fell into silence again, and the elusive dance rose and fell with the wind. Somewhere a man was taking one of the titles of his clan, with music and dancing and a great feast. (52–53)

The leisurely sentences—of heat, natural sounds interspersed with silences, and faint drumming in the distance—leave a visceral impression because of what remains unstated. As Achebe narrates it, someone in a neighboring village is being honored with the *ozo* chieftaincy title, even as the young boy Ikemefuna is about to be sacrificed on the outskirts of Umuofia. In this way, the *ekwe* drumming in the distance becomes soundtrack to a peaceful ceremony and a violent act. Achebe reveals this duality precisely through the emotionless narration, and thereby turns pathos into wrenching criticism. What the novel presents is the implacable duality that sustains organized society, whose surface order exists alongside the possibility of violence rationalized by the logic of, or demand for, sacrifice.

Set on the eve of Kenya's independence from British settler colonialism in December 1963, Ngugi's *A Grain of Wheat* explores an ambivalence built into human affective interactions in contexts of social struggle and change. Ngugi uses the eyes, proverbial windows to the soul, as index of embattled humanity in the throes of change. One of the novel's principal characters, Kihika is a young man from a respected family who joins the Kenya Land and Freedom Army guerrillas in the forest to fight against the British. Kihika sees the struggle of the Gikuyu peasants against colonial dispossession in terms of sacrifice. Alongside Kihika, Ngugi poses taciturn Mugo as an enigmatic figure at the heart of this novel of clear political sides. Mugo's outsider status endears him to the other major African characters. They recognize him as hero and project their desire for agential certitudes upon him. At the novel's end, we discover that Mugo is the one who betrayed Kihika to British forces. Mugo's strange behavior throughout the novel—which the villagers saw as evidence of his suffering and sacrifice for the struggle—turns out to be based on guilt. In a paradoxical twist, he condemns and redeems himself by confessing to the gathered crowd at the celebration of Uhuru. Having contributed to Kihika's capture, Mugo sacrifices his own future by confessing at the novel's end, knowing he will be punished for betraying the people's hero:

> "You asked for Judas," he started. "You asked for the man who led Kihika to this tree, here. That man stands before you, now. Kihika came to me by night. He put his life into my hands, and I sold it to the whiteman. And this thing has eaten into my life all these years." ... Throughout he spoke in a clear voice, pausing at the end of every sentence. When he came to the end, however, his voice broke and fell into a whisper. "Now, you know." ... And still nobody said anything. Not even when he walked away from the platform. People without any apparent movement created a path for him. They bent down their heads and avoided his eyes. Wanjiku [Kihika's mother] wept. ("It was his face, not the memory of my son that caused my tears," she told Mumbi later.) (218)

In this passage, the crowd's reaction goes deeper than astonishment and suggests something closer to religious awe. Ngugi's handling of the moment of Mugo's confession empowers us to read the villagers' silence as a paradox of sanctification and abjection, fear and anger. Mugo is the scapegoat who is both abhorred and sanctified by the crowd's silence. The villagers detest Mugo for his betrayal, but equally so for his confession. By confessing, Mugo forces everyone to ask whether they had also betrayed the struggle in smaller ways. More poignantly, he forces them to ask whether, put in his position, they would have had the strength to act differently. In this way, Mugo serves the society's need for heroism by outing himself as antihero. He helps the process of healing by pushing the characters to confront shared vulnerability: the secret of less spectacular betrayals. And so, the novel gives us the perspective of Wanjiku, Kihika's mother and the character who should detest Mugo more than anyone else. While the crowd avoids Mugo's eyes, Wanjiku registers the materiality of Mugo's face: "'It was his face, not the memory of my son that caused my tears', she told Mumbi later" (218). By her strength and admission to Mumbi (Kihika's sister), Wanjiku reconfigures the politics of the moment. The mother of the betrayed sheds tears because of the betrayer's face, rather than the memory of her son. At this critical moment for Wanjiku, Kihika has become narrative—memory that needs to be recalled—whereas Mugo's face is concrete and immediate in its visceral demand. Ngugi thereby reflects on sacrificial logic by making Mugo's body—his face, his eye—the materiality that provokes the assembly's discomfort and registers his ambivalence as subject-object of sacrifice.

Askar, the protagonist of Nuruddin Farah's *Maps* is giving voice to what we have to interpret as his creator's authorial anxiety when he mulls over the word *sacrifice* as uttered by his aunt Salaado:

> He repeated the word to himself, like a blind man touching the items surrounding him, a man familiarizing the senses of his body with what his mind already knows. And he *saw*. He *saw* Misra divine, he *saw* her stare at a freshly slaughtered goat's meat, and he *saw* her tell a future when the meat quivered. The scene changed. Now he *saw* her open a chicken, he *saw* her give him an egg which she had salvaged from the dead fowl's inside and he *saw* her talk of a future of travels, departures and arrivals. Again the scene changed. And he *saw* a horse drop its rider, he *saw* a girl kidnapped, he *saw* the girl grow into a woman ripe as corn, he *saw* the hand that had watered the corn pluck it, then eat it—he *saw* the man-of-the-watering-hand murdered. Sac-ri-fice! . . . In short, life *as* sacrifice. In short, life *is* blood, and the shedding of one's blood for a cause and for one's country; in short, life is the drinking of enemy blood and vengeance. Life is love too. (257, emphases in original)

The sequence of visions—the tableaus that Askar "saw" in this passage—reels back for us the events of the novel itself. Some of the events are experienced directly by Askar while others are related to him by Misra, his adopted mother. If he sees all the memories as pointing to a single lesson that life is an implacable cycle of sacrifice, that conclusion is immediately juxtaposed to the paradox that life is also "love." In the caesura between the sacrifice and the love, Farah worries about the cold apprehension and possible wrong choice by such characters as Askar, in fiction and in politics.

The foregoing examples from Achebe, Ngugi, and Farah suggest the sense in which the deployment of the topos of sacrifice in African literature has always been ambiguous. In turn, this ambiguity alerts us to the possibility that the writers' most enduring gift to us is not in the ways they replenish or replicate the ideology of national belonging and the pieties of sacrifice. Rather, it lies in the way they entice and equip us to reflect on the ambivalences immanently lodged into the concept, as much at the ethnographic level of worldview as at the political level of collective belonging. One line of inquiry I pursue in the chapters to follow is that African literary texts do not just deploy sacrifice as theme but also reflect critically on it. In this sense, the texts are more contradictory and suggestive than the writers themselves sometimes intend. The best of African writing—from the black whitemen, through the Pan-Africanists, to canonical figures such as Achebe and Soyinka—reject sacrificial violence (in pagan or modern societies), even as they celebrate the *rhetoric* of sacrifice in social relations. As we shall see, Bishop Ajayi Crowther condemns pagan rituals even as he celebrates Christian sacrifice and self-abnegation. The black Atlanticists C. L. R. James, Richard Wright, and Peter Abrahams reject religion even as they poeticize symbolic sacrifice (by, for instance, arguing that the tribal past should be sacrificed in the name of modernization and nation-statehood). Likewise, Achebe and Soyinka reveal deep contradictions in the way they use the trope in their works.

There is nothing original in emphasizing that as rhetoric or politics, sacrifice is ethically complicated and rarely a self-evident social good. As many commentators in cultural theory have argued, the metaphor of sacrifice as social good needs to be interrogated because it is fundamentally narcissistic: it elides affective political interest with religious and secular altruism, even as it disavows the conceptual operation. For my purposes, what is important is that the ambivalent ways in which the trope emerges in African writing testifies to a self-reflexivity that invites greater attention. Likewise, the tendency to figure change simply in terms of crisis needs to be rejected, so that literary globalism may be better placed to return African agency to the table. Even as the texts I examine enact or replenish the logic of sacrifice explicitly or implicitly in their rhetoric, they also open it up to interrogation and critique. The many guises of sacrifice in African writing therefore alert us to what civil wars make clear in the real world: namely, in addition to its aesthetic possibilities as trope, sacrifice should unsettle us as inherently ambiguous. In this way, the contradictory ways that the topos of sacrifice emerges in African writing constitute an instance of particularity that carries universal implications.

One final matter of full disclosure remains. From the past of the slave trade to the present of globalization, the necropolitics that has marked Africa's modernity imposes on us the obligation to scrutinize constructions of selfhood and nationhood. Beyond professional and civic-moral commitment, my concerns in this book derive from a perspective on African identities that may have to do with my own family background. Born and raised in Nigeria, I immigrated to the United States, first as graduate student and thereafter a teacher of literature.

Anyone familiar with African history will know that the source of my last name is likely to be a former missionary benefactor or mentor for one of my ancestors. On both paternal and maternal sides, I am a descendant of former slaves and Christian converts who came from Brazil and Sierra Leone in the nineteenth century to settle in what later became Nigeria. Over the years as I worked on this book, some colleagues have asked whether it is some sort of paean to my lost roots, as it were. My own understanding is that this book is not about roots; rather, it is about why a neglected part of Africa's recent history should interest Africanists and scholars of postcolonial literature. According to the family stories, my paternal grandfather, Josiah Marcus Obayanju George, was a church organist who apparently remained a chain smoker even as he lay on his deathbed in 1947. This stern Methodist, descendant of Sierra Leonean immigrants to the Ìta Àkànní area of Lagos Island, chose to marry an ardent Roman Catholic—Louisa Silva, my paternal grandmother—laundress and daily communicant of the Holy Cross Cathedral built by the Afro-Brazilian community, also in Lagos.

On my maternal side, I am especially fond of a little story about my great-grandfather, Joachim Castilho, as my mother (his granddaughter) tells it. Apparently middle-aged when he arrived and settled in Lagos in the area that came to be known as Popo Aguda (Brazilian Quarters), he acquired the nickname Bàbá kòṣéẹ́ (roughly, Mister Not Acceptable) for his mildness and strange way of speaking the Yoruba language. As my mother tells it, the phrase "kòṣéẹ́" (this is not acceptable) was the old man's guilt-ridden response whenever customers tried to beat down his price for the nails and chisels he sold in his retail shop in central Lagos. Because his Yoruba was acquired late in life, Joao Castilho spoke with a heavy accent that displayed late second-language acquisition. And so, the strange accent with which the old man demurred—and my mother often took mischievous pleasure in vocalizing the strangeness—earned him his mellow nickname.

"Mister Not Acceptable" died decades before I was born, but I find his story of good-natured renaming instructive. What it tells us easily gets buried under the narratives of crisis, religious hatreds, and ethnic divisions that dominate discussions of Africa's modernity. Growing up as a descendant of Afro-Brazilian and Sierra-Leonean forebears in the city of Lagos, I did not suffer any discrimination or hurtful exclusions. Other than occasional jabs at my pretentious anglophilic surname by playmates on soccer playgrounds, my slave roots was never interesting, for them or for myself, as a *politicized* matter. This is both a plus and a minus. It is a minus because the convenient bracketing of the creolization at the very foundation of Nigeria's major city reveals the society's failure to truly engage the past of African complicity in the Middle Passage. But it could be redeployed as a plus in the service of ongoing historicity. This is for the simple reason that, while it is always necessary to engage the past, conflating the past with the present in order to divide by politicizing identities is never a good thing.

A remarkable feature of contemporary politics in many African societies is that such a misuse of the past will continue to gain ground in tandem with the continent's economic problems. The fact that ex-slaves from the New World and Sierra Leone participated in the making of Nigeria tends to be buried under the declamations of primordial princely lineage in this demonstrably young and mongrel society. In this way, Western reification of black Africa as a place of ahistorical collectivities feeds into—and is in turn reinforced by—the growing popularity of ethnic retrievals on the continent.⁹ This book redirects thinking about Africa by reading a small selection of writers of African descent. In the current climate, examining various ways in which figures of African descent have represented its failings and possibilities is one way of repositioning African literature within postcoloniality and literary globalism.

Attending to the microlevel of individuals and the stories they have told, my concern is with utterly human intensive uses of language to advance justice. I am concerned, in other words, with the human in "humanities." And as I will demonstrate as this book unfolds, many have preceded me in this commitment, from the Bible-quoting black whitemen to the self-avowedly secular novelists and internationalists. My task is to reflect on what these precursors teach me and what they stand to teach literary globalism and African humanities at the present time.

Notes

1. The term *black whitemen* is my translation of a Yoruba coinage that was used to refer to the Westernized Africans: *Òyìnbó aláwọ̀ dúdú* (literally, white person with black skin). In current criticism, of course, the image of a disconnect between skin and culture—or color and class—inevitably recalls Frantz Fanon. But it should be stressed that unlike the Fanonian "black skin white masks," the Yoruba designation *black whitemen* was supposed to be culturally descriptive and not pejorative. See Crowther, *A Vocabulary of the Yoruba Language, Compiled by the Rev. Samuel Crowther*. In English, they were also called black Victorians and black Englishmen. See Emmanuel Obiechina, *Culture, Tradition, and Society in the West African Novel*, 10.

2. See Hobsbawm, *The Age of Extremes*; and Badiou, *The Century*.

3. A comprehensive list is of course impossible. But for a sampling, see Cooper, Ferguson, Mamdani, Peel, and Comaroff.

4. See Barber, Desai, Hofmeyr, *Gandhi's Printing Press*; Jaji, Newell, and Tissières.

5. Mbembe, "African Modes of Self-Writing," *Public Culture* 14, no. 1 (2002): 239–73. A lively set of responses from a range of Africanist scholars in the humanities and social sciences appears in a subsequent issue of the journal, alongside Mbembe's rejoinder. See *Public Culture* 14, no. 3 (2002).

6. See Diagne, "Keeping Africanity Open," *Public Culture* 14, no. 3 (2002): 621–23.

7. See Gavin Kitching, "Why I Gave Up African Studies," *African Studies Review and Newsletter* XXII, no 1 (June 2000): 21–26. See also Danny Postel, "Out of Africa: A Pioneer of

African Studies Explains Why He Left the Field, and Provokes a Firestorm of Debate Within It," *The Chronicle of Higher Education*, March 28, 2003.

8. For a general anthology on the discourse of sacrifice in relation to religion, see *Understanding Religious Sacrifice: A Reader*, edited by Jeffrey Carter. For recent discussions of violence in relation to modern European intellectual history, see Chow, "Sacrifice, Mimesis, and the Theorizing of Victimhood (A Speculative Essay)." *Representations* 94 (Spring 2006): 131–49; Kessler, "Review Essay," *Religion and Literature* 37, no 3 (Autumn 2005): 109–15; and LaCapra, "Fascism and the Sacred: Sites of Inquiry After (or Along With) Trauma."

9. Much can be said about internal distinctions and rivalries among the returnee population itself. In addition to differences based on class and even language, some were Protestant, others were Catholic (from Brazil and Cuba), and still others converted to Islam rather than Christianity. This is not the place to enter into an analysis of the intricacies of social hierarchy and relative privilege within and between these demographic subgroups. For historical and ethnographic accounts of the returnees, see Herskovits; Laotan; Lindsay; Mann, *Marrying Well* and *Slavery and the Birth of an African City*; and Matory. For a fictional text about Afro-Brazilians in Lagos, see Antonio Olinto's novel *The Water House*.

AFRICAN LITERATURE AND SOCIAL CHANGE

1 Crossing Currents: Postcoloniality, Globalism, Diaspora

MUCH HAS HAPPENED in Anglo-American literary theory and cultural criticism over the last four decades. Most recently, arguments about paradigms of world literature, transnationalism, and diaspora have accompanied institutional changes and redirections. This development testifies to events in the world at large and is symptomatic of larger social anxieties. With the emergence of literary theory in the 1970s, literary criticism was challenged to reconsider established traditions of narrow formalism and ahistorical aestheticism.[1] But theory did not just happen because literary scholars suddenly looked inward and had a change of heart. Theory occurred within a broad ferment of world-historical developments, such as civil rights and antiwar activism in the United States, the anti-apartheid movement, and guerilla resistance against Portuguese colonial holdouts in Africa. The conceptual advances opened up in the first wave of theory—that is to say, theory as it took shape in the 1970s and 1980s—thus emerged in an atmosphere of real political and institutional overdetermination. In turn, theory feeds into, even as it is reshaped by, critical paradigms designed to address the particularity of non-white populations and non-normative sexualities.[2]

The postcolonial theory of the 1980s and 1990s is to be located squarely within these institutional developments. Diverse and internally contentious as the postcolonial eruption into critical theory was, we will find beneath the chaos of methods and vocabularies some version of the following: (1) a deconstruction of origins and essentialized identities, (2) a critique of colonial epistemic violence, and (3) an attempt to grapple with the fecund ruins of a delegitimized Eurocentric humanism. More specifically, postcolonial theory pushed further these poststructuralist tenets in order to consolidate a critique of cultural-nationalism and statist ideological formations.

If postcolonial theory emerged within the ferment of theory in the late twentieth century, the recent turn to paradigms of global literary study—what I will henceforth call literary globalism—is one consequence of theory's exertions. At this point, my story gets more interesting, for the turn to literary globalism is often implicitly posed as evidence of the obsolescence of postcolonial theory. On this view, literary globalism constitutes a step beyond the embattled paradigm of postcoloniality.[3] In effect, confronted with real-world developments that appear to make twentieth-century anticolonial politics obsolete, literary globalism becomes a way of sublating postcolonial studies. I endorse the intellectual possibilities of literary globalism but argue that the rubric of postcoloniality still has good work to do. Consider this illustration of the way postcoloniality gets set up in antithetical relationship to literary globalism: during a campus visit by a graduate student finalist for a position, one interviewer informs the candidate that Kazuo Ishiguro is not a "postcolonial" writer. Presumably, Ishiguro is a "British," "cosmopolitan" writer, and to be these things is to escape the postcolonial label. In this way, the interviewer is saying that postcoloniality is a *being*, not a doing-in-the-world, still less a writing-in-the-world. This simplistic opposition takes us back to the old false binary, whereby particularity is posited as antithetical to universality. Students of African and Caribbean literatures will be familiar with this uninteresting line of thought. Once upon a time, critics quarreled over whether Christopher Okigbo is an African writer or V. S. Naipaul a Caribbean writer—especially because both men insisted they didn't see themselves as African or Caribbean writers, respectively. It should by now be enough to put the false opposition to rest by saying that postcolonial literature is a site of expression where postcoloniality exerts its force field, not an aestheticized monument to non-Western being. Located within a global political and intellectual conjuncture, postcoloniality is not an identity but a category of social existence and knowledge production. Properly grounded, postcoloniality is a problematic in the good Althusserian sense. It is not a political position to be construed as logically coextensive with the problematic that occasioned it. Despite the polemical arguments of the 1990s—between Marxists and poststructuralists, culturalnationalists and postnationalists, or realists and postrealists—postcoloniality in the sense I am suggesting is not a subjective moral affair. It is rather the name of a set of historical entanglements and epistemic quandaries. Postcoloniality indexes a shared global context, necessarily local and inherently international, constituted by what Edward Said famously called "overlapping territories, intertwined histories." Understood this way, postcoloniality is not just a "method" of close reading, still less a moment in the old-fashioned literary history that begins with European desire flowing outward.

Here, then, is the moral of the story I've been sketching. The injunction to move beyond the postcolonial rubric in order to reach the global is a distraction. The best it does is to smuggle in a discredited version of universalism through the backdoor: in this case, the postcolonial is the particular that globalism claims to sublate in order to ascend to a spurious universalism. Hoary and dehydrated, this discredited approach to literature and culture might yet survive the sustained poststructuralist and postcolonial critiques of the 1980s and 1990s. Wherever agency is approached in abstraction from particular articulatory moments wherein all meaning—another word for agency—necessarily takes shape, the old Eurocentric universalism is getting ready to roll. I come at these issues from the perspective of postcolonial African literary studies. I start with a truism that repays constant reiteration: namely, the usefulness of a theory does not lie in what its defenders or critics say about it but how it equips us to analyze cultural problems in innovative ways, or use literature to challenge theory itself. I've been suggesting that the problematic of postcoloniality cannot be dissolved into the backwash of literary globalism and world literature—at least not without significant losses. A productive approach is to begin by contextualizing both currents in order to retrieve the intentionality of their interrelated emergence. Where postcolonial studies serve in literature departments to expose the elisions of Eurocentric literary criticism, globalism seeks to overcome the covert cultural nationalism at the heart of traditional literary studies. What postcolonial theory shares with globalism is thus the attempt to overcome narrow cultural nationalisms disguised as liberal aesthetic attentiveness. Approached in this way, the confluence of postcolonial studies and literary globalism might allow us to rethink the relationship between the local and the global, the national and the transnational.

This book positions Africa, construed as a geopolitical and subjective signifier, within ongoing discussions about *both* postcoloniality and literary globalism. I am broadly interested in the discourses that have worlded the signifier Africa, but my primary object of analysis is what Africans, or figures who identify themselves as such, have had to say about the continent's past and future.[4] It is easy to show that the best of African literature has always been internationalist in outlook. The central preoccupation of African literature has been to insert Africa in the global march toward the promise of progress and justice in modernity. And yet, the literature often serves cultural nationalism by laying claim to the glorious duty of combating stereotypes about the continent. In this unremarked imbrication of the national and the global lies a key question: how might the struggle in the realm of culture and representation avoid becoming detached from the political contradictions being played out in the continent's affairs? It is stating the obvious to observe that the bloodshed and economic distress in contemporary Africa expose the failures of the continent's nation builders. For my purposes, the challenge to be faced is that the continent's problems compel a reconsideration of the protocols of literary globalism and African humanities scholarship. My concern in this book is to pursue such reconsideration by exploring points of intersection and divergences between different kinds of writing about Africa by figures of African descent. This chapter presents a first step in that direction by exploring fault lines and continuities in mainstream theory, from its rise to influence in the 1970s to its afterlives in our post-9/11 world. My aim is to think about literary globalism against a background of two historical and discursive energies: namely, mid-twentieth-century black internationalism and postindependence African literature.

The argument of this chapter unfolds in three steps. In the first section, I conduct a summary stocktaking of Anglo-American literary and cultural criticism over the last few decades. I do so by examining the intersection of postcolonial studies and poststructuralist theory as it took shape in the 1980s. I then turn to current conversations about literary globalism and world literature: at that point, I suggest that taking seriously the discursive consequences of transatlantic slavery and black diasporic thought are crucial to any genuine understanding of Africa's epistemic particularity on the global stage. I conclude by drawing out how the chapter's stocktaking can serve to enrich our approach to literary globalism and postcolonial studies at the present time. The task of explicating African literature, I argue, should specifically involve a pedagogical investment, such that the reading and teaching of literature is informed by utopic projection of subjectivities in the making. As we shall see, I call these subjects of the future our "readers on the ground."

Some Consequences of Theory

This section's subtitle evokes the collection of essays edited by Jonathan Arac and Barbara Johnson titled *Consequences of Theory* and published in 1991. In evoking this exemplar of the theoretical conversations of the 1980s, I want to suggest that many things have changed, even as other things remain the same three decades later. One thing that remains unchanged is the signifier "Africa" within the vicissitudes of theory. In their Introduction to *Theory after "Theory,"* coeditors Jane Elliott and Derek Attridge (2011) make the valid judgment that a "range of discourses and practices, initiatives and projects . . . may be seen to descend from the 'Theory' of the 1970s." They conclude that in all these theoretical developments and new fields is a "lively sense of a continuing debate about fundamental issues such as life, representation, contingency, subjectivity, and freedom and at the same time a vigorous conversation about wholly practical questions relating to political change, living conditions, institutional practices and so on" (14). I argue that one of the tasks of the new theoretical developments should be to explore the resubjectification of colonialism's racial others—their performances of autonomous agency as raced and sexed subjects in real time. In the case of African letters, this resubjectification sought to redress the denigration of the African under the sign of the subhuman. It is well known that this racist objectification also had violent dimensions and was neither confined to the domain of representation nor simply epistemic. In the spirit of Elliott and Attridge's closing rally, "'Theory' is dead; long live theory" (14), I want to revisit some instructive scenarios that theory has thrown up in the last couple of decades. One comes from the poststructuralist debates of the 1970s and 1980s, the other from our contemporary moment of globalism.

I begin where theory as we now know it began, as sign and tension, to adapt a formulation by V. Y. Mudimbe from a different context.⁵ In an early essay from 1967 titled "Criticism and Crisis," Paul de Man reflects on the recurrent tendency in Western letters to resort to the rhetoric of crisis. De Man's essay takes up the notion of crisis as an anxiety that seems to haunt literary criticism as a matter of routine. His examples speak primarily to the issue of formal experimentation and the panic this seems ritually to generate, but his argument carries larger epistemological and political implications. That the revelation of his wartime journalism earlier in his career generated a crisis of its own, one that engulfed literary studies, contains a sobering irony, of course. But my interest in this essay comes from, first, his reflections on the challenge of knowledge production and, second, his privileging of literary knowledge as such. Reading Husserl's "The Crisis of European Humanity and Philosophy," de Man notices the contradiction in Husserl's invocation of a civilizational other. He finds Husserl's gesture particularly intriguing in a text that purports to reflect on philosophical demystification: "Husserl speaks repeatedly of non-European cultures as primitive, prescientific and pre-philosophical, myth-dominated and congenitally incapable of the disinterested distance without which there can be no philosophical meditation. This, although by his own definition philosophy, as an unrestricted reflection upon the self, necessarily tends toward a universality that finds its concrete, geographical correlative in the formation of supratribal, supernational communities such as, for instance, Europe. Why this geographical expansion should have chosen to stop, once and forever, at the Atlantic Ocean and at the Caucasus, Husserl does not say" (15). De Man is interested in how a notion of crisis figures in the rhetoric of Husserl at a time of the broader political crisis that Nazism signals. For him, Husserl's thinking about crisis performs a truth that the thinker is himself unaware of within the logic of his performance. For the frame of the civilized as opposed to the primitive that governs Husserl's text is precisely at the root of the epochal crisis driving Husserl's sincere critical attention.

Unlike Husserl, it is the blindness of ethnocentrism that structuralism sought to overcome. De Man reads Claude Lévi-Strauss's structuralism as nothing less than a dethronement of the old, transcendent subject of positivistic science. The problem is that Lévi-Strauss can only do so by installing "reason." This new apparatus of cognition is a "virtual focus" (19) that shores up the credibility of knowledge. In this way, structuralism commits Lévi-Strauss to the rigorous felicity of science, as opposed to the void of poetry. His virtual focus is fictional to the extent that the stability of cognition assumed in it is a fantasy. In de Man's words, "The 'virtual focus' is, strictly speaking, a nothing, but its nothingness concerns us very little, since a mere act of reason suffices to give it a mode of being that leaves the rational order unchallenged. The same is not true of the imaginary source of fiction" (19). Much to the contrary, for de Man, literary discourse does not seek to restore the rational order that the notion of "virtual focus" serves to reconstruct. The fiction that literature constructs reveals itself as a construction, one that harbors nothing beyond its own interiority. In the world made available in fiction, "the self has experienced the void within itself and the invented fiction, far from filling the void, asserts itself as pure nothingness, our nothingness stated and restated by a subject that is the agent of its own instability" (19). Earlier in his discussion of Rousseau, de Man writes: "The self-reflecting mirror-effect by means of which a work of fiction asserts, by its very existence, its separation from empirical reality, its divergence, as a sign, from a meaning that depends for its existence on the constitutive activity of this sign, characterizes the work of literature in its essence. It is always against the explicit assertion of the writer that readers degrade the fiction by confusing it with a reality from which it has forever taken leave" (17). This characteristic de Manian formulation invited polemical reactions, and got a good dose of them.[6] Put simply, the most common critique that was leveled against deconstruction is that it cannot make possible a critical accounting of the relative gains of various ways of construing and representing reality and the mind's endeavor to grasp that reality in literature. This problematic enters into discussions of postcolonial literature through the debates between Marxists such as Aijaz Ahmad, Benita Parry, and Epifanio San Juan on the one hand and poststructuralists such as Gayatri Spivak or Homi Bhabha on the other hand. What interests me is the question of *crisis* that supplies de Man with the ground of his discussion. The debates around theory, or about poststructuralist postcolonial studies, were often framed in terms of crisis: for example, the crisis of the humanities, the crisis that political nihilism portends, and so forth. Current literary and cultural criticism has not moved beyond such metaphorics of crisis as characterized the theory debates of the late twentieth century. As indicated earlier, the claim that postcolonial studies has been rendered obsolete by new problems and crises is itself evidence that we are still within the historical space of postcoloniality. Whether it is attributed to the corporatization of the university, the loss of prestige of the liberal arts in favor of quantifiably useful knowledge, or even the so-called lowering of standards by political correctness, the idea that humanistic studies are in crisis is an old complaint. I suggest that the complaint tells us more about unresolved problems within literary studies than about the tyranny of university administrations and science, technology, engineering, and mathematics (STEM) disciplines. A productive response to the anxiety is to grasp it as sign of ongoing change within literary studies and on the social terrain. Understood this way, what comes across as "crisis"—in politics as much as in the humanities—may also be approached proactively as challenge and possibility.

In a 1977 colloquy, Meyer H. Abrams had suggested that the fate of deconstruction is that it would be sublated in the Hegelian sense: "it will pass on; but it won't pass away. In the Hegelian term, it will be *aufgehoben*; that is, it will be canceled, yet survive at another level" (Abrams, 333). From one perspective, it would be correct to say that Abrams's prediction did come to pass with the emergence of postcolonial theory, queer theory, and African American and Ethnic American studies. Assessing the debates about postcolonial theory in the 1990s, Stuart Hall formulates the intervention of the postcolonial paradigm in cultural theory as a periodization and "renarrativization," one that "displaces the 'story' of capitalist modernity from its European centering to its dispersed global peripheries" ("When Was 'the Post-Colonial'?, 250). For Hall, postcoloniality is "the retrospective re-phrasing of Modernity within the framework of 'globalisation' in all its various ruptural forms and moments. . . . In this way, the 'post-colonial' marks a critical interruption into that whole grand historiographical narrative which, in liberal historiography and Weberian historical sociology, as much as in the dominant traditions of Western Marxism, gave this global dimension a subordinate presence in a story which could essentially be told from within its Western parameters" (250). Hall's definition equips us to grasp postcoloniality as a category of knowledge production whose epistemological promise, grounded as it is in specifiable time and space, resides in temporal circumscription. To see things this way is to recognize that the "global" cannot negate the "postcolonial" and be anything but hollow reification. Likewise, postcolonial literature would be the name we use to identify a problematic that the literary text engages through its act of language—that is to say, a name for what the text actually performs—rather than the author's being or advertised intention.[7]

To play devil's advocate for a moment, it is true that the end of the Cold War has ushered in new geopolitical alignments and new conflicts. In the age of digital media and global networks, nineteenth- and twentieth-century conflicts of class, nation, or race have undergone shifts that should compel cultural criticism to reinvent itself by resetting its foci. It is also true that to be fixated on a dyadic colonial/postcolonial frame is to preserve a colonized outlook because colonialism—as much in linguistic representation as in political practice—was premised on such simplistic temporality and line of difference.[8] However, these observations actually suggest the continued relevance of postcoloniality. Far from disqualifying the postcolonial paradigm, these historical observations confirm its epistemological challenge. For one, globalization cannot in any interesting sense be dissociated from the imperialism of the nineteenth century. The West's colonization of others in the name of mercantile and industrial capitalism exacerbated the deterritorializations, the immigration flows, and the international corporatism of globalization. Second, without the cultural-nationalism of writers, critics, and all-round engaged intellectuals from the non-Western world, there would today be no archive with which literary globalism has to deal, even in a gesture of disavowal. As Edward Said (1993) argued in *Culture and Imperialism*, without the cultural and political work accomplished during the decolonization era of the mid-twentieth century, there would be no textual trace of hearts and minds witnessing to the eventness of the moment. At the level of historicity and materiality of intellectual work (here, the creation of an archive), postcoloniality is at once lived experience and intellectual response. It is a condition of possibility for the contemporary advent of globalism as an angle of vision in literary and cultural criticism. It is not the only or most important condition of possibility, but neither is it negligible.

The reasonable conclusion to draw from the foregoing, then, is that literary globalism *cannot* be an advance beyond postcoloniality because the latter is the sign of a conjuncture through which we are still living. In the last decade or so, we are witnesses to a remarkable fact of Anglo-American literary studies, namely, that continental thinkers come and go in waves of brandings and rebrandings (from the moment of, say, Althusser, Derrida, Foucault, and Deleuze in the 1970s and 1980s to Giorgio Agamben, Alain Badiou, Jacques Rancière, or Slavoj Žižek at the turn of the twenty-first century). This may in part be due to the inevitable time lag that comes with foreign-language texts hitting the Anglo-American academic market in translation. However we choose to explain it, a risk attaches to the phenomenon that needs to be strongly underlined. The risk is that in the midst of theory's dance of succession, old questions return under the mask of fresh answers, even as old blindnesses persist without being recognized as such. As long as literary globalism is framed as substantive advance beyond the intensities of postcoloniality, contemporary literary and cultural criticism cannot adequately grasp what the African example has to offer.

In the chapters that follow, we shall see the sense in which selected black missionaries and writers we associate with African literature—authors of what Achille Mbembe has called "African self-writing"—elaborate particularities of voice and vision that can be harnessed by everyone who takes the patience to read closely and humbly. For now, my point is that the discrediting of spurious universalisms that drove theory's passion in the late twentieth century should continue to be on the agenda, precisely because theory always carries the risk of new false universals. To be productive, theory will not seek to regulate particularities or "elevate" them to some realm of unblemished abstraction. From my perspective, this point can never be overstated, and an instructive illustration can be found in Alain Badiou's *Saint Paul. The Foundation of Universalism*. Badiou approaches Pauline religious fervor as an epistemological drama whose ethical core is a universalism of the good kind. According to him, truth in Saint Paul's writings is singular. Saint Paul's truth unfolds as declaration of an event whose radical newness defies preconstituted structure as such. For Badiou, the event of truth cannot be claimed by subsets of identity or established parameters of legitimation because truth is "of the order of what occurs" (*Saint Paul*, 14). Understood this way, truth as radical event cannot be authorized by identity, insofar as identity needs to posit an outside to delineate itself: "Truth is diagonal relative to every communitarian subset; it neither claims authority from, nor (this is obviously the most delicate point) constitutes any identity. It is offered to all, or addressed to everyone, without a condition of belonging being able to limit this offer or this address" (*Saint Paul*, 14).

Badiou sets himself against Nietzsche's critique of Pauline Christianity as a thanatological discourse rooted in ritualization of sacrifice, what Badiou defines as "eventalization of the hatred of life" (*Saint Paul*, 65). For Badiou, Nietzsche dismisses Pauline Christianity because of a mistaken assumption that a direct line of thought connects Saint Paul to Hegel, the grand evangelist of civic morality, so to speak. It is Hegel, after all, whose dialectics positions death as the meaning that gives moment and substance to life. Badiou writes: "We know how much the Hegelian apparatus owes to Christianity, and how dialectical philosophy incorporates the theme of a Calvary of the Absolute. In that case, resurrection is nothing but the negation of the negation, death is the decisive time of the Infinite's self-externalization, and suffering and martyrdom possess an intrinsically redemptive function, which, it has to be said, corresponds to a Christian imagery that has been omnipresent for centuries" (*Saint Paul*, 65). Badiou wants to rescue Saint Paul from the sort of reading, such as Nietzsche's, that makes a plodding Hegelian of him. He argues against Nietzsche's derision of Saint Paul as father and author of Christian self-abnegation, a theorist of death as redemption (*Saint Paul*, 72–73). As Badiou would have it, dialectical thought makes the daring of death-in-life the predication of earthy life itself or, posed differently, of historical becoming. Change and fulfillment are thereby rendered inconceivable outside of ritualized, hypostasized agonism. Time is desultory, driven only by such hope as sacrifice inspires. Against this, Badiou locates Saint Paul's achievement, not in the pathos of sacrifice but in the exuberance of a new epoch and its uncharted possibilities. For Badiou, what needs to be emphasized in Saint Paul is his robust universalism, one that is properly purged of the hypostasis of death that always threatens to tarnish the evental unfolding of truth:

> Every name from which a truth proceeds is a name from before the Tower of Babel. But it has to circulate in the tower. Paul, we have insisted, is not a dialectician. The universal is not the negation of particularity. It is the measured advance across a distance relative to perpetually subsisting particularity. Every particularity is a conformation, a conformism. It is a question of maintaining a non-conformity with regard to that which is always conforming us. Thought is subjected to the ordeal of conformity, and only the universal, through an uninterrupted labor, an inventive traversal, relieves it. (*Saint Paul*, 110)

In sum, for Badiou, Saint Paul's thought is universal and committed to life; meanwhile, Hegel's universalism is Christian to the core, and this is because his dialectical thought is actually a misdirection of Saint Paul's epochal iconoclasm. What interests me is the logic of Badiou's account of the universalism he wants to endorse. I want specifically to isolate two ideas: (1) that the "universal is not the negation of particularity" and (2) that the universal is rather "the measured advance across a distance relative to perpetually subsisting particularity" (*Saint Paul*, 110). These formulations interest me because Badiou follows a different train of reasoning in the interview with Paul Hallward, first published in 1993 in *Angelaki* and later appended to *Ethics: An Essay on the Understanding of Evil*. In this discussion, Badiou uses the historical example of negritude poetry, "as incarnated by Césaire and Senghor" to illustrate the gap between culture and politics. To be fair, *Ethics* is addressed to students and general readers. Likewise, the context of conversation during which the example of negritude comes up is relatively light. At one level, it would be unfair to generalize about Badiou's universalism based on his tangential commentary about negritude in a freewheeling conversation about politics and internationalism. But at another level, this is exactly the point. Badiou's aside about negritude is instructive precisely because it occurs as a side note, a casual illustrative case in a conversation that construes itself as expansive and internationalist.

Badiou refers to the lesson of negritude poetry in responding to Peter Hallward's question on "the relation between politics and culture" and the related problem of defending ethical universalism (moving beyond identity, so to speak) while also taking account of the fact that "where people are oppressed, they are oppressed as women, as black, as Jewish or Arab" (*Ethics*, 107). Badiou invokes negritude as a necessary cultural movement that worked as aesthetics but cannot serve truly emancipatory politics. From Badiou's perspective,

> *Négritude* . . . consisted essentially of reworking exactly those traditional predicates once used to designate black people: as intuitive, as natural, as primitive, as living by rhythm rather than concepts and so on. It's no accident that it was a primarily poetic operation, a matter of turning these predicates upside down, of claiming them as affirmative and liberating. I understand why this kind of movement took place, why it was necessary. It was a very strong, very beautiful, and very necessary movement. But having said that, it is not something that can be inscribed as such in politics. I think it is a matter of poetics, of culture, of turning the subjective situation upside down. It doesn't provide a possible framework for political initiative. (*Ethics*, 108)

Badiou overlooks the basic fact that resistance can only proceed on the very ground of the categories being resisted: the oppressed can most tellingly contest their oppression by getting hold of the categories wielded by the oppressor. Truth, as we saw earlier, can only unfold in the tower of babel, and the task of thought is to work through "conformism" in order to reach "nonconformity." It is no longer interesting to say that historically, black people were thought of as intuitive, as primitive, as natural, and so on. What would be interesting is recognizing that blacks are still represented as such in the popular domain of the everyday, and carefully considering what that means for our understanding of true universalism in cultural criticism.

The problem might be that in this instance, Badiou positions culture too far away from politics. As scholars ranging from Gregson Davis to Abiola Irele, Kwame Anthony Appiah, Paulin Hountondji, Lilyan Kesteloot, and Christopher Miller have shown, the event of negritude was at once cultural and political. It emerged from and spoke to an international context. It is not accidental that the two figures named by Badiou were also elected politicians: Césaire served as mayor of Fort-de-France and, later, president of the Regional Council of Martinique, while Senghor was the first president of independent Senegal. Badiou's disavowal of negritude's materiality invites a simple question: what exactly does it mean for a discourse to "provide a framework for political initiative"? Could the understanding of framework itself—what we accept as its basis and scope—be precisely what is at stake in political struggle? In his interpretation of the universalism of Pauline thought Badiou insists that truth as event—which is to say, truth that witnesses to and participates in change—cannot be contained within any existing religious, political, or epistemic structure. On Badiou's terms, whether we understand the new truth in terms of governance, art, or philosophy, it is the event and the knowledge that beholds it as such that will articulate a new shape and content. Against this background, his rejection of the possibility of universality in negritude cuts directly against his own definition of universality in the context of Saint Paul's thought.

In suggesting that negritude poetry necessarily closes off universality, Badiou recapitulates Jean-Paul Sartre's (1948) famous critique developed in "Orphée Noir"—his preface to *Anthologie de la nouvelle poésie nègre et malgache de langue française*. In that essay, Sartre had argued that negritude's poetry of origins is an "anti-racist racism" that needs to surpass the necessary moment of negation to realize its emancipatory potential.[9] According to Sartre, negritude has to die in the very thrust of will and language that would defeat racism and herald the triumph of the truly universal. The raced self and its predication of struggle need to dissolve, so the universal society might crystallize in a shimmering new light. Half a century after Sartre's well-intentioned universalism, Michael Hardt and Antonio Negri say something quite similar in *Empire*. Hardt and Negri conclude that the knowledge contained in Homi Bhabha's or Edward Said's theories of postcoloniality cannot unfold on their own terms but only as symptoms of passage from an outdated regime of truth and sovereignty: from the colonial paradigm to the new terrain that they christen Empire. If Badiou's attempt to retool

Marxism leads him to the false universalism beneath his critique of negritude, Hardt and Negri read postcolonial theory as epiphenomenal to postmodernism. This positioning prepares the ground for their sublation of postcolonial theory and anticolonial nationalism as simple moments that do not escape Empire but can only be symptomatic of the concrete passage going on. Like Sartre, they argue that movements like negritude or other forms of cultural-nationalism appear to succeed in the short term because they are destined to fail in the long term, obedient as they are to the logic of Empire. They see liberation (as opposed to emancipation) in the era of globalization as an agglomeration of desires, an embodied "creative force" that would be adequate only if it escapes old formations and categories: "The Third World, which was constructed by the colonialism and imperialism of nation-states and trapped in the cold war, is destroyed when the old rules of the political discipline of the modern state (and its attendant mechanisms of geographical and ethnic regulation of populations) are smashed. It is destroyed when throughout the ontological terrain of globalization the most wretched of the earth becomes the most powerful being, because its new nomad singularity is the most creative force and the omnilateral movement of its desire is itself the coming liberation" (363). In passages like this, what Hardt and Negri present as self-evident critique of postcolonial theory is in fact an articulation of its problematic. In the last instance, Hardt and Negri and Badiou—like Sartre before them—seek a principle of universality that would operate without the encumbrance of racial or other culturally constructed identity. For them, it is the social-structural locations and mobilizations—Deleuzian, rhizomatic, and deterritorialized—that will yield true liberation.

We are back, then, to the old problem of universality in interplay with particularity, back to the problem of construing one without suppressing the other. We are back, that is, to what may ruefully be called the class-or-race-delirium: how to articulate the struggle for racial equality without a universalizing theory that accords primacy to class as objective structural location. As is well known, Frantz Fanon balked at such limited options in his riposte to Sartre's essay in *Black Skin, White Masks*. For him, Sartre's reading grants the particularity of black yearning only to contain its full implications, to choke it in the crib as it were. Adapting Sartre's original metaphor of poetry as a nourishing spring, Fanon complained that the spring risks being drained by the epistemic violence of idealist abstraction. "'Black Orpheus,'" Fanon writes, "marks a date in the intellectualization of black *existence*. And Sartre's mistake was not only to seek the source of the spring, but in a certain way to drain the spring dry" (*Black Skin, White Masks*, 113, emphasis in original). He concludes his engagement of Sartre by declaring, "My black consciousness does not claim to be a loss. It *is*. It merges with itself" (114) ("Ma conscience nègre ne se donne pas comme manque. Elle *est*. Elle est adhérente à elle-même" [129]).

Fanon's quarrel with Sartre is an old story, and by the time Sartre came to write the preface to *The Wretched of the Earth*, some of the rift had been mended. I bring it up to emphasize that Fanon's perspective saw negritude's limits in order to redirect black struggles in modernity, not subsume it within a universalism that presumably escapes particularity. There is no blanket rejection of particularity here. What Fanon sought to recover is the specific iteration of particularity that negritude and bourgeois nationalism represent in different ways. He grasps both negritude and bourgeois nationalism as articulatory moments ripe with possibility and danger, conjunctures where an authentic "inventive traversal," to echo Badiou, may or may not take hold. Just as Badiou's rescue of Saint Paul traverses Nietzsche and Hegel to recover what he wants to preserve as the theoretical truth of Pauline thought, Fanon worked *through* negritude, not around it. And so he writes: "I define myself as absolutely and sustainedly open-minded. And I take this negritude and with tears in my eyes I piece together the mechanism. That which has been shattered is rebuilt and constructed by the intuitive lianas of my hands" (*Black Skin, White Masks*, 117).

To be sure, where the issue of what comes after anticolonial struggle is concerned, Fanon gets many things wrong. I will say more about this in relation to nationalism, bourgeois governance, and modernization in chapter 4. Here, what I am after is the interplay of particularity and universality that his definitive critique of negritude apprehends and enacts. In their most promising vectors, critical theory and globalism in literary studies are regulative ideals. Both envisage universals, by which I mean horizons of ethical value and disciplinary commitments. They are ideals we do well to seek, but with the awareness that the search is itself an aspect of the goal. To delude ourselves into believing we have theorized universality, wholly and without residue, is to fear the newness of truly generative thought. The universal can only be glimpsed in the particularities of event, human choices, failures, or triumphs. It is not a state of transcendent grace that thought attains, beyond and aseptically apart from specifiable particularity and subject position.

Africa in the Moment of Literary Globalism

So far, I have been elaborating the case for the relevance of postcoloniality in literary globalism. The fact that influential theorists such as Badiou or Hardt and Negri are challenged to talk about negritude or postcolonial theory, however tangentially, is evidence that something has indeed occurred. This thing that has occurred includes, to restrict our purview to the twentieth century, the passion in their own words of figures like Fanon, Amílcar Cabral, W. E. B. Du Bois, Edward Said, Henry Louis Gates Jr., or Gayatri Spivak. I now want to turn to the specific problem that African literature poses to mainstream theory and criticism. Two critical studies drawn from separate (and ostensibly opposed) fields of literary criticism will serve to develop my argument here. Michael Echeruo's (1977) *Victorian Lagos: Aspects of Nineteenth Century Lagos Life* was a landmark contribution at a time when the social sciences dominated Africanist area studies and cultural nationalism dominated African literature and literary criticism. Steven Knapp's (1993) *Literary Interest: The Limits of Anti-Formalism* was a head-on engagement of deconstructive and New Historicist approaches in Anglo-American literary criticism. Knapp, we will recall, coauthored with Walter Benn Michaels the controversial essay "Against Theory" (1982). A polemical rebuttal of the enterprise of literary theory as it took shape in the 1970s, "Against Theory" made its case from the standpoint of American pragmatism.[10] If with Echeruo we are on the terrain of African studies from the humanities side, with Knapp we are dealing with a participant in the theory wars of the 1980s. Read together, the major Africanist critic and the pragmatist language theorist relate a story worth telling.

Echeruo's *Victorian Lagos* provides an intellectual history of Anglophone West Africa by examining editorials and press reports that appeared in Nigerian newspapers in the second half of the nineteenth century, specifically from 1863 to 1900.[11] Echeruo shows that the elite who led the nationalist movement in Anglophone West Africa came to consciousness as a class in the nineteenth century. This class, he argues, was Victorian in taste and self-understanding. Echeruo locates his study in the city of Lagos, the commercial heart of modern Nigeria. In the period that concerns him, Lagos "was not then thought of as the capital of a homogenous and independent territory, much less a national, entity. In consequence, the 'negro' community of Lagos—which saw itself as living in a cultural outpost of a larger negro world that, among other places, included Liberia and the United States—came to see Lagos city also as a part of a larger administrative complex" (110). *Victorian Lagos* demonstrates that the Lagos of this period, like the entire west coast of Africa, was run and spoken for by this numerically small elite who were culturally in the minority, even though they had greater political power than the rest of the population:

> The fact that these members of the Lagos elite were Africans is not for us as important as the fact that they were, in effect, a new kind of African. True, some of them were descendants of slaves. But many factors—for instance, the emancipation of Brazil, the independent State of Liberia, the colony of Sierra Leone, and the establishment in these two states of institutions of education (through the University of Liberia and the Fourah Bay College)—placed them at a considerable advantage over most of the Nigerians on the spot. That, in any case, was to be expected. What gave a special character to these new Africans was the fact that they were in a profound, not a polemical sense, Africans of a Victorian persuasion. (110)

It is interesting that in putting forth his thesis that the African elite of this period, the "new Africans," were of a Victorian outlook, Echeruo immediately adds that his claim is "in a profound, not a polemical sense." Clearly, Echeruo is anticipating the possibility that his characterization of the nineteenth-century African elite may automatically be read as deriving from a polemical intent. His caution regarding the phrasing points to an ideological frame that the conventional construction of African literary history tends to marginalize, one that needs to be highlighted and thought through. Why would it be self-evidently polemical to recognize that the nineteenth-century African elite—the so-called black whitemen—were Victorian in outlook and self-understanding? The reason is only marginally related to the general pejorative connotation that Victorianism carries. More relevant is the fact that the category African has a specific discursive connotation whereby, to acquire or retain felicitous meaning, it has to be the binary opposite of things Victorian. In the inherited and still operative constructions of Africa, the continent designates radical alterity. Consequently, to categorize something as "African" and "Victorian" is to violate a discursive frame. It is to conjure up a value-laden oxymoron and thereby initiate a polemic, hence Echeruo's rhetorical reticence.

Echeruo is measured in his account of the missionary zeal of the Victorian Africans. In his concluding remarks, he assesses the Christian missionary dimension of the task that the West African elite set themselves. These men undertook, in his words, "on behalf of Africa, the civilizing duties of Victorian England." To this end, "Sierra Leone, Liberia, the West Indies, the United States and Brazil were the training and recruiting grounds; the hinterland of Africa was their vineyard" (113). Echeruo perceives the irony in their self-perception:

> To the extent that they had the privilege of education they seemed very determined to save other Africans from the predicament of illiteracy and godlessness; to the extent, however, that they were black, they realized that they shared a common dilemma with everyone who was not just African, but black. Hence, though they had no common territorial roots in Africa, they felt a common racial obligation to it. What they lacked was not the sensibility of the condition of the African, the black man, but the sense of the ordinary, the indigenous African mind and experience. (113)

Echeruo here struggles with the threat of destabilization that the Victorian Africans pose to dominant notions of Africa, or the black subject and its so-called authentic experience. If, as Echeruo acknowledges, many of the christianized elite were born in Sierra Leone, in what sense can their location be posed in implicit opposition to something called the "indigenous African mind and experience"? The crucial reason is that African-ness in his account is both ontology and historical sedimentation. It is ahistorical identity over which one has no control (i.e., one is born into it). But it is somehow also a *datable* mode of being, a condition of mind that one acquires or fails to acquire. Obviously, the two meanings are neither coextensive nor compatible. The former is absolute and nonhistorical: individuals inherit it simply as a consequence of birth. By contrast, the latter denotes historical process and concrete experiences in time.

The point of these examples is not to belabor some ideological vector that is unique to *Victorian Lagos*, lodged in the interstices of its prose. What I am getting at cannot be understood on an individual level; neither should it simply be waved away as essentialist identity politics. Echeruo's account points us to a discursive frame that exceeds the individual dimension. This discursive frame is still alive, as much in popular culture as in academic literary studies. In "The Embarrassment of Victorianism: Colonial Subjects and the Lure of Englishness," Simon Gikandi explains why this has been the case: "For the colonized . . . the Victorian age represents such a powerful reminder of colonial domination and cultural alienation that it is hard to associate it with a discourse of freedom or moral progress. It is much easier to privilege the narrative of decolonization and to read it as the process by which African subjects overcame the colonization of their consciousness than to posit it as the source of the cultural grammar that enabled decolonization" ("Embarrassment," 160). After the advent of poststructuralism, after the so-called subversive value of hybrid identities, psychic indeterminacies and liminal locations have been theorized, there remains a rhetoric of pure arrival and voluntarism in much of current criticism. By this I mean a framing of theoretical as well as political engagement in terms of purity and contamination, crisis and the call to restoration. We have gone beyond the critical language that takes subject-positions like black or African as self-evident givens. But we have not entirely overcome the assumptions—about collectivity, engagement, and agency—that subtended those essentialisms in the first place.

From a different direction, Knapp's book is concerned with canonical English studies. However, he reaches out toward the postcolonial by way of a reading of Achebe's *Things Fall Apart*. In its encounter with this novel, Knapp's book instances a discursive frame that complements Echeruo's. Knapp is arguing against what he sees as the hasty politicization of literature in theory and criticism. De Manian deconstruction and New Historicism are the critical currents he engages, but much of cultural studies and theories of postcoloniality would qualify as targets of his critique of what he calls "antiformalism." For him, "there is no need to personify historical and social formations in order to convert them into appropriate objects of literary interest" (104). Knapp is not arguing for a value-free understanding of literature and criticism. Unlike traditional formalism, he insists that literary texts dramatize issues of an ethical or political nature, and that reading can help to make these ethical or sociopolitical issues explicit and usable in the world. According to him, literary representations put before us "complex scenarios." They make available a multiplicity of responses to specific situations posed within the interior logic of the representation itself. The reader can grasp these situations and responses as allegorical of specific values in society. He or she invests affective energy in the values that the complex scenario puts forth. Likewise, the reader draws ethical consequences from the process of allegorization and emotive investment. But the ratification of the ethical/political choices cannot validly be said to reside, immediately and one-dimensionally, in the representation itself: "Perhaps . . . the moral benefit of literary interest lies not in any capacity to tell us which values are the right ones, but far more modestly, in the way it helps us find out what our evaluative dispositions *are*" (100). This is another way of saying that to the extent that the representation is truly a complex scenario, what it promises is a cognitive or emotive state for the engaged reader. But the precise shape of this cognitive or emotive state, the evaluative or political choices it elicits, is not hardwired into the representation itself. Or, more accurately, it should not be hardwired into the representation itself, otherwise the latter has not attained the status of a complex scenario. The implication of this argument should by now be clear. For Knapp, there are complex and noncomplex scenarios, complex literary performances and noncomplex ones. In the language of the streets, there is good literature and there is inferior literature.

To illustrate this thesis, Knapp turns to *Things Fall Apart*, literary globalism's great African novel. In turning to the novel, Knapp joins literary scholars, world leaders across the ideological spectrum, and teenagers from Detroit, United States to Seoul, Korea. But Knapp is too sophisticated a reader to repeat the dogma that *Things Fall Apart* reveals traditional Africa to the world or gives savages the dignity of language and culture. Rather, Achebe's novel offers what Knapp calls an "impressively stark instance" of a complex scenario. In the novel, says Knapp, the representation of colonial aggression does not permit one-dimensional moral certitude: "The European intervention into traditional Ibo culture is presented . . . as a cruel act of aggression and as the only available answer to the often extreme injustices of Ibo custom. (Thus the first converts to Christianity are precisely the victimized and marginalized members of Ibo society, including . . . women who have borne twins . . . and morally disaffected people like the protagonist's own son, unable to reconcile himself to the ritual murder of a hostage who had become, in effect, his adopted brother.)" (99). Knapp has identified a central issue in the novel. A reprehensible cultural practice becomes the excuse for a colonizing mission whose tactics are in turn violent and unjust. In addition to Achebe, various non-Western writers have taken on this dialectic. The reason they do so is because they are interested in exploring a historical process that took an epochal turn in the nineteenth century and is still ongoing. Knapp is not interested in pursuing such specific historical coordinates and implications. Rather, he takes from Achebe's novel an abstract moral dilemma: "to regret the passing of the Ibo way of life is by implication to tolerate the extreme subordination of women, the exposure of twins, and the murder, if the oracle so commands, of an adopted child; but to condemn those practices is, in the terms of the novel, to align oneself with the invading missionaries and colonialists" (98–99).

Knapp's framing of the moral complexity of *Things Fall Apart* constrains the novel's full scope. The moral complexity becomes a grand aesthetic abstraction because Knapp positions the reader outside the time of the novel's drama and characters. He locates conflict and character at a temporal distance from the moment of the reader's encounter with the novel. His analysis suppresses the contemporaneity of the reader with the characters and event—the bodies and history—represented in Achebe's novel. In this way, *Things Fall Apart* serves as mirror in which the West can view otherness while sketching the contours of its own discreet normativity. This evacuates Achebe's novel of ethical or theoretical issues it might otherwise raise for us at a discursive juncture shared by Africa and the West. Because Knapp's interest is universal literariness, "complex scenarios" rescued from the skepticism of postmodernists, Achebe's novel will be handy only to the extent that its datable human element and political passion are given short shrift. Africa, understood as the narrative signs of the Igbo world as Achebe represents it, has to be exterior to the novel's readership. It has to be a phenomenological other that enables the reader-as-self to be reconstituted in real time and space. The implied reader has no social identity yet exists in the present, but Africa is located in an abstract past, one that is also the eternal present of imaginative literature. By contrast, a reading that is attentive to the coevalness of the world of Achebe's fiction and our contemporary anxieties would emphasize that the novel begins with the sacrifice of an unnamed virgin and the young boy Ikemefuna in exchange for a woman from Umuofia—the protagonist Okonkwo's village—who had allegedly been killed by the people of Mbaino. As we saw earlier in the introduction, *Things Fall Apart* begins with an "us versus them" conflict that has nothing to do with race or British colonial designs. It begins, rather, with an alleged violent act and its redress through sacrifice, a transaction that affirms the border between Umofia and Mbaino: the border, that is, between two African collectivities. In this most widely read and translated African novel, the inaugural conflict is between two neighboring tribes, not races or "civilizations." This sort of reading will also notice, in the narration of Ikemefuna's murder, a meditation on the sanctioned violence that holds up routinized daily life. To frame Achebe's work solely within hegemonic racial or civilizational anxieties—West versus non-West, black versus white—is therefore to constrain its epistemological possibilities.

Echeruo and Knapp exemplify aspects of a Eurocentric frame in which Africa carries epistemic connotations that make an imagined Western world intelligible by being its antithesis. One achievement of the most interesting theoretical developments of the last few decades is that this discursive frame has been discredited. But it would be inaccurate to suppose that we have surpassed it. Writing in the 1990s, Knapp is drawn to *Things Fall Apart* because its setting makes it a good candidate for thinking about morality and representation in the midst of the era's theory debates. His account of literariness may be old fashioned, but it is too easy to convict him of formalism and leave the conversation there. At core, his notion of complex scenarios is unexceptionable: we can ignore or be embarrassed by it, but we cannot seriously *refute* it. Posed more strongly: no argument for the relevance of literary studies in the face of shrinking research funding and loss of undergraduate majors can refute Knapp's account without lapsing into incoherence. It is as old as Hamlet's injunction to the Players or Keats's defense of "negative capability"; and it is as recent as Erich Auerbach on the vagaries of mimesis from antiquity to Woolf or Franco Moretti's turn to the quantitative sciences to reanimate literary studies on a global scale. The crucial question then becomes: who is the reader presupposed in any universalizing account of literature in the contemporary world? This question may be repressed or sidelined, but it doesn't go away: any coherent accounting of the relevance of literary studies in the academy depends on it. For our purposes, one way to move beyond Echeruo's untheorized Africa and Knapp's Eurocentric formalism is to revisit two things: (1) the question of the reader's positioning and (2) the problem of Africa as inherited signifier.

In a reaction to the theory debates of the 1990s, Henry Louis Gates Jr. made the counterintuitive claim that our lived reality and the scholarly knowledge that apprehends it may never *earn* the label of postcolonial. Gates is arguing against the tendency to conscript Fanon's writing for disparate theoretical agendas while ignoring the fact that Fanon had his own self-conscious agenda. In his words:

> Of course, discarding the imperial agenda of global theory also means not having to choose *between* or *among* Wright and Léopold Sédar Senghor; Césaire and Senghor, Spivak and Said; Greenblatt, Pease, and Porter; Bhabha and JanMohammed, Parry and Fredric Jameson and Aijaz Ahmad; or even Fanon and Memmi. Rather, it means not representing the choice as one of epistemic hygiene. And it requires a recognition that we, too, just as much as Fanon, may be fated to rehearse the agonisms of a culture that may never earn the title of *post*-colonial. (*Tradition and the Black Atlantic*, 112, emphasis in original)

The passage may sound pessimistic, but Gates's caution is actually quite worldly. To the extent that the problems of postcolonial African states are only comprehensible if placed in relation to the legacies of colonial rule, the present will always contain the trace of the colonial past. To be historically grounded and conceptually coherent, the global has also to be postcolonial. Gates's caution, made in reaction to the theory debates of the 1980s and 1990s, is apposite in the current climate of literary globalism. If the 1980s and 1990s were characterized by debates around multiculturalism and culture wars, the anxieties that animated those debates persist in current discussions of failed states, unwanted immigration of unskilled labor, and religious extremisms. The reappearance of Goethe's and Marx's "world literature" as impetus to new methodological directions should therefore be historicized against this background. Let us now turn to three recent contributions to the conversation about world literature, from David Damrosch, Jonathan Arac, and Peter Hitchcock. In doing this, I aim to tease out paths toward a robust appreciation of the lessons of African self-writing in the modern era.

In *What Is World Literature?* Damrosch (2003) proposes "elliptical refraction" as one of three properties that characterize forms of world literature. The other two are world literature as "writing that gains in translation" and world literature as "mode of reading: a form of detached engagement with worlds beyond our own place and time" (281). It is worth our while to put pressure on the formulation "worlds beyond our own place and time." Perhaps our place and our time are neither self-evident nor so easy to delineate. Within the United States, there are postmodern spaces such as Fredric Jameson famously theorized, alongside industrial-age spaces of indentured labor, sexual traffic, and Giorgio Agamben's bare life. But setting these qualifications aside, there is something worth pursuing in Damrosch's proposition that world literature might be thought of as "an elliptical refraction of national literatures" (281). On this model, the literary text is situated within a loop where a text's local conditions occupy one end, while its reception in a global setting (including the transformations brought upon it as a condition of that reception), constitute the other end. If we apply this criterion to the case of African literary discourse, its locality would constitute one end, while its reception and reconstellations within the Anglo-American academy (among various other sites) constitute the other. For the elliptical refraction to be truly generative, however, the local end of the loop needs to be properly elaborated; it should at least be as expansively elaborated as its reception in a global frame.

In his 2002 *New Left Review* essay titled "Anglo-Globalism," Arac grants the significance of Franco Moretti's reconsideration of novel studies to renew literary studies in a global frame.[12] But he is worried by Moretti's emphasis on quantitative methods for synthesizing themes with production and circulation patterns across cultures. For Arac, in dispensing with original language of composition and the microlevel analytical attention it makes possible, Moretti's model renews the idea of world literature by eschewing traditional close reading. The vast cross-cultural purview of distant reading also relies on the imperialism of the English language even as it claims comparative accretion. With the collaborative design of distant reading, Moretti's readers, says Arac, "read closely in all the various languages of the world, and present the findings to the global synthesizer" (45). In this way, the synthesizer can remain monolingual and global, yet secure in the hegemony of English or the major European languages. I would go further. A significant cost of Moretti's model is that quantitative information cannot illuminate the vicissitudes of human actions in their rigorous existential particularities. Data about where and when certain kinds of novels emerged or resurfaced certainly promises important insights. But such information cannot yield much about human interiority that would be adequate to a world struggling to rectify past errors. Lagos, the commercial center of modern Nigeria, sits on the edge of the Atlantic Ocean. That some of the earliest African novels emerged from the city (and others like it on the West African coast—Accra, Abidjan, Dakar) conforms to the model of contact zones as fertile grounds for the novel as form. After granting this, we would still do well to think about the trade in human beings that flourished on the same coast through the first half of the nineteenth century, or the unimaginable poverty that continues to be reproduced even as I write.

Arac's essay takes us to the paradigm of postcoloniality by underscoring the importance of Erich Auerbach's *Mimesis* in Edward Said's sense of intellectual vocation. Said's valuation of Auerbach was designed to work as a rebuke of what he saw as the degeneration of criticism into postmodern nihilism. We will remember that for Said, the circumstances that surrounded Auerbach's writing offer an illustration of the potential of exile and marginality to enable proper critical appreciation of cultural products and the societies that make them possible. Beyond this, Said values *Mimesis* as important literary criticism because he saw in it an account of literary representation that celebrated the humane potential of literature. Where poststructuralist critiques of teleological narratives and inherited notions of literary tradition would fault *Mimesis* for its linear narrative of consciousness and Western literature, Said sees its subtending humanism as something worth celebrating. Arac does not entirely buy Said's defense of Auerbach's traditional humanism as a kind of starting point that only requires redirection from within. For him, Said's model of the critic as some sort of virtuoso of the textual detail can sustain old-school elitism, or "isolate the critic as irrevocably as the new-critical model isolated the text" (44). Nonetheless, as alternative to distant reading, Arac prefers the humanism and critical cosmopolitanism associated with Said, for whom literature is indissociable from the force field of history and politics. It is there, where language and form disclose issues of social rupture, that Arac poses a question I would like to quote at length:

> The language-based criticism residually familiar in the American academy emerges from a deep history but has not actually long existed. For this is *literary* criticism, and it therefore coexists with the modern sense of literature, only some two centuries old. In their different ways both Plato and Aristotle practiced something that we recognize as theory, but not language-based analysis of authors or works. The skills of what would become such a literary criticism emerged first and were long elaborated in rhetorical analysis and religious exegesis. When these came together in classical philology in late eighteenth-century Germany, it was the moment of explosive nationalist

emergence. Language-based criticism of modern literatures rose and flourished with the modern nation-state. Moretti's essay tacitly acknowledges this history but does not address the further question posed by the globality of world-literature and the diminishing place of the nation-state in our times: what can the future hold for a mode of critical performance that is losing its home base? Must it learn the arts of diaspora? (45)

My answer to Arac's question is a resounding yes, and one central claim of this study is that Anglophone African literature was all along, like black-Atlantic internationalism, an "art of diaspora."

I shall have more to say on this claim in the next section. For now, I want to take up Peter Hitchcock's innovative use of Mikhail Bakhtin's defamiliarization of genre. Citing Neil Lazarus's (1999) work on cricket and Afropop in *Nationalism and Cultural Practice in the Postcolonial World* as well as Achille Mbembe's (2001) anatomization of governance in *On the Postcolony*, Hitchcock argues that such work "do not just expand the substance of postcolonial inquiry; they also suggest that such analysis bends towards cultural studies and away from many of the logical prescriptions of literature *sui generis*. The English department has been the bastion of genre, and what questions genre also questions its raison d'être" ("The Genre of Postcoloniality," 309). Like Arac, Hitchcock uncovers the Hegelian emplotment of literary history that continues to govern literary criticism even after the various isms have left their imprints. The temporal and hierarchical devolution of cultures inherited from Enlightenment thought has been discredited in theory, but it is not set aside. It is instead dispersed onto a spatial disciplinary topography, such that what used to be called "the English Novel" now becomes "the Novel in English" or "the Global Anglophone Novel." For Hitchcock, as long as the centrality and ideality of the category "novel" remains intact, theorizing its limits actually amounts to rehabilitating its limitless possibilities. And this direction will not get some of us where we need to go. As he puts it:

> "Literature" as a subject has consistently obfuscated the logic of its categorization and the means of its subsistence. The history of literature in that regard is deeply imbricated with the logic of genre and its discriminations. . . . It is interesting, however, that once the weakness of generic identification has been proved, and especially so with the novel, the genre persists, as if to thumb its nose at those who would deign to dislodge it. . . . There is politics enough in the troubling of the category, perhaps, but that effort must therefore remain modest where a politics of culture is concerned. ("The Genre of Postcoloniality," 313)

Hitchcock cautions against literary globalism that devolves around predictable reinventions and idealizations of "literature" inherited from the European eighteenth century. By contrast, he turns to Bakhtin who famously undermined bourgeois genre systematization through the concept of novelization. The notion of "postcolonial form" invoked in the title of his book *The Long Space. Transnationalism and Postcolonial Form* suggests a certain elusive distinctiveness. In this book, Hitchcock deploys Bakhtin's concepts of novelization and the chronotope to formulate what might be distinctive about form in transnational postcolonial fiction.

As is well known, novelization is Bakhtin's concept for what he saw as the active singularity of the novel form: not just the eighteenth-century European novel that we have come to know but also fiction from Greco-Roman antiquity. The novel in this powerful transcultural sense is a dialogical antigenre, and it always takes shape at the margins of high cultural, official discourses. The cultural work that the novel form performs is for Bakhtin a novelization of preconstituted discourses and ways of knowing. "Novel" appears, not simply as a literary-historical genre, but as an event of novelization—that is to say, a category of datable epistemic impact or possibility.[13] Following Bakhtin, postcoloniality emerges in Hitchcock's account as the chronotope that gives distinctiveness to the serial works of Wilson Harris, Nuruddin Farah, Pramoedya Ananta Toer, or Assia Djebbar. His deployment of the concept of novelization thus allows him to move beyond a tendency in literary globalism to smuggle in discredited Eurocentric perspectives that can grasp difference only as a belated version of the same. For Hitchcock, the serial novels of Farah, Harris, Pramoedya, and Djebbar elaborate a distinctive perspective on the modalities of modern existence: "In writing through the moment of decolonization their eventness entails wresting the form from itself. It is not just a question of reclaiming that which the novel has been in its long history, but of articulating *what it could not have been* until the great struggles of national independence and anticolonial revolution in the second half of the twentieth century" (*The Long Space*, 27, emphases in original).

One way of thinking about the problem with which Arac and Hitchcock are grappling is in terms of the relationship between literature and the academic criticism that speaks to it and learns from it. Thanks to Eurocentric emplotments of literary history, non-Western literatures emerge only as belated replications or satellite extensions of a modular Western European beginning. Eurocentric literary history allows literary globalism to remain narrowly fixated on the literary statement as emblematic of the totality of culture, implicitly erecting a hierarchy between "literary" and "nonliterary" uses of language. But what if we approach the literary text as act of will and mode of thought, like other speech acts in social context? In the chapters that follow, I read nonfictional as well as fictional texts but not to reconfirm aestheticist ideas of literature as cultural achievement. Rather, I read both kinds of writing as acts of language, inscriptions of will, and provocations to thought. The point is not to deny that "literature" construed in the strictest of terms—that is, as an aesthetic object to be distinguished from other kinds of writing—has its uses. What needs to be rejected is a different kind of claim with which it often gets conflated: namely, that the universality of imaginative literature is best served when abstracted from the historical imbrications that delimit literature's very emergence in society. The error is the idea that removal of imaginative literature from historical embeddedness frees us to more powerfully experience ethics and aesthetics. To my mind, the direct opposite is true: it is when we follow the social embeddedness of a text all the way, so that we emerge on the other side—that is, through and beyond the social, not abstracted away from it—that we are best placed to be enriched by the literary. History and society are not mere threshold and predication of the literary image. Much more interestingly, history and the embodied subjects that live it emerge *through* and *beyond* the occasions of literature. In this sense, the literary is language at work in the world: as bearer of humanistic knowledge, it is neither higher nor lower than other emanations of expressive culture.

In chapters that follow, I will be exploring the sense in which the texts achieve what we may call novelization effects through their engagements with inherited knowledges about Africa. I extend the concept of novelization to cover ethnographic accounts and letters of missionaries in chapter 2, the memoir and fiction of black diasporic figures in chapter 3, and novels by two Nigerian writers in chapter 4. Deployed in this broader sense, novelization exceeds the domain of literary form (i.e., "literariness" as technique, ethic, or sensibility) and offers a way of articulating how the texts participate in providing richer vistas on the contingencies of cultural encounter. The texts dialogize hegemonic or official discourses of their different eras: the ethnocentric missionary gaze of the nineteenth century, the colonial paternalism of the early twentieth century, and the myopic instrumentalism of the late twentieth century. The poetic human reality that is Africa is neither the positivist's social scientific referent nor the nationalist's one-dimensional object. It is better understood as a mediated inheritance with which representation is condemned to work. Formerly, this used to be Africa as signifier of savagery and devil worship; currently, it is Africa as signifier of failed states and unrelenting crisis. The texts I examine simultaneously replicate and complicate this image. By means of the representational dynamic I invoke through the idea of novelization effects, the texts engage and reinvest the inherited racialized image of Africa. In doing so, they challenge us to reposition Africa in faithfulness to the demand of our time: as sign of ongoing change and universalizable particularities.

The Black-Atlantic Detour

In the preceding sections, we saw different illustrations of the perennial tension, in literary criticism, between universalism and particularism. Against Knapp's untenable universalism and Echeruo's reification of something called African identity we may pose Arac's suggestion of arts of diaspora and Hitchcock's use of Bakhtinian novelization. To explore both directions fruitfully, it is necessary to move the question of identity closer to the heart of the conversation. In this section, then, I take up that possibility by considering the internationalism of the early and mid-twentieth century. I start with Pan-Africanism and move on to discuss contributions from Édouard Glissant and Kenneth Warren. My argument is that the black whitemen are the forerunners of what later became black internationalism. In turn, modern African writers in the European languages are continuators of the internationalism that was a condition of possibility for the midcentury decolonization movement, inheritors of and participants in the historic dynamic that Glissant theorizes as *Détour*.

Let me proceed by way of Paul Gilroy. Writing about Richard Wright, Gilroy argues in *The Black Atlantic* that the novelist's lifework "constitutes another fragmentary part of the history of the international social and political movement known hazily and inadequately by the label Pan-Africanism" (151). Gilroy identifies the tag "Pan-Africanism" as a loose and inadequate umbrella label for the ferment of transnational black collaborations and dissentions that dates from the nineteenth century and extends into the twentieth. The movement, he writes, "like the anti-slavery organising on which it was built, challenges our understanding of modern politics precisely because it overflows from the confining structures of the nation state and comprehensively queries the priority routinely attached to those structures in historical and sociological explanations of social and cultural change" (151).

Introducing the anthology he edited in 1979 under the title *Ideologies of Liberation in Black Africa 1856–1970*, political scientist J. Ayo Langley characterizes W. E. B. Du Bois as "father of Pan-Africanism" (55). In a retrospective discussion with St. Clare Drake held on May 1, 1987 in Amherst, Massachusetts, George Shepperson shared his reminiscences about Pan-Africanism: "If Pan-Africanism in the English-speaking world was started by intellectuals from the Caribbean, Afro-American intellectuals were not far behind" (2). But of course, the transnational reach of Pan-Africanism included as well French-speaking and Spanish-speaking Caribbean and African intellectuals, as attested to by those cultural movements that soon came to be known as *negritude* and *negrismo*. The First Pan-African Congress held in London in July 1900 had Trinidadian lawyer and activist Henry Sylvester-Williams as general secretary and Du Bois as chairman of the address committee. Between 1900 and 1945, five other gatherings were held: Paris (1919); Brussels, London, and Paris (1921); Lisbon and London (1923); New York (1927); and Manchester (1945). If at the turn of the twentieth century the guiding spirits of the movement were diasporic blacks, by the moment of the Manchester conference of October 1945, African leaders were central participants in the planning and vision of the organization. These are the charismatic, flawed "big men" who would later enter African history books as the inaugural leaders of their respective nation-states at independence: Jomo Kenyatta, Hastings Kamuzu Banda, Obafemi Awolowo, Julius Nyerere, and Kwame Nkrumah—recalled in a fleeting line of epic rhapsody in Ngugi wa Thiong'o's *Petals of Blood* as "Kwame of the eagle's eyes" (311). Also present at the Manchester meeting was the South African exile Peter Abrahams, to whom we shall be returning in chapter 3. In 1958, another Pan-Africanist gathering took place in Ghana in a renamed incarnation, the "All-African People's Conference." Convened by Nkrumah and his adviser George Padmore, the conference was symbolic as it took place in the independent nation of Ghana, the first sub-Saharan African country to attain independence from Britain. In attendance was, among others, Patrice Lumumba, whose assassination barely three years later constitutes a tragic heralding of the trend of regional secessions and imperialist interference based on cold war politics: the overall militarization of structures of governance that came with colonial rule and continues to plague African states.

These few sketchy examples illustrate a complex ferment that was transnational in scope, racial in its focus on black anticolonial struggle but emphatically nonracialist in its vision of a possible constituency of suffering humanity—that is to say, all of Fanon's "wretched of the earth." For ease of reference, I will henceforth refer to this discursive formation simply as Pan-Africanism. Somewhat schematically, we may think of an uneven, wide-flung phenomenon like Pan-Africanism as inhabiting two levels: the political and the cultural. My concern is with the cultural dimension of the moment, its traces in the discursive formation that contemporary cultural criticism variously calls "black Atlanticism." One powerful watershed event for revisiting Pan-Africanism in its complex cultural ramifications is the First International Conference of Negro Writers and Artists held in France in September 1956. Hosted by the journal *Presence Africaine* and its editor Aliounne Diop, the significance of this meeting for my purposes resides in its implications for theory at the present time. In the United States, the academic and public service organization American Society of African Culture (AMSAC) emerged out of the conference as affiliate of the Societé Africaine de Culture. AMSAC spawned the short-lived academic quarterly *African Forum*. Edited by political scientist John A. Davis, *African Forum* ran for just three years from 1965–68; its purview spanned the cultural as well as political domains. As Davis puts it in his inaugural editorial statement, "AMSAC was from the first concerned with the political, social, and economic aspects of the new African nations. Since AMSAC was itself formed just before most of the nations of the sub-Saharan Africa began to obtain their independence, it is obvious that we should plan our programs to encourage greater understanding of the new and developing nations of Africa, singly and as a whole. Moreover, free cultural development is not possible without political freedom" (4). *African Forum*'s editorial board included James S. Coleman of University of California, Los Angeles; Gray Cowan, then of Columbia University; St. Clair Drake; Kenneth Dike, then vice-chancellor of the University of Ibadan in Nigeria and one of the founding figures of the Ibadan School of History; and Davidson Nicol of Fourah Bay College at the University of Sierra Leone. South African writer and cultural critic Es'kia Mphahlele is listed as one of the regional consultants. The first issue of the journal is dated summer 1965 and featured articles by Nnamdi Azikiwe, Jomo Kenyatta, and Julius K. Nyerere, then presidents of newly independent states of Nigeria, Kenya, and Tanzania, respectively. The essays they contributed centered on the question of what they each refer to in their titles as "African unity."[14] Howard University historian and activist Rayford W. Logan contributed an essay under the title "The Historical Aspects of Pan-Africanism: A Personal Memoir," in which historical documentation is enlivened by the human sheen. The issue featured as well a review of Chinua Achebe's *Arrow of God* (which had appeared in 1964) by the African American critic Saunders Redding, then of Hampton Institute, later of Cornell University, and a review of Senghor's *Négritude et Humanisme* by James W. Ivy of *The Crisis*.

The First International Conference of Negro Writers and Artists of 1956 might be read as one instance of the black-Atlantic structure of feeling in the midst of the political and epistemic decolonization agendas of the mid-twentieth century. Present at the conference were Americans James W. Ivy, Horace Mann Bond, and Richard Wright. Also present were the West Indians Fanon, George Lamming, and Jean Price-Mars; the painter and sculptor Ben Enwonwu from Nigeria; and the writers Amadou Hampaté Bâ from Mali and Jacques Rabemananjara from Madagascar. With characteristic verve, Henry Louis Gates Jr. writes of this gathering:

> Here, gathered in the Amphitheatre Descartes, itself one of the West's most sacred and lavishly conspicuous icons of and tributes to the triumph of Reason and the spirit of Enlightenment over the dark worlds of superstition and pagan beliefs, sat the authors of third world liberation, world-historic theorists of colonial resistance, forging new ideologies, new "weapons of theory" out of Négritude, Marxism, psychoanalysis, African communalism, you name it. Remember, it was 1956 and these were the heady days of grand theory for the black world. Never had the promise of a genuine politics of culture seemed more real, more realizable. (*Tradition and the Black Atlantic*, 3).

The 1956 Paris conference, the American Society of African Culture, *African Forum*, the journal that AMSAC spawned—these are chosen here as examples of a discursive juncture where many others would equally well serve.[15] Speech acts by black subjects from the abolitionist era onward have come down to us under a range of labels. In current usage we may call it black internationalism to keep things simple, or black Atlanticism after Paul Gilroy, or a *practice* of diaspora as Brent Hayes Edwards theorizes it. In this book, I will be referring to discourses of black internationalism under the umbrella of black Atlanticism, after Gilroy. By this term I do not claim historical coverage or scientific sociological reference. What is being described is profoundly irreducible to quantitative sociological categorization or neat historicist capture. I understand the term *black Atlanticism*, rather, as a multilayered pattern of textual and intersubjective relations, set in play as structures of feeling in the sense made memorable by Raymond Williams. We will recall that for Williams, the concept of structures of feeling is more interesting than what he called "more formal concepts of ideology or worldview" because of the weight it gives to the ancient category of feeling. Here, feeling becomes at once internal and external, objective in the wake of its subjective predication, so that thinking undergoes a counterintuitive sublation into the domain of the felt. In Williams's formulation, what he is after is "not feeling against thought, but thought as felt and feeling as thought: practical consciousness of a present kind, in a living and interrelating continuity" (132). Understood in this way, black Atlanticism indexes a specifiable and datable structure of feeling, interpretable in hindsight precisely because it is serially textured, played out in multiple settings, ebbs, and flows. What we have here is not so much a movement as a problematic: a discourse that *had to be* transnational because its propagators had no nations with which they could unproblematically identify. Where blacks in the Americas and Europe could only be second-class citizens in their own countries, black Africans were yet subjects of colonial empires, products of tribal-ethnic communities from which the benefit of Western education had inevitably alienated them. Whatever else it does, Western education necessarily recomposes any romanticist affect they may wish to harbor for community as natural filiation.

It is time to revisit that era in order to reposition its problematic and discursive legacy. The writers and intellectuals who made cultural-nationalism compatible with interracialism in that earlier moment—flawed and idealistic as they were—might yet have something to tell us in the present of globalism. At the least, they demonstrate that contemporary literary globalism, with its investment in expansive communities beyond the metaphysics of filiation, is predated—by some considerable distance in time—in black-Atlantic internationalism. In turn, this equips us to approach the contributions of writers like Chinua Achebe and Wole Soyinka as something more interesting than the cliché that they rehabilitate some wounded African self in order to facilitate modernization. If literature by African American, Caribbean, and black British authors is diasporic in the primary historical sense, African letters might profitably be construed as diasporic because of its epistemic pedigree in black Atlanticism. In the preceding section, we came upon Jonathan Arac's suggestion that current Anglo-American criticism might want to learn the arts of diaspora. My claim is that the best of African writing from the nineteenth century on can with benefit be read as one recombinant instance of the arts of diaspora.

Of course, examples of massive group migrations within the continent of Africa are not on the same scale as the Jewish diaspora, the Middle Passage, and other cases such as James Clifford sketches in "Diasporas."[16] My contention that African letters in the European languages should be read as a case of the arts of diaspora is not in this established sense of coerced or voluntary group migrations. Rather, it is in the sense in which Martinican poet Édouard Glissant formulates the distinctiveness of Caribbean discourse in modernity. In his much referenced theory of détour set out in *Le Discours Antillais*, Glissant argued that black writers and thinkers had to use Africa as detour in order to get a handle on the specificity of the black diasporic experience. For Glissant, détour (as opposed to retour/return) is what displaced or marginalized cultures engage in as a way of understanding their historical situation and expressing themselves in idioms that, though marginalized, have a generalizable inner logic. This inner logic is a longing for a return to the point of encounter, the moment of the historical event, what Glissant calls *Relation*. Return in Glissant's theory is not a return to some phantasmatic origin (as in "back to Africa") but rather, a return to the historical entanglements that made the New World possible. Glissant draws on fellow Martinicans Césaire and Fanon as exemplars of the dynamic he is theorizing. According to Glissant, Fanon the revolutionary and Césaire the poet of negritude both illustrate a possibility that could be shared if properly identified: "The poetic word of Césaire, the political act of Fanon, led us *somewhere*, authorizing by diversion (*détour*) the necessary return to the point where our problems lay in wait for us" (*Caribbean Discourse*, 25). Glissant formulates his notion of detour as follows: "We must return to the point from which we started. Diversion [*le Détour*] is not a useful ploy unless it is nourished by reversion [*le Retour*]: not a return to the longing for origins, to some immutable state of Being, but a return to the point of entanglement, from which we were forcefully turned away; that is where we must ultimately put to work the forces of creolization [*les composantes de la Relation*], or perish" (26).[17]

As Christopher Miller has argued, Glissant's concept of detour allows him to reject any nostalgia for origins or singular essentialized identity. Glissant anchors his concept in history and present aspirations; its vision is of a present defined by Relation, shared by a convocation of the descendants of oppressors and oppressed alike. Miller concludes that "return with a little r is thus for Glissant a nondelusional, nonromantic act of consciousness *and that return and detour need each other*" (341). African thinkers and writers were also engaged in a version of detour in Glissant's sense, although this discursive agonism is too often misrecognized as rehabilitation of a phantasmatic African authenticity. Posed differently, what is to be found in Cheikh Hamidou Kane, Senghor, Achebe, Soyinka, or Ngugi—to cite the big men of African literature—is not pristine Africa but a point of entanglement, one that is shared with the Western world. The Africa of African letters is a construct of language and desire, the detour that allowed the pioneering generations of African westernized elite to explain themselves to themselves and the world. Glissant's concept thus equips us to go beyond traditional idealist criticism as well as Eurocentric emplotment of literary and social history. In the 1980s, Jürgen Habermas rejects poststructuralist and Adorno's critiques of Enlightenment rationalism by arguing for a reorientation of thinking in the light of historical evidence. He is not persuaded by Derridian emphasis on aporia or Adorno's fixation on the moment of negativity in the dialectic of thought. As Habermas puts his complaint in *The Philosophical Discourse of Modernity*, "anyone who abides in a paradox . . . is not just taking up an aporetic position; one can only hold that place if one makes it at least minimally plausible that there is *no way out*. Even the retreat from an aporetic situation has to be barred, otherwise there is a way out—the way back" (128). In my terms, "the way back" is not to an eighteenth century that has been abstracted away from its constitutive exclusions but to that era as a point of entanglement in Glissant's sense. At the bloody sites of this entanglement, secular enlightenment shows itself to be in coeval time with Christian evangelism, New World chattel slavery with Africa's precolonial conquest states, the making of the black diaspora with Africa's colonial subjugation.

This reconstellation of Glissant's concept of detour to apprehend African letters equips us to address the relative absence of continental African contributions when such discourses as Pan-Africanism and black Atlanticism are discussed. Among others, Laura Chrisman has pointed to this absence as one of the weaknesses in Gilroy's theorization of the black Atlantic. Edwards's *The Practice of Diaspora* remedies Gilroy's relative neglect of Africa and does so without reconstituting an essentialized "black identity." His concept of *décalage* recasts Senghor against the grain of the latter's modernist primitivism and allows him to explore black internationalism in the interwar years as material practice, as articulation of "difference within unity." In Edwards's sense, "*décalage* is the kernel of precisely that which cannot be transferred or exchanged, the received biases that refuse to pass over when one crosses the water. It is a changing core of difference; it is the work of 'differences within unity,' an unidentifiable point that is incessantly touched and fingered and pressed" (14).

Where Edwards stresses discontinuity as one way of charting a shared historical moment in the black-Atlantic archive, Kenneth W. Warren's *What Was African American Literature?* argues against mystifying that archive. For him, such mystification may in fact sideline historical unfolding even while claiming to be attentive to the past. Warren's provocative argument is directed at the institutional construction of African American literary history within the broader field of American Studies. But he offers a suggestive avenue of critique, one that I should like here to press. Warren argues that African American literature is a historical achievement whose conditions of production have been transformed and whose possibilities at the moment of globalization should no longer be uncritically tied to the past of slavery, Jim Crow, and racist state policy. For him, "with the legal demise of Jim Crow, the coherence of African American literature has been correspondingly, if sometimes imperceptibly, eroded as well" (2). Warren suggests that contemporary discourses of diaspora and black Atlanticism routinely invoke the ghost of the past in order to lay claim to a vanguard role in the social-political demands of the present. In this regard, he recalls Paul Gilroy's work and Ian Baucom's *Spectres of the Atlantic: Finance Capital, Slavery, and the Philosophy of History*. Warren recalls Walter Benjamin's "Theses on the Philosophy of History," specifically thesis VI, in which he describes history as evanescent images from the past flashing up at moments of social stress in the present. For Warren, Benjamin's image of history is "especially attractive" but could also be tricky, positing as it does "a dynamic relation between past and present that almost obliterates history, thereby casting the present-day historian in the role of potential hero, or even freedom fighter, on behalf of a past that almost magically becomes our contemporary in terms of what it needs or demands from us" (82).

Warren criticizes the tendency to invoke history primarily in ritualized rejection of its injustices. For him, this might be a covert way of making the intellectual—the literary critic or theorist—the hero in the battle of books in the academic marketplace. He writes:

> The recent recourse to history in discussions of African American life and culture has tended to make discrete periodizations beside the point, and to attach a taint of injustice to periodization itself, which by its very definition has to be concerned as much with discontinuity as continuity and has to insist on some distinction between past and present. Accordingly, to proclaim the "was-ness" of something so recent as the last century of African American literary production carries with it an almost sinister cast. Nonetheless, at the risk of courting the sinister, it is my contention here that to understand both past and present we have to put the past behind us. (84)

The claim here is that we learn most from the past by putting it "behind us"—that is, by not *conflating* it with the present. But at the same time, we cannot have a proper understanding if we don't *relate* the past to the present. The challenge is recognizing the pastness of the past in order, precisely, to grasp its present-ness as relational. Understood this way, the past is a case of otherness. The logic of Warren's claim would then be that we respect the otherness of the past by distinguishing it from our present, even as we recognize its relational proximity to us as immanent and constitutive.

These are complex issues that I cannot engage in any depth here.[18] However, I should like to touch on the issues of categorization and periodization that Warren raises. His argument is a bold way of negotiating the pull of national literature ("American literature") on the one hand and ethnic or cultural particularity (African American, Latino American, etc.) on the other hand. Warren sometimes overstates the case in that he seems to presuppose that contemporary writing by people designated black within the United States needs to be either American literature or African American literature and cannot be both at once. In my view, this does not have to be the case. As markers of literary traditions, the entanglement of "American literature" and "African American literature" conveys their relationality and contingency. In terms of conceptualization and categorization, therefore, each can be thought of as distinct, even as both are contingent, congruent, and mutually incomplete in their relational alignment. Precisely because literary histories—whether national, ethnonational, or continental-hemispheric—are always institutionally constructed, the categories of identification generated by them can be multiple, interlayered, and in productive tension.

Literary histories are also, of course, products of institutional twists and turns and, ultimately, instruments of pedagogy. Warren's account is best appreciated as a periodizing argument for American literature as well as African American literature. He articulates a vision of the possibility of a candidly self-scrutinizing community, based on pragmatic social commitments rather than easy self-congratulation. In this sense, *What Was African American Literature?* is most compelling when approached from the perspective of concrete classroom goals in particular and the production of American subjects more broadly. In a passage I quoted earlier, Warren states, "to understand both past and present we have to put the past behind us" (84). The "we" in this formulation would at the least include the community of academics, part of whose professional obligation is to interpellate students for future careers of social responsibility. Unlike the unmarked reader of formalism or the stable class subject of Eurocentric Marxism, the reader here is multiply positioned: formed in relation to race, nation, ethnicity, gender, and sex. Adapting from Ernesto Laclau's theory of radical democracy, the reader is agential subject insofar as she/he occupies multiple yet determinate subject positions. For Laclau, we are always multiply positioned in social interactions. Identity is best understood as a rupture of becoming: it is not an unchanging referent, a static repository of meaning but an articulation. Laclau's understanding of democratic politics "wholly accepts the plural and fragmented nature of contemporary societies but, instead of remaining in this particularistic moment, it tries to inscribe this plurality in equivalential logics which make possible the construction of new public spheres" (*Emancipation(s)*, 65). In the narrative terms that make theory most productive, we could say that my particularity (as, say, black, male, heterosexual, middle class) holds no intrinsic meaning, except within this or that social context where some collectivity strives to accomplish a social good. Such collectivity may involve one or more of the subject positions we identify as black, male, heterosexual, middle class, and so forth. To grant this much is to grant that each of these markers of identity cannot be closed in upon itself, that is to say, intrinsically meaningful and agential. The predication of each as subject position can acquire social agency only on the condition of openness to some other identities and subject positions. As Laclau puts it,

> Difference and particularisms are the necessary starting point, but out of it, it is possible to open the way to a relative universalization of values which can be the basis for a popular hegemony. This universalization and its open character certainly condemns all identity to an unavoidable hybridization, but hybridization does not necessarily mean decline through the loss of identity: it can also mean empowering existing identities though the opening of new possibilities. Only a conservative identity, closed on itself, could experience hybridization as a loss. But this democratico-hegemonic possibility has to recognize the constitutive contextualized/decontextualized terrain of its constitution and take full advantage of the political possibilities that this undecidability opens. (65)

A recent example among many others: the coalition that Barack Obama put together to win reelection in November 2012 is one articulation of political linkages toward a possible liberal hegemony: college-educated whites, people of color, suburban middle-class women, the millennial generation, and so forth. These different groups articulated a specific political statement as a layered bloc of collectivities. In a different context—let us say, on the question of abortion; lesbian, gay, bisexual, transgender, and queer (LGBTQ) rights; immigration laws; or affirmative action—the same groups will not necessarily constitute an agential bloc or pursue congruent agendas. At the heart of Warren's intervention is a vision of the proper role of academics in the age of neoliberalism and self-righteous American imperialism. I want to direct attention, then, to one such role: namely, the formation of students as citizens of a state and the world. African American authors write at once as African American and American, even as they write multiple other identities or anti-identity. Following Laclau's account of multiple subject position, it is when every discrete subject position is open to dislocation by other discrete positions that alliances become possible and collectivities can be formed in unforeseen and unpredictable ways. Along these lines, the categories "American literature" and "African American literature" can interlayer and reconstellate each other in enabling ways, even as each is positively ruptured and reconfigured on the grounds of gender and sexuality studies, hemispheric studies, or diasporic studies, to name just a few.

What connection may we draw between Warren's contribution and my own concerns in this study? The opening sentences of *What Was African American Literature?* transcode historical suffering through a casual metaphor of purposive labor: "Historically speaking, the collective enterprise we now know as African American or black literature is of rather recent vintage. In fact, the wine may be newer than generally acknowledged, which is to say that it was neither pressed on the African continent nor bottled during the slave era" (1). I have been arguing that no such wine press exists, if by that we mean a preconstituted sensibility based on racial community—in the manner, for example—of Senghorian negritude or Nkrumah's "African personality." Stuart Hall puts the matter in the following way: "The original 'Africa' is no longer there. It too has been transformed. History is, in this sense, irreversible. We must not collude with the West which, precisely, normalizes and appropriates Africa by freezing it into some timeless zone of the primitive, unchanging past. Africa must at last be reckoned with by Caribbean people, but it cannot in any simple sense be merely recovered" ("Cultural Identity and Diaspora," 117). To restate what should by now be a truism: the very category Africa is sign of textual construction and phenomenological entanglement. Like all constructions, it has been deployed to serve many purposes, some of them unhelpful or noxious. Precisely for that reason, it can be resignified to mean differently in specific discursive contexts. Like the Caribbean and black British artists about whom Hall was writing, African writers are themselves engaged in "reckoning" with Africa as signifier of many things, some of which would include geography, reconfigured identities, and poetic abstraction. I call this reckoning the black-Atlantic detour because it is a cognitive exertion they share with New World blacks, albeit from a different vantage point, that of having been acculturated in settings on the continent itself.

To extend this logic to the domain of literary production and reception, a given text constitutes its audiences at multiple levels depending on context. A play by Soyinka, for instance, can be for one group of readers (what in the language of Stanley Fish we might call an interpretive community) a "Yoruba" text, but in another context, the same play functions as a "Nigerian" text, and yet for another context, an African, a postcolonial, or a "world literature" text. In this way, the same text elicits complex permutations of identification, depending on the context of interpellation within which it conscripts and is conscripted. Inducements for identification, the cultural work of textual representations, are always multivalent and cannot be preempted or circumscribed except through interpretive imposition. For the different interpellative moments to escape epistemic violence, therefore, each should thematize the immanence of other possible permutations, the proximate demand of the other. The interplay of race, nation, and tribe in African literature challenges us to take identity seriously as a problem for literary studies. The question is: how might literary globalism make thinkable a collectivity of readers, defined by a sense of identity that is complexly layered, grounded and forward looking, not static or restorative? With this question, we are on the terrain of desire, pedagogical praxis, and uncertain possibility. And it is a good place to be.

Reader on the Ground

In *Death of a Discipline*, Gayatri Spivak's critique of globalization and Anglocentric "world literature" opens out to the kind of literary globalism I find persuasive. Spivak reads Jacques Derrida's elucidation of the paradoxes of friendship to work out a notion of collectivity and the intellectual's limited role in working toward it. She identifies the task of comparative literary studies in the age of postcoloniality to reside in commitment to a "future anterior, where one promises no future present but attends upon what will have happened as a result of one's work . . ." (*Death of a Discipline*, 29). In the aftermath of the cold war, and during the first phase of postcolonial theory to which her work was a foundational contributing voice, the social-scientific disciplines—especially political science and anthropology—were on the defensive. Humanities scholars criticized social scientists on ethical grounds for their complicity with imperialism and cold war politics. At this moment, Spivak urges that to properly learn from postcoloniality, literary studies should build interdisciplinary alliances with area studies scholarship and American Ethnic Studies. Such interdisciplinary exploration equips literary globalism to move beyond restrictive Eurocentric understandings of literature and history. As she puts it, the challenge is to work to prepare the ground for potential subjects to come, or what she calls readers of the future: "I ask us to imagine ourselves outside the top-heavy German/Romance Comparative Literature, scrabbling for control, rationalizing sanctioned ignorance, pointing at European intellectual enclaves already present in earlier colonial formations as 'history,' toward those readers of the future. . . . It is with careful accounting for time lags that effective collectivities are formed" (*Death of a Discipline*, 31). This subject-to-come should be understood as multiply placed and constitutively split, as Laclau has taught us. Intellectual work can provide for those readers of the future, who will have been our students on the ground, possible vistas on to the world that controverts the prosaics of prescripted identities. In this way, we teach students to think their way out of and beyond parochialisms, not simply accept and mimic them for lack of alternatives. Spivak writes, "All around us is the clamor for the rational destruction of the figure, the demand for not clarity but immediate comprehensibility by the ideological average. . . . Anyone who believes that a literary education should still be sponsored by universities must allow that one must learn to read. And to learn to read is to learn to dis-figure the undecidable figure into a responsible literality, again and again" (71–72).

Spivak's *Death of a Discipline* looks forward to a reader of the future, but that reader is most appropriately theorized as reader on the ground because the future is always too soon upon us. As Spivak realizes only too well, literary studies cannot enable the building of rural clinics and the access roads to them. But it can conscript the agency of the literary to accomplish something else: namely, equip social agents to conceive the possibility of change. More concretely, we can as teachers equip students to go out into the world thinking poetically, critically, and deliberately, even as they go into the trenches to build clinics and access roads, whether as nongovernmental organization workers or as doctors and engineers. This is a less tangible, more humble project but an important one nonetheless. This book recalls previous transnational moments, the missionary moments identified in the chapters to follow, as iterations of what we now recognize as the ethic of literary globalism. To paraphrase Spivak, each of the black diasporic and African intellectuals I examine have been ministering, through their writings, to what will have happened as a result of the writing. Speaking in terms of collectivity, our students can become one significant dimension of what will have happened. In this commitment, things can never be too early or too late.

There is one final antecedent example of futurity, and it is on this that I should like to close this chapter. In his essay on C. L. R. James's *Beyond a Boundary*, Kenneth Surin suggests that James's achievement exceeds autobiography or the Hegelian materialist mode that otherwise governs his thinking.[19] For Surin, *Beyond a Boundary* anticipates a political future through its analytical motions and ethical desire. Surin characterizes the vision exhibited in James's book in terms of the "future anterior" in the sense articulated in Jacques Lacan's "The Function and Field of Speech and Language in Psychoanalysis." For Surin, "James always seemed, in many very practical ways, to want another kind of politics—a politics beyond 'actually existing' socialism, a politics beyond that of an independent Trinidad under Eric Williams, a politics of a new kind of Pan-Africanism, and so on. A politics that is yet to come, the politics of new and different imaginative capacities. . . . *Beyond a Boundary* is a cartography of singularities and multiple becomings which move restlessly, in the mode of a 'future anterior,' into the practical and conceptual 'spaces' of this politics that is yet to come" (201). Of course, James is better known for dealing with the grand historical questions of socialist revolution and literature writ large (i.e., literature the Romantic and Victorian way). In chapter 3, I will discuss his less well-known account of Kwame Nkrumah's rise and fall. There, I will suggest that a robust pedagogical path reveals itself in the interstices of his rhetoric of modernization. That path is the revisiting and reconstitution of just what the signifier Africa might be made to mean in the present of "failed states" right alongside the ethic of literary globalism. At this point, I only emphasize that the sense of futurity Surin identifies in *Beyond a Boundary* extends to James's oeuvre as a whole. James imagined the future as at once audience and consequence of his address. In this, he is very much like the black whitemen before him and the idealistic Pan-Africanists of his generation. In his preface to the first edition of *Black Jacobins*, James wrote:

> The violent conflicts of our age enable our practiced vision to see into the very bones of previous revolutions more easily than heretofore. Yet for that very reason it is impossible to recollect historical emotions in that tranquility which a great English writer, too narrowly, associated with poetry alone. . . . Tranquility today is either innate (the philistine) or to be acquired by a deliberate doping of the personality. It was in the stillness of a seaside suburb that could be heard most clearly and insistently the booming of Franco's heavy artillery, the rattle of Stalin's firing squads and the fierce shrill turmoil of the revolutionary movement striving for clarity and influence. (xi)

James dates the sense of urgency to the eve of World War II and the Pan-Africanist ferment concurrent with that world-historical eruption. Students of James will recall that he ends *Black Jacobins* by connecting the lessons of the Haitian revolution with the Pan-Africanist yearnings of his own moment in the 1930s. Today, we can no longer speak of things like "the great revolutionary movement"—at least, not with such poetic solicitude as James was able to muster. Yet, if we set aside his assumption of a singular revolutionary movement and destination, James could have been writing about any number of violent upheavals in the last half century. Replace the names fascism and Stalinism with any number of belligerent isms in our globalized age, and this passage remains as fresh as when James penned it in the middle of the twentieth century.

Whether his idealism at the moment of his writing—what he calls "the fever and the fret" (xi)—has been proven wrong by history may legitimately be debated. However, the results of the assessment are not relevant to my point here. My claim is that James is an *event* in the sense that Surin proposes. His work expresses critical thinking toward a politics to come—"*becomings other*" that are still in process and only as such. James and the other diasporic and African intellectuals in the chapters to follow are events that opened up spaces for imagining a possible future, "striving for clarity and influence" (xi). From our vantage point more than a half century later, the future for which James worked includes our current global challenges. As critical thinker and writer, James is generative for many reasons, not least of which is his habit for the resonant line of prose. The permanent achievement of writing like *Black Jacobins* is precisely the interpellation of Spivak's readers of the future, an achievement that is tangible in the present, yet on the move as the future moves. This book is one attempt to work toward that future by revisiting the epistemological event that James and his generation articulated. In the chapters to follow, I claim the role of the pacifist foot soldier in pursuit of James's future-anterior subjects: readers on the ground in classrooms devoted to postcoloniality or African literature. And so, my engagements in the chapters to follow consider the writers as events and their texts as encodings of this eventness.

Notes

1. See Jonathan Arac, *Critical Genealogies*; Paul de Man, *Blindness and Insight*, 20–35 and *The Resistance to Theory*, 3–20; Fredric Jameson, *The Political Unconscious*; and Edward Said, *The World, the Text, and the Critic*.

2. As examples, we may think of the following: the vernacular theory in African American Studies associated with Henry Louis Gates Jr. and Houston Baker; the work in feminist Ethnic Studies of Gloria Anzaldúa, Norma Alarcón, and Trinh Minh-ha; and in queer theory the contributions of Eve Sedgwick, Lee Edelman, and Judith Butler.

3. In the last decade or so, the debates about literary globalism and world literature have proliferated such that it is impossible to give anything like a comprehensive list. But a number of significant critics and theorists may be isolated whose work contains fruitful perspectives. For work that advances the concept of "world literature" following Goethe's lead with, of course, qualifications to bring the idealism up to date with our postcolonial present, see Pascale Casanova, David Damrosch, and Franco Moretti. For work that is less concerned with retooling the "world literature" aspect but instead understands literary globalism as postcolonial worldliness, see Emily Apter, Wai Chee Dimock, and Bruce Robbins. Later in this chapter, I take up the contributions of a number of other scholars who are in productive dialogue with "world literature" and literary globalism: specifically, Jonathan Arac, Peter Hitchcock, and Gayatri Spivak.

4. The sense of worlding I deploy here, which will be operational in my investigations in this book, is not the Heideggerian concept in its becalmed phenomenological stasis but Gayatri Spivak's transcoded materialist version. For an elaboration of Spivak's notion of worlding, see *A Critique of Postcolonial Reason*, especially 198–311, 423–31.

5. V. Y. Mudimbe is writing, in *The Idea of Africa*, about the constitution of academic anthropological knowledge about the continent and its peoples. Here are his words: "I understand truth as a derivative abstraction, as a sign and a tension. Simultaneously uniting and separating conflictual objectives of systems constituted on the basis of different axioms and paradigms, truth is neither pure idea nor a simple objective" (39).

6. See, for example, Stanley Corngold, Rainer Nägele, M. H. Abrams, and John Guillory.

7. It is helpful to clarify my use of the terms *postcolonial studies*, *postcolonial theory*, and *postcoloniality*. So far, I have been using them interchangeably, but it is the concept of postcoloniality that most immediately speaks to my argument. In line with Stuart Hall's perspective, I use *postcoloniality* to refer to postcolonial periodization in social history as well as in the humanistic disciplines. My particular interest is in the implications of what Hall calls renarrativization of social history for literary and cultural criticism.

8. This is, of course, a caricature of postcolonial theory as it took shape in the 1980s. The caricature is sometimes willful but more often based on inadequate understanding of what was really going on. Prominent voices in the field were actually arguing *against* Manichean constructions of the past or of collective belonging. Generally poststructuralist in orientation, scholars like Homi Bhabha, R. Radhakrishnan, Abdul JanMohamed, Stephen Slemon, and

Robert J. C. Young rejected identitarian binarisms, which they saw as dominant in nationalist discourses or nation-centered approaches to literature. Indeed, this is why other critics saw the theory as an offshoot of poststructuralism, part of the hegemonic mainstream rather than a path to thinking beyond it (see George, *Relocating Agency*). For critics of the poststructuralist, antinationalist vector of postcolonial theory, see Timothy Brennan, Laura Chrisman, Arif Dirlik, Neil Lazarus, and Epifanio San Juan Jr. For recent discussions about the obsolescence or otherwise of postcolonial studies, see "Editor's Column: The End of Postcolonial Theory?" *PMLA* 122, no. 3 (2007): 1–32; Chakrabarty, "Postcolonial Studies and the Challenge of Climate Change"; Gandhi; George, "Postcolonial Contraventions"; Mbembe, "Provincializing France?"; and Young.

9. See Sartre, 291–330.

10. "Against Theory" originally appeared in *Critical Inquiry* 8, no. 4 (1982). It is reprinted, together with critical responses as well as the authors' rejoinders to the responses in Mitchell, *Against Theory*.

11. Needless to say, no such thing as "Nigeria" existed as a formal juridical state until the British amalgamation of three formerly separate administrative protectorates and the colony of Lagos in 1914.

12. See Moretti, *Graphs, Maps, Trees* and *Distant Reading*.

13. See Bakhtin, 3–40. In the introduction, Holquist describes the innovativeness of Bakhtin's perspective on the category of the novel as follows: "'novel' is the name Bakhtin gives to whatever force is at work within a given literary system to reveal the limits, the artificial constraints of that system. Literary systems are comprised of canons, and 'novelization' is fundamentally anticanonical. It will not permit generic monologue. Always it will insist on the dialogue between what a given system will admit as literature and those texts that are otherwise excluded from such a definition of literature. What is more conventionally thought of as the novel is simply the most complex and distilled expression of this impulse" (Bakhtin, xxxi).

14. Nnamdi Azikiwe, "Realities of African Unity"; Jomo Kenyatta, "African Socialism and African Unity"; and Julius K. Nyerere, "The Nature and Requirements of African Unity." See *African Forum. A Quarterly Journal of African Affairs* 1, no. 1 (1965).

15. A somber photographic record of the gathering appears on the back pages of the special issue of *Presence Africaine* devoted to presentations at the conference, captioned: "The delegates at the First Conference of Negro Writers and Artists." In this photograph, it is possible to read a range of self-exhibitions, as though the faces and postures are silently giving body to the words by and about some of the more canonical names. We may read, for instance, a tantalizing range from the brooding intensity of Fanon, who stands third row, fourth from the left, and Wright on the second row, fourth from the right, to the easy charm of statesmen Senghor (front row, fourth from the right) and Césaire (second row, fourth from the left). If this is no more than a figment of my own imagination as they say, it is because the brooders and the statesmen made it possible to be so imagined, half a century after their exertions. See *Presence Africaine* 8–9 (June–November, 1956).

16. See Clifford. See also Tölölyan.

17. See Glissant, 36. The English translation from which I have quoted is *Caribbean Discourse: Selected Essays*, translated by J. Michael Dash.

18. For a sampling of critical responses to Kenneth Warren's book from diverse perspectives, along with the author's reply to his critics, see the section titled "Theories and Methodologies. What Was African American Literature?" *PMLA* 128, no. 2.

19. See Surin.

2   Mission Tide: Bishop S. A. Crowther and the "Black Whitemen"

THE EXPANSION OF European mercantile interests into sub-Saharan Africa from about the eighteenth century was accompanied by the spread of Christianity and Western letters. In the last five decades, Africanist scholars in the humanities and social sciences have investigated the implications of the dual advance of mercantile and industrial capitalism side by side with Christian missionary activity in Africa.[1] These studies have shown connections between processes of Christian conversion, Western education, and the formation of nation-states and the intellectual elite in modern Africa. Like all contexts of religious conversion or what presents itself as such, the engagement with Christianity and Western literacy by Africans inevitably comes with complications of ways of knowing, cultural identity, and social alignments. Here, religious conversion becomes indissociable from political conversion or, at the least, rupture; the former acquires meaning and becomes real within the ferment of the latter and vice versa. In the initial stages of the missionary enterprise in West Africa, British, French, and German missionaries were at the vanguard.[2] However, a class of Westernized blacks emerged as an aftermath of the Atlantic slave trade and its abolition by England in 1807. Variously called "native agents" in British writing about missionary work in Africa, or "black whitemen" among the indigenous Africans among whom they worked, this class played a significant role in the incursions of Christianity on the western coast of the continent.

The story of the emergence of the black whitemen is, of course, also the story of the transatlantic slave trade and the politics of its abolition. The American colony of Liberia was founded by emancipated slaves from the United States in 1821 and became independent in 1847, while the British colony of Freetown in Sierra Leone was founded by antislavery philanthropists in 1787 (Fyfe; July; Sanneh). The colony soon became home to maroons from the West Indies, Nova Scotian blacks, and Africans liberated by British ships that patrolled the Atlantic Ocean to intercept and confiscate slavers not protected by treaty. Many of the so-called black whitemen were thus emancipated slaves or their descendants from the New World and Liberia. Others were the enslaved Africans who were "liberated" from slave ships in the Atlantic Ocean by antislavery squadrons. After their liberation, which was also their recapture, they were trained in Sierra Leone and then sent to work in (or, on their own initiative, emigrated to) the interior of West Africa as traders, artisans, catechists, or teachers. In the Yoruba language spoken in the southwestern part of Nigeria, the returnees from Sierra Leone are referred to collectively as *Sàró*, and the black Brazilian returnees as the *Àgùdà*. Through the late nineteenth and early twentieth centuries, these returnees and their descendants generally considered themselves part of a transatlantic "Negro" collective and formed the political elite in what was to become Nigeria. As they saw it, their mission linked them to blacks in the Americas and the wider world.[3]

If the African religious conversion was to generate unprecedented complications in the traditional society as a whole, the ambivalent location of the black whitemen who aided the missionary organizations—the native African or foreign-born figures from the New World—adds an entire new layer to the complications of cultural imperialism and religious conversion. Over the years, historians have discussed this process, demonstrating its roots in a complex interplay of trends in Western Europe, the Americas, and black Africa.[4] If we turn from the academic field of history to that of literary studies, the situation is very different. In Anglophone postcolonial literatures scholars have examined the implications of British colonialism for our understanding of the effects of colonial encounters on identities, epistemic orders, and linguistic representations. And in black diasporic studies, scholars have shown various ways in which both colonizer and colonized, black and white, are impacted by historic moments such as the slave trade or the nineteenth-century scramble for Africa. Notwithstanding these developments in black-Atlantic and postcolonial studies, the case of blacks who served missionary organizations in Africa remains understudied. Eighteenth-century figures (e.g., Phyllis Wheatley, Olaudah Equiano, Quobna Cuguano) and twentieth-century black internationalists (e.g., Léopold Sédar Senghor, Frantz Fanon, Aimé Césaire, W. E. B. Du Bois, C. L. R. James, Richard Wright) have extensively been written about, but the black whitemen of Anglophone Africa remain unknown in literary and cultural criticism. Even in the disciplinary enclave of African literary studies, these figures have received very little scholarly attention, in contrast to the canonical twentieth-century writers—that is to say, the Achebes, the Soyinkas, and the Ngugis.[5]

My concern in this chapter is to make up for this neglect. I aim to do so by demonstrating what we stand to gain from subjecting the words of a thinker such as Samuel Ajayi Crowther to the labor of reading and critique. The black missionaries and their texts can teach us much about the text of Africa, the contingencies of history, and the vagaries of desire—social and individual. As black subjects who participated in the epistemic, cultural, and political capture of their racial kin, the black whitemen offer a provocative layer to our appreciation of the ferment of religion, colonialism, and nationhood in black Africa. This chapter concentrates on the writings of Crowther, arguably the most renowned missionary of the nineteenth century with an African background. My discussion concentrates on three main kinds of writings Crowther produced: first, the missionary travelogue, written with a public audience in mind; second, the quarterly field report, written for a limited audience of the Church Missionary Society (CMS) committee on foreign missions; and third, the personal letter, addressed to his English spiritual mentor Henry Venn (1796–1873), scion of the Clapham circle Venns. My claim in this chapter is that Crowther's work not only sheds light on the body of literary texts we read and teach as "African literature," but it also adds a unique inflection to ongoing discussions of issues of diaspora, transnationalism, and globalism.

Playing in the Archive

To set us on our way, let me begin with some thoughts on the place of textual access and recovery in the argument I am developing. The end of the twentieth century and the post–September 11 world ushered in a resurgence of debates about literature and politics, identity and culture, meanings and exclusions. As we saw in the preceding chapter, one version of the debates involves paradigms of world literature and transnationalism. My argument in this book is that key issues raised by these recent paradigms need to be differently nuanced if the work of African writers is to make any meaningful contribution to the discussions—if, that is, Africa is to be more than mere epiphenomenon, whose particularities get subsumed under narrowly Eurocentric temporality and anxieties. At their best, the theorizing of, say, Paul de Man and Fredric Jameson in the first wave of theory, or Giorgio Agamben and Alain Badiou in the second, derives from a historical emplotment, a sense of event and positionality, that *cannot* be shared by the likes of Chinua Achebe, Ngugi wa Thiong'o, or Nuruddin Farah, still less the black whitemen of this chapter. It is at the point that we grant differences in intentionality that we are challenged to account for the social density that calls forth and circumscribes the representer's efforts. This is the point at which we have to encounter concrete as well as epistemic sedimentations from the past. What we stand to gain from our analysis of Crowther, then, is the adventure of a sentient being in time and space, the presentness of the past.

In her classic *Imperial Eyes: Travel Writing and Transculturation* (1992), Mary Louis Pratt has defined what she calls autoethnography or autoethnographic expression to refer to "instances in which colonized subjects undertake to represent themselves in ways that *engage with* the colonizers' own terms. If ethnographic texts are a means by which Europeans represent to themselves their (usually subjugated) others, autoethnographic texts are those the others construct in response to or in dialogue with those metropolitan representations" (7). Crowther's work can indeed be said to belong to this category, but he also exceeds it. On his own self-understanding, Crowther is writing in furtherance of an order of knowledge and a vision that is fundamentally Eurocentric. Crowther is condescending toward traditional African entrenched values, but it is precisely in this wholesale acceptance of a Eurocentric perspective that he complicates European missionary writing.[6] Therein, I want to argue, lies the specificity of the black whitemen: their writings accomplish, despite themselves, what I am calling novelization effect. As I indicated in the first chapter, the notion of novelization effect invokes Mikhail Bakhtin, for whom the term *novel* implies something broader than what we conventionally mean when we refer to a literary-historical genre, as Georg Lukács uses it in *The Theory of the Novel* (1920), Ian Watt in *The Rise of the Novel* (1957), Fredric Jameson in *The Political Unconscious* (1981), or Franco Moretti in *Modern Epic* (1996). Bakhtin reads the novel form in terms of events of novelization that always emerge and perform cultural work at the margins of official discourses. From this perspective, Crowther's textualization of Africa registers what I construe as novelization effects. Governed though he is by familiar missionary ideology, he nonetheless enacts a drama of culture and subject positioning, thereby yielding insights that can productively enrich our analyses of African letters in relation to postcoloniality and globalism.

This approach to Crowther and the black whitemen allows us to locate him within the problematic of postcoloniality and black Atlanticism. In turn, this equips us to discern in his prose the specificity of the signifiers *Africa* and *black*, properly grasped as raced and sexed categories, within literary globalism. In Crowther's writing, the category "African" exists as the other—inherited and actively reproduced—that allows him to demarcate the self. There is an extensive nineteenth-century archive on this African, and Hegel condenses it in a passage such as this:

> Under the heading of substantial objectivity, we must include God, the eternal, justice, nature, and all natural things. When the spirit enters into relations with substantial things such as these, it knows that it is dependent upon them; but it realises at the same time that it is a value in itself in so far as it is capable of such relationships. But the Africans have not yet attained this recognition of the universal; their nature is as yet compressed within itself: and what we call religion, the state, that which exists in and for itself and possesses absolute validity—all this is not yet present to them. The circumstantial reports of the missionaries fully bear this out, and Mohammedanism seems to be the only thing which has brought the negroes at all nearer to culture. (177)[7]

Hegel's magisterial confidence in the truth of missionaries' circumstantial reports is embarrassing, of course. But my purpose in citing this passage has nothing to do with the predictable issue of the bad things people used to say about black people. Indeed, to be endlessly stuck on Hegel's reverie constitutes a disservice to Crowther's legacy. It should by now be completely trite to point to

Hegel's ignorant condescension toward the human beings he deemed to be savages. I point to the passage, then, simply as paradigmatic of an extant archive, inside of which Crowther worked to understand his moment and work toward a future. When therefore we encounter Hegel's reference to the "circumstantial reports of the missionaries," we need, by this point, to be able to say that some of those missionaries were the offspring of those savages, and some of what they wrote demands attention on its own terms. In other words, the savages were doing their own savage things even as Hegel was writing about them, and what they did included giving birth to other savage offspring, some of whom later came to be called black whitemen. Where Bakhtin's concept of novelization speaks to the disruption that the novel form performs on preexisting and concurrent forms, Crowther's texts (like the other writings I study in this and subsequent chapters) are on my reading exerting effects of novelization on received discourses about African savages and their dazed, nonhistorical, being.

According to Foucault in *The Archaeology of Knowledge*:

> The analysis of the archive, then, involves a privileged region: at once close to us, and different from our present existence, it is the border of time that surrounds our presence, which overhangs it, and which indicates it in its otherness; it is that which, outside ourselves, delimits us. The description of the archive deploys its possibilities (and the mastery of its possibilities) on the basis of the very discourses that have just ceased to be ours; its threshold of existence is established by the discontinuity that separates us from that which we can no longer say, and from that which falls outside our discursive practice; it begins with the outside of our own language (*langage*); its locus is the gap between our own discursive practices. In this sense, it is valid for our diagnosis. (130–31)

Foucault's view on the otherness of the archive is useful for my purposes, but it is crucial to set aside the metaphor of diagnosis activated within it. This stance of the diagnostician derives, to be sure, from Foucault's need in *The Archaeology of Knowledge* to signal some distance from structuralism and the ethnology that fed colonial knowledge production. I am not diagnosing Crowther as a contaminated relic of the past, still less an object lesson with which to deride the limitations of the present. My view is that the otherness of the black missionary archive "delimits" a horizon of black yearning in modernity but not from an ungraspable exteriority; rather, its delimitation also interpellates and incriminates. My aim is to recognize the challenge of that incrimination, to look it in the eye and enlist it for interpretive purposes.

As I indicated earlier, this study is not a search for ancestors or nostalgia for origins. But there is a personal aspect to my fascination with Crowther and the black whitemen of Nigeria. I was born and raised in central Lagos Island, where he lived after he became bishop of the Niger. I grew up in the area called

Popo Aguda (Brazilian Quarters), where returnees from Brazil and Cuba settled when they started arriving in the nineteenth century. The recaptives from Sierra Leone were concentrated to the west of Popo Aguda in the neighborhood called Olowogbowo.[7] The site of Crowther's burial used to be the Campos Square Cemetery (Itẹ̀ òkú ígboro) on Ajele Street, until 1971 when the cemetery was moved to Ikoyi in what was then the affluent part of Lagos Island. As a little boy, I attended the Holy Cross Elementary School, about three blocks from Crowther's old burial site. By the time I started elementary school, the Campos Square Cemetery was no longer in use; it had become an open field where children went to play soccer or torment one another. I joined my peers to run around Crowther's burial site, and found myself in one or two planned after-school fights. As a scrawny eight-year-old, I carried a private anxiety that playing with other kids on what used to be a graveyard was a terrible crime. This crime, as I suffered its guilt, was worse than merely disobeying God's injunction not to follow the bad crowd by running around or fighting after school. My crime was far worse: I was rudely stamping on the prostrate bodies of dead people, one of whom was no less a figure than the great Crowther. It is for this childishly powerful reason that my reading of Crowther's archive cannot be from a position of cognitive mastery in the manner of simple ideology critique, where the analyst diagnoses with certitude and control. In this sense, my position cannot simply be the Lévi-Straussean ethnographic or orthodox Marxist eye. As we shall see, more serviceable for me would be the figure of the excitable reader. Beyond my little boy neurosis about childhood transgression and the turbulent repose of the dead, therefore, Crowther's archive invites us to face squarely the dimension of diaspora in African letters. He is an early example of diasporic investment in African letters, in the company of such other black whitemen as Tiyo Soga, Thomas Birch Freeman, Kwegyir Aggrey, Magema Fuze, Charles Reindorf, Samuel Johnson, Aaron Sibthorpe, and Sol T. Plaatje.[8] To repeat: this study is not a search for ancestors or nostalgia for origins. My purpose is to argue against such nostalgia.

The significance of a broad black-Atlantic approach can be illustrated if we consider J. D. Y. Peel's important book *Religious Encounter and the Making of the Yoruba* (2000). Writing from the disciplinary perspective of historian and social anthropologist, Peel bases his discussion on unpublished journals and letters of the native missionaries and pastorate of the CMS in Nigeria from the nineteenth century through to the twentieth. His focus is the encounter of the Yoruba of southwestern Nigeria with Christianity. Precisely because the ethnic category "Yoruba" is Peel's object of analysis, it has to be presupposed in his reconstruction. In other words, the social anthropologist's focus on the Yoruba cannot allow a comprehensive engagement of the complexities of nationhood in relation to tribe and ethnicity in contemporary Nigeria. Even less so can Peel take up the interactions of nationhood and tribe on the one hand and race on the other hand. Peel shows that "Yoruba" as a category of culture and identity is datable and that the people so designated are in motion. He also shows that the problems of tribe and nation, self and other, that lie at the heart of the Yoruba wars of the nineteenth century—the era he calls the age of confusion in Yorubaland—are still very much around, complicated now by the challenges of the nation-state. Yet, *Religious Encounter* frames its narrative within the problematic of Europe's encounter with the Yoruba, thereby presupposing the signifier *Yoruba* as a fait accompli of sorts. Peel succeeds magnificently in shifting the locus of analysis and implied agency from Europeans to the native missionaries like Crowther. But his analysis can admit of only two cultures at the moment of encounter: the Europeans and the Yorubas. *Religious Encounter* is therefore not adequately alert to the Pan-African, black-Atlanticist dimensions of the story. My argument is that, because it involves questions of conversion and print culture, the story of the "making of the Yoruba" can be enriched if, in addition to Europe's presence, we bring in local factors (i.e., internal tensions and power struggles), as well as racial slavery and capitalism's power-knowledge nexus.

For Peel, the Yoruba inculturation set in motion by missionary work makes it necessary to speak of the Yoruba as a nation without a state (i.e., Nigeria). Likewise, the cultural nationalism analyzed by the Ibadan school historians J. F. Ade Ajayi and E. A. Ayandele is, on his reading, productively contradictory because it serves nationalist yearning for statehood, even as it consolidates Yoruba ethnicity (Peel, 278–83). Indeed, on Peel's persuasive reading Wole Soyinka's cultural nationalism operates similarly; it reflects the passion of the elite. Much evidence can be marshaled in support of this line of argument, but I have to set it aside for now. Later in chapter 4, I address its implications for the way we read a Yoruba writer such as Soyinka. Here, my point is simply that Peel cannot deploy a pan-ethnic "Nigeria" as object of analysis or "Africa" as locus of interrogation. This is as much a consequence of disciplinary priorities as it is of methodological difference. If we shift the angle of analysis from an anthropological to a literary-critical one, we are better placed to rectify the elision of a specifically black-Atlantic problematic in Peel. Recent work by literary scholars David Attwell and Leon de Kock on the South African Xhosa missionary Reverend Tiyo Soga (1829–71) is relevant here. Working on modern South African literatures, Attwell and de Kock draw from Soga's writings a cluster of issues that are relevant to my purposes.[9] Attwell and de Kock show that Soga was a protonationalist—although they seem to weigh differently the extent and meaning of Soga's nationalism. De Kock shows the ways in which Soga's acquiescence to Eurocentric understanding of the place of Africa is accompanied by a critique—sometimes implicit, at other times explicit—of racist denigration of Africans. Attwell is less concerned with identifying Soga as a cultural-nationalist pioneer. He reads Soga in a more conventionally poststructuralist mode. He is more concerned with the contradictions in Soga than the solidity and certitude of discernible positions. I should like to place my discussion of Crowther less on the terrain of whether he is a cultural nationalist avant la lettre than on the question of societal change and the human subjects that make them. In terms of old-fashioned intellectual history, Crowther is located in a direct line of descent with the figures we will consider later from the twentieth century. But my primary concern is less ambitious than intellectual history and more conceptually perverse. I want to revisit the discursive path from the missionaries to the contemporary era of globalism in order to demonstrate that we are at a distance—politically and epistemologically—from the missionary moment that the black whitemen exhibit. But our moment constitutes in its own way a missionary moment, an iteration of a related logic of turbulence and change. Our positionality as products of and witnesses to globalization places us at a distance from the likes of Crowther but also binds us to them in ways we will benefit from unpacking.

Slave Boy, Test Case, Author

As a young boy of about thirteen, Ajayi, later Bishop Samuel Crowther, was captured from his birthplace, Oshogun, in the midst of the prolonged civil wars that bedeviled southwestern Nigeria through most of the nineteenth century.[10] Sold into slavery, he was purchased and taken on a slave ship bound for the Americas. He was rescued when the ship was intercepted in the Atlantic by a British naval squadron. He was subsequently trained in Sierra Leone and returned to Nigeria as agent of the CMS. Ordained in 1843, he was one of the pioneer CMS ministers who established Anglican stations in western Nigeria and, later, the Niger valley. Along with Rev. Henry Townsend, he founded the Egba mission at Abeokuta in 1846, a year after both men established the first Anglican church in Nigeria at Badagry with Rev. Charles A. Gollmer (Ajayi, *Christian Missions*, 25–52). He became bishop in 1864 and headed the so-called Niger Mission composed entirely of "native" agents. He translated many of the books of the King James Bible into Yoruba and compiled a primer on the grammar of a number of West African languages. He accompanied three British expeditions (1841, 1854, and 1857–59) that opened up the River Niger to foreign trade, Christianization, and colonization. His journal of the 1841 expedition was published with that of the senior missionary on the expedition, Rev. James Frederick Schön, as *Journals of the Rev James Frederick Schön and Mr Samuel Crowther* (1842). He published his journals of the other two expeditions in 1855 and 1859: *Journal of an Expedition Up the Niger and Tshadda Rivers* (1855) and *Gospel on the Banks of the Niger: Journals and Notices of the Native Missionaries Accompanying the Niger Expedition of 1857–59* (1859). Appended to the 1842 publication is a short account of his life that he wrote in 1837 at the request of the CMS.[11]

Crowther worked for the CMS for more than five decades. After his rescue in the Atlantic Ocean, he was transported with others to Freetown where he enrolled at Fourah Bay College, established for the purpose of educating the recaptives and preparing them to work as teachers, catechists, and artisans in the fledgling settlement.[12] Henry Venn, general secretary of the CMS mission and Crowther's mentor, was influenced by the ideas of Sir Thomas Fowell Buxton elaborated in *The African Slave Trade and Its Remedy* (1839). For Buxton, the surest way to end the slave trade is to encourage "legitimate trade" with the tribes in West Africa. Venn was also a firm believer in the concept of native agency; so close was he to Crowther, and so dear to him was the vision of native agency, that his death in 1873 opened the Niger Mission to political pressure and intrigue, which ultimately led to Crowther's fall from grace within the CMS toward the end of his life and career. Venn believed that the best way to spread the gospel in West Africa was to groom native priests who would in time be able to lead an independent church. For him, the future of the Anglican Church in Africa would require the withdrawal of European leadership at some point, so that Africans can take charge. Venn's vision is for future native control of their churches as satellites of the Church of England. Obviously, this is an uncanny prefiguration of what would later become the colonial ideology of indirect rule in the political sphere. In both cases, the idea is that Europeans should plan to leave natives to run their own affairs—church and state—after they've been given necessary tutelage to do so with some measure of competence, as it were.

The work of historians has served to detail the developments that led to Crowther's falling out of favor with the CMS home office in London, where he came to be seen as a weak administrator who could not control his fellow African clergy. He was also accused of being a charlatan for what was deemed his dabbling in trade and politics in the Niger valley area (Ajayi; Ayandele; Loiello). He resigned in August 1890, a year before he died on December 31, 1891. His resignation precipitated a crisis within the Anglican mission in West Africa, leading ultimately to secession from the church led by Crowther's son, Dandeson Crowther. Charges of racism and European arrogance were thrown around, but as Ajayi, Loiello, and others have shown, the specter of race had been lurking all along, even if Crowther and his supporters in London were too idealistic or in denial to recognize it as such. When he became bishop in 1864, his diocese was awkwardly delineated to include the whole of British West Africa where the CMS had a presence, with the exception of the colonies of Lagos, the Gold Coast, and Sierra Leone. The exclusion of Lagos from Crowther's sphere of authority can only be explained on the basis of race because it is the place where Europeans in the area resided or were likely to visit for any extended period. Ajayi (*Missions*, 206) indicates that another reason for the delineation of Crowther's diocese is that "European missionaries had not declared themselves willing to be placed under his jurisdiction." Excluding Lagos from Crowther's bishopric effectively prevents him from having direct pastoral or supervisory authority over European worshippers and missionaries. The result is a comical situation that Ajayi (*Missions*, 206) describes as follows: "Crowther was not bishop over Lagos; nor over Abeokuta or Ibadan, where European missionaries [i.e., Townsend and Hinderer] happened to be; but he was bishop over Otta—midway between Lagos and Abeokuta—where European missionaries happened not to be." In other words, at his consecration as bishop, Crowther was to be spiritual shepherd to only African converts and African clergy.

The foregoing details of historical context are interesting, and much work remains to be done to subject them to the labor of close reading. I focus here on the motions of Crowther's thinking as the archive might be made to yield. The decade and a half between the first major expedition of 1841 and the third of 1857 conveniently delimits the time span of Crowther's writing on which I primarily focus in this chapter. In the first expedition, he was a young catechist under the supervision of Rev. Schön. The second expedition was financed jointly by Liverpool businessman MacGregor Laird and the British government. The third expedition was in part aimed at exploring the feasibility of expanding the influence of the CMS to the eastern Niger region. The 1857 expedition marks the formal beginning of the Niger Mission, and Crowther signals this by leaving Christopher Taylor, a catechist returnee from Freetown, at Onitsha to begin work establishing the station. To appreciate the significance of Crowther for postcolonial and black diasporic thinking in the era of globalism, consider the following: the missionary Crowther and the novelist Chinua Achebe, to cite an obvious name, are two Africans who are separated by a significant distance in time, vision, and genre. But beneath and beyond this distance, both have functioned as paradigmatic "African voices" in their spheres of discursive address and reception. For Crowther, this sphere of address and reception is the Victorian bourgeoisie satirized with gendered smugness in such characters as Mrs. Jellyby of Charles Dickens's *Bleak House*, or Marlow's naïve aunt in Joseph Conrad's *Heart of Darkness*. For Achebe, the audience is us, willy-nilly grounded in the present and responsible to possible futures. What, then, is distinctive in Crowther's location and voice?

Crowther elaborates three lines of thought that also serve as moments of self-construction. At the most obvious level, he speaks in the voice of the universal Christian humanist. But precisely in this role, he emerges as a cultural worker who provides an inchoately articulated version of racial uplift. Crowther and the black whitemen are ambivalent subjects whose search for a "civilized" African voice is, at the moment of their labor, an oxymoron. To the extent that they are seen as sharing racial kinship with Africa, they need to represent "the African" in the register of notional possibility, a potential Christian and "Negro" self. For it is this self—notional and yet preexistent—that missionary rhetoric always promises to deliver. Crowther is especially exemplary because he is a gifted user of language, but also because he lived and worked with the CMS most of his life—from his recapture in 1821 to his death in 1891. For most of the nineteenth century, he was the face of the CMS in West Africa, the embodiment of the notional African in Anglican evangelical circuits. Very precisely, Crowther is the quintessential "slave boy" who got interpellated by the CMS as a social experiment. But within this entrapment, he still managed to impose a trace of authorship and desire that exceeds the circumscription of his employers. Authorship is here to be taken in two senses. Crowther is author in the sense of simultaneously acting in the world while also rendering an account of the acting. He is also author in the sense that he envisioned himself inaugurating a new kind of society and a new subject of the law, divine and secular. As we will see, there is in Crowther a great deal of naïveté and idealism. We can also discern in his prose a reasoned pragmatism that outpaces and complicates simple religious felicity. Crowther *thought* and wrote of his thinking. It is to his credit, and our profit, that his thought imagined a reshaped order.

Because the reshaped order that Crowther imagines is supposed to be Christian/not pagan and yet somehow "modern"/not irrational, it is easy to read him as a version of what has come to be called colonial discourse in cultural criticism. He believed in the cultural inferiority of the native tribes and the moral superiority of Christianity. However, the missionary zeal of his writings compels him to rely on a discourse of universal Christian community, one that is not only desirable but also possible. Conceptually, he is caught between an ontological view of culture and identity and a historical, agential, vision. Crowther's writing persistently shows this oscillation between a racialist and a universalizing grasp of native Africans and their cultures. For him, the tribes he encounters on the banks of the Niger live in spiritual darkness. Bringing civilization and the Christian God to them will encourage them to give up the trade in slaves and turn to legitimate trade with British commercial interests. An important goal of the 1841 expedition was to set up a trading station at Lokoja—the confluence of the Niger and Tshadda (now called Benue) Rivers. After Mungo Park, Hugh Clapperton, Richard and John Lander, and many others, the mystery of the source of the Niger River had finally been laid to rest. Thereafter, the objective was to explore trading opportunities with the interior regions of Africa.

The availability of palm oil in the delta regions of present-day Nigeria particularly interested the expedition parties of 1854 and 1857–59. So, too, did the availability of cotton, sorely needed in industrializing Britain. This interest is signaled, for example, in this passage from a communication to the British trade office by the Manchester Cotton Supply Association: "English capital and skill are waiting to be employed in the establishment of cotton-presses and gins on the banks of the Niger, more particularly at Rabba, provided there be a certainty of the passage through the delta being kept open by the regular and frequent passing of steam vessels" (Crowther, *The Gospel*, vii–viii). Against this background, a crucial role of missionaries like Crowther was to pave the way for the incursion of European capitalist interests into the interior of West Africa. They accompanied the trading and exploratory expeditions on free passage in order to bring the light of the Christian God, alongside what they saw as the material benefits of encroaching capitalism, to the native communities.

As the expeditions arrive at each native community on the banks of the Niger, the ritual was routinely to announce this dual intent. In his journal entry of Sunday, July 23, 1854, Crowther (*Journal of an Expedition*, 21) notes that he made his first pitch for Christianity to one of the local chiefs after they had concluded discussions relating to trade: "When Captain Taylor [leader of the expedition] had done with him, I took the opportunity to speak with him at length on the subject of the Christian religion, Simon Jones interpreting for me. The quickness with which he caught my explanation of the all-sufficient sacrifice of Jesus Christ, the Son of God, for the sin of the world, was gratifying." The sequence whereby talks about trade jostle with talks about Christ and the light of God indicates that Crowther's missionary discourse is at every point along the way in competition with a more mundane, secular concern. Crowther's travel writing also signals this jostling in the way he reflects on the progress of the expedition. He records the changes in the dress patterns or lack thereof of the native tribes between 1841, when the first expedition took place, and 1854, when the second returned to the same tribes. "There is another striking change in the habits of the people themselves. In 1841, very few of them were to be found with any decent articles of clothing; I spied to-day [sic] among a group of about forty people on shore, fifteen who I could distinctly see had English shirts on. This is an evident mark of the advantage of legal trade over that in men" (Crowther, *Journal of an Expedition*, 11).

Crowther's gratitude that natives are putting on "decent articles of clothing" because of mercantilism and the contact with Europe is often burdened by a religious ambivalence toward surface appearances and worldly acquisition. He records with delight and hope that natives are becoming civilized, putting on clothes, and engaging in "legitimate trade" rather than the abjured "trade in men." But he is also wary that their taste for trade and material possession may corrupt them. In *The Gospel on the Banks of the Niger*, his account of a local chief Aje stresses the latter's "covetousness" in language that suggests that primitive culture has the virtue, in its impoverishment, of being protected from the corruption of property: "Aje manifested his covetous propensity to-day beyond description: his conduct on board disgusted everybody, his own attendants not excepted. His familiarity with Europeans from his youth, and the kind indulgence he has ever met with from them as a son of Obi [King], have completely spoiled him. His tenacity in keeping his attention fixed on any object he cast his eye upon, or which entered into his brain to ask for, was beyond conception" (14). In this passage, Crowther's investment in the spiritual state of the native reveals itself in tension with the secular mercantilist project that the expedition simultaneously advances. At moments like this, his discourse shows itself split from within, poised on a recurrent tension between two aspects of the civilizing mission he inherits and propagates.

If there is one absolute sign of the debasement and evil of heathen life in missionary rhetoric, it lies in the practices of human sacrifice and cannibalism attributed to natives. Crowther of course repudiates both practices, but the understated language of the repudiation is intriguing. In *Journal of an Expedition*, he writes of the information he is given in one village that members of a neighboring tribe were cannibals. Let me quote the passage at length:

> We were told that the Mitshis were cannibals and they devour the bodies of their enemies killed in war. But I am inclined to believe that this act of savageness is only practiced in time of war, to terrify their enemies, and is not an habitual thing. When the Ijebus invaded Abeokuta some years ago, and were defeated, some bodies of the Ijebu slain, were cut in pieces by the Egbas, and boiled in large pots, that the Ijebus might have the greater dread of the Egbas. Ikumi, the chief of the Ijaye, performed a like barbarous act when one of his wives was put to death, either for revenge, or to terrify others from committing themselves in like manner. (63)

Crowther suggests the possibility that the case of cannibalism in question might appear to be radically unchristian but is actually a tactic meant to intimidate antagonists. The effect is to shift the affective valence of cannibalism away from the register of ontological or cultural predisposition to one of relational political calculation and misogynistic anxiety. The pressing need Crowther faces is to remind his readers that the native is a fallen mortal like all non-Christians, pushed to the extremities of politics and war. On these terms, cannibalism turns out to testify to the African's membership in, not distance from, the community of fallen man. His figure of the warring native is not quite the familiar one codified in racist discourses about savages and headhunters. Rather, Crowther's version testifies complexly to two civilizational codes: primitive difference and unchristian worldliness. Where the former depends on racial hierarchy, the latter dissolves it or, at the least, logically carries the possibility of its dissolution.

In his biography written in 1837, he had gestured in a similar direction by describing how, like the other slaves rescued in the Atlantic Ocean by a British naval squadron, he was initially afraid that they had been forcibly liberated from their slavers in order to be consumed for food. Describing their reaction to the skinned hogs they saw on the ship that rescued them, Crowther writes:

> It was not long before we six were conveyed into the *Myrmidon*, in which we discovered not any trace of those who were transshipped before us. We soon came to a conclusion of what had become of them, when we saw parts of a hog hanging, the skin of which was white—a thing we never saw before; for a hog was always roasted on fire, to clear it of the hair, in my country; and a number of cannonshots were arranged along the deck. The former we supposed to be the flesh, and the latter the heads of the individuals who had been killed for meat. But we were soon undeceived, by a close examination of the flesh with cloven foot, which resembled that of a hog; and by a cautious approach to the shot, that they were iron. ("The Narrative of Samuel Ajayi Crowther," 313; *Journals of Schön and Crowther*, 382).

By indicating that they initially mistook what they were seeing for dismembered remains of fellow slaves, Crowther suggests the otherness, so to speak, of the practice of cannibalism to his experience, even before his conversion to Christianity. And with the reference to "cannonshots" that he thought were the heads of African slaves who had been cannibalized, he links the *Myrmidon* to its function as a vessel of war. Intentionally or not, Crowther ties an aversion to cannibalism to an aversion to war and its ammunitions in his narrative of 1837. When, about two decades later, he explains dismemberment and cannibalism by invoking the calculations and extremities of war, the rhetorical effect is to depict the native as a fallen mortal whose sin is secular warfare, not racialized debasement. In our era of so-called failed states, crazed warlords, and rampaging tribal mobs, the passage also affords us a glimpse of how Crowther reformulates crisis as moment and phase. Reformulated this way, crisis is to be understood as a conjuncture—datable, thinkable, and passable—precisely because it is open to the play of contingent forces.

As previously mentioned, the 1837 biographical statement was first published as appendix to *Journals of the Rev. James Frederick Schön and Mr Samuel Crowther*. So impressive was Crowther's account to his employers that he was asked to write another one, and the unpublished copy of this new version is now located in the Cape Town Diocesan archives.[13] The first version included in *Journals* is richer in terms of its literary qualities. From the moment of his capture in Oshogun, Crowther writes of being taken toward the coast and the town that became the city of Lagos. Once in Lagos, he is sold to a Portuguese slave trader and put aboard a Brazilian ship, *Esperanza Felix*, that carried a cargo of 187 slaves ("The Narrative of Samuel Ajayi Crowther," 312). The narrative describes the interception by an antislavery squadron consisting of HMS *Myrmidon*, commanded by H. J. Leeke, and HMS *Iphigenia*, captained by Sir Robert Mends.

We may imagine the rescue scene. Crowther writes of the evening they were put on board the slave ship *Esperanza Felix*: "On the very same evening, we were surprised by two English men-of-war; and on the next morning found ourselves in the hands of new conquerors, whom we at first very much dreaded, they being armed with long swords. In the morning, being called up from the hold, we were astonished to find ourselves among two very large men-of-war and several other brigs" (*Journals of Schön and Crowther*, 381; "The Narrative of Samuel Ajayi Crowther," 312). Here are men and women of varying ages, cut off from familiar surroundings, saved from transportation to the New World but without any power to choose their own movements or modes of life thereafter. After the rescue, the Africans are kept waiting, ignorant of the fate that awaited them, while their rescuers decide their fate through a court hearing in Bathurst—a returnee and recaptive settlement in Sierra Leone. These individuals constitute a historical instance of Agamben's "bare life." Their status is sui generis, suspended as they are between the legal nonpersonhood of the slave as property and the yet-nameless status of the "recaptured"—a faceless mass whose historical trace in the archive is as collective *object* of British philanthropy and Christian soul making. From this perspective, Crowther's biographical essay is an account of the loss of one identity (pagan) and the providential taking on of another (Christian, civilized). And so he ends the narrative by announcing his wedding to "a Christian woman," invoking the providence of God, and praying for continued guidance in the propagation of the gospel.

The "Christian woman" Crowther married is Susan Asano Thompson, but he does not name her in the narrative—a strange omission, surely, and also a provocative symptom. Crowther frames his autobiographical account by announcing that he was asked to write it and apologizing that some of its details might be boring. Let me quote the narrative's opening gambit at some length:

> As I think it will be interesting to you to know something of the conduct of Providence in my being brought to this Colony, where I have the happiness to enjoy the privilege of the Gospel, I give you a short account of it; hoping I may be excused if I should prove rather tedious in some particulars.
>
> I suppose some time about the commencement of the year 1821, I was in my native country, enjoying the comforts of father and mother, and the affectionate love of brothers and sisters. From this period I must date the unhappy, but which I am now taught, in other respects, to call blessed day, which I shall never forget in my life. I call it unhappy day, because it was the day in which I was violently turned out of my father's house, and separated from relations; and in which I was made to experience what is called to be in slavery—with regard to its being called blessed, it being the day which Providence had marked out for me to set out on my journey from the land of heathenism, superstition, and vice, to a place where His Gospel is preached. ("The Narrative of Samuel Ajayi Crowther," 298–99; *Journals of Schön and Crowther*, 371–72)

Every time I teach the text, my students comment on the strangeness of this beginning. Students are especially struck, and not a little bit put off, by Crowther's apology for telling the story he was invited to tell. Raised in a discursive context where the faces of Mahatma Gandhi, Martin Luther King Jr., and Nelson Mandela have become totemic and iconic, students find it difficult to relate to his meek announcement that he has been *taught* to understand his enslavement as an "unhappy day" that is also a "blessed day." My response is often to point out that whether we explain the odd passage as a consequence of stylistic clumsiness or sheer cringe-worthy obsequiousness, it is memorable in ways neither Crowther nor his benefactors could have imagined. The commissioned autobiography, which reads paradigmatically like eighteenth-century slave narratives, can productively be grasped in terms of a novelization effect it registers—its dialogical interface with canonical narratives of spiritual growth and consciousness.

Young Crowther, then in his twenties, leaves on the surface of his text a clear understanding of a grotesque official assumption: namely, that the narrative's meaning—as far as his missionary employers are concerned—does not reside in his personal story as mortal being with anxieties and desires. Rather, his account is expected to function as allegory of God's providence and purpose. Whatever else his account does, the one thing it cannot not do is convey his conversion and appreciation of missionary work among African heathens. And yet, in order for the allegory's objectification of Crowther to have affective force, it needs a bedrock of his specific human drama. Posed differently, the abstraction of Crowther as allegory requires the particularity of his singular human experience. And so, serving the public purpose of testifying to the good deeds of the CMS, Crowther cannot but inscribe the pulsing trace of his own narrative of independent subjecthood. By independent subjecthood I mean the unfolding of a specific interiority, separate from the surface layering of official Christian intention. The narrative, then, is an intrusion into the archive's order of sanctioned silencing. It exceeds its own missionary ideological framing and records an official "beginning"— Crowther's conversion—only insofar as this beginning is preceded by a prior collision of desires—that is to say, his bucolic family life and the interruption of war: "For some years, war had been carried on in my Eyo Country, which was always attended with much devastation and bloodshed" ("The Narrative of Samuel Ajayi Crowther," 299; *Journals of Schön and Crowther*, 372).

As already indicated, the 1837 biographical narrative was originally included as appendix to his and Schön's published journal of the 1842 expedition. The historian Philip D. Curtin has written of the varied interest groups and stakeholders—commercial, religious, governmental—in England. The political debates and partisanships of the various interest groups preceded the commencement of the expedition in 1841 and continued beyond its abrupt conclusion in 1842. The reverberations famously influenced Dickens's "Borrioboola-Gha" and his portrayal of Mrs. Jellyby in *Bleak House*. According to Curtin, although it became associated with costly failure and needless loss of lives, the expedition's objectives were not entirely unfulfilled:

> To a point, it [the expedition] all worked according to plan. The ships sailed up the river. The Commissioners signed treaties in the recommended form. The scientists and observers gathered a great deal of new information. Everything else failed in the face of high mortality. Forty-eight of the Europeans died during the first two months in the river, and 55 of the 159 who went along died before the expedition returned to England in 1842. In fact, this mortality was no higher than should have been expected; but it was higher than the planners had anticipated, and the disaster was magnified in the public mind by the false hopes of the enthusiasts. (*The Image of Africa*, 303)

Read alongside Schön's journal, Crowther's account is remarkable for its relatively dispassionate tone in the midst of the demoralization and feverish dejection of the European members of the expedition. Schön understandably dwells on the sickness and death experienced by the European expeditioners, emphasizing their courage and purity of motives. Crowther's account shares Schön's dejection but on a lower key. It may well be that Crowther is simply less expansive with language, but perhaps his terse prose and quiet detachment has a different kind of source.

For Schön, the costly mission of 1842 is a test of the perseverance of the CMS in staying true to its founding vision. The subtending theme is civilized, Christian sacrifice. For Crowther, it is an illumination, a promise of what could be, what ought to be. Instead of being the cause of British withdrawal from its "noble" objectives in the non-Western world, the self-sacrifice of the 1842 dead should be seen as inspiration to do more. Sacrifice in the service of a cause, it would seem, can fully be honored by increased commitment to the cause, keener poeticization of sacrifice. In our twenty-first-century environment of permanent surveillance and remote warfare, the logic here should be familiar. When the expeditionary party arrives at Cape Coast Castle where the eighteenth-century African missionary Philip Quaque (1741–1816) is buried, Crowther notes the testament to Quaque's career on his headstone. In the letter he composed to accompany his journal of the expedition (published as appendix I), he makes a deeply meaningful connection. Quaque was a relative of a middleman for European trading companies in the Gold Coast who was sent to England for education and subsequently ordained as priest of the Church of England in 1765. He returned to the Gold Coast as "Missionary, Catechist, and Schoolmaster to the Negroes on the Gold Coast in Africa" in November of the same year (Carretta and Reese, 9). He was employed by the Society for the Propagation of the Gospel (SPG), an affiliate of the Anglican Church, but the terms also put him in the service of the Company of Merchants Trading to Africa (CMTA). The trading company

CMTA replaced the Royal African Company after the latter's dissolution in 1750, and Quaque served as chaplain to its European employees at Cape Coast Castle. Quaque's salary and upkeep were thus paid for at the conjunction of religion and commerce—the SPG and the CMTA.

Crowther closes his letter to CMS secretaries by summarizing the lesson of the expedition in a way that endorses the view of native agency promulgated by T. F. Buxton. As indicated earlier, native agency refers to the policy, influential before the discovery of antimalaria prophylactics, to deal with the high mortality of European missionaries in tropical Africa by relying on blacks from the New World and native converts who were thought to have natural immunity against malaria. Crowther endorses Buxton's vision by recalling his visit to Quaque's burial site and the monument that adorns it: "When I saw the engraving which I inserted in my Journal at Cape Coast Castle, I could not but think how many African Missionaries, whose constitution is suited to the climate, might now be employed in this part of the Lord's Vineyard. Who the individual was, I know not; neither have I heard anything of him, except from his monument" (*Journals of Schön and Crowther*, 349–50). Crowther's invocation of Quaque as precedent and ancestor thus has a subtext that is crucial to our understanding of the place of the black whitemen. His homage to Quaque's efforts years before is a restatement of the validity of the native agency idea, as though a line of descent leads from the eighteenth-century Quaque to the black whitemen of the nineteenth century.

If in the 1840s the issue was native agency in the promulgation of the gospel, the stakes would become higher a couple of decades later. Under the stewardship of Henry Venn as general secretary, the question now devolved into the possibility of a native church that will ultimately be independent. And so, three decades after his visit to Quaque's monument at Cape Coast Castle, Crowther finds occasion to position his work in terms of a linear continuity with the 1841 expedition. In a November 20, 1874 letter to Schön, Crowther assures him that the sacrifices of 1841 were not in vain:

> Could you visit the Niger once more and see the establishments of mission stations in different parts of the country, as well as mercantile trading factories at Ndoni near Aboh, at Osomara, at Alenso, at Oko, at Onitsha, at Lokoja, at the confluence and at Eggan, to which six steamers and three steam launches are plying to and fro, taking goods up and bringing down produce to Bonny, six, eight, some ten ships during the season, you will not regret your hazardous expedition to the Niger in 1841 as having been in vain and strength spent for naught. (Original Papers CA3/04/461)[14]

Crowther's rhetoric is thus an instance of missionary indoctrination and incipient colonial discourse, but it also carries unique inflections. His specific location as a native missionary and the purpose for which he was writing—namely, the conversion of native Africans—combine to generate in his prose a specific rhetorical configuration. He understands his situation to be that of a black subject called up by history to influence the course of African history. For him, he was saved by providence from the debased state of the native tribes among whom he worked and about whom he wrote. Yet, his rhetoric cannot but motion in directions that complicate the subject-object stasis of this self-apprehension. To gather the support and resources to pursue the experiment with native agency, Crowther and his mentors need to represent the native as being at once fully benighted and potentially savable. The native has to be the other of Christian Europe but also just another mortal: humanity in its fallen state, waiting for the light and largesse of the Christian God. Consequently, Crowther's text cannot but be caught between an ontological account of racial and cultural identity and a historical, agential account.

On the evidence of Crowther's writing, we are empowered to dare to think the following: just as his moment testifies to political crises of various stripes that the missionaries harped on, the various crises in contemporary Africa are signs of social energies—good and bad—that necessarily accompany change. Through his account of kings, chiefs, and conflicts in Yorubaland, Crowther performs an immanent questioning of the traditional systems of power into which he had been born and which he now seeks to transform. In his account of the power-hungry sycophant Aje whom we encountered earlier, we saw one illustration of the traditional power structure that the missionaries' arrival threatened, suppressed, or conscripted. In Crowther's quarterly reports to his employers back in England, he records anxieties and political strategizing by the traditional kings or chiefs with whom he has to interact. For instance, on a missionary visit to Ketu, the king (the "Alaketu of Ketu") welcomes Crowther with an instructive gesture of language: "*awó rí awo.*" As Crowther records the encounter, the king "looking attentively on me said, for he had been acquainted with my name, Crowther, awó rí awo, Crowther, awó rí awo, meaning friends long known by mutual understanding only, have at last seen each other" (MS CA2/031/128). A better translation of this greeting, which is also a stylized threat, is as follows: one cultic initiate meets another. The Yoruba word "*awo*"—which Crowther translates as "friends long known by mutual understanding"—refers to an initiate in a powerful cabal. The cabal could be related to secret cults of religious deities, but it could just as well be a vocational caucus (e.g., the hunter's guild). To force a contemporary translation, a "made man" of HBO's *The Sopranos* would be an *awo* of organized crime, and a member of the president's cabinet would be an *awo* of official matters of state. By welcoming Crowther as fellow *awo*, the Alaketu recognizes the arrival of a new and different order of power, even as he conscripts it by declaring the possibility of alliance or, failing that, antagonism.

Another illustration is provided in MS CA2/031/6, where Crowther narrates the reaction of the populace one frightening night when a crowd of devotees of a local deity known as *Orò* (the bull roarer) parades the town to intimidate the new Christian converts. To protect her family, a recently converted mother instructs her children—who have started attending the mission school—to recite the alphabet. Alone with her children in the middle of the night and afraid of the anger of the *Orò* cult, the woman calls on the power of a new knowledge. Believing that the Latin script encodes some sort of metaphysical incantation, she names the Christian dispensation as a new kind of occult practice. For the mother, the written script is a site of power, concretely and in terms of symbolic capital. That the woman is absolutely correct in her interpretation of the newly emerging dispensation is borne out by the Alaketu's splendid rhetorical conscription: "*awó rí awo.*" Confronted by Crowther and what he represents, the king's greeting asserts—and Crowther records it for CMS secretaries back in London—that one cult of power is being confronted by another on God's vineyard in Africa.

If Crowther is a hands-on person in terms of pragmatism and energy, he is also something of a bookworm. Ajayi has suggested that although Crowther is generally acknowledged in historical literature as a tireless fieldworker, what has not been fully appreciated is that he is first and foremost a reader and a thinker. There is some truth to this, and I would like to elaborate it by looking at two occasions in his letters to Henry Venn. In his letter of April 15, 1852, Crowther recounts political challenges and intrigues confronting the Egba mission. Concluding the letter, Crowther writes:

> In the midst of political excitement, trials and difficulties, and opposition, we have a hiding place wherein we may quietly retire and commune with the disposer of all things, who has assured us that no weapon which is prepared against us and his cause shall prosper. Surely we should not suffer present trials to weigh more in our hearts than past mercies to cheer up our spirits and animate our hopes. O for that faith even like a grain of mustard seed, which asks for great things, the removal of mountains, and plucking up of Sycamore trees. Lord increase our faith. (MS CA2/031/20)

Combined in this passage are notions of faith, retreat, and contemplation. All three notions are connected fundamentally to solitary communion or silent reading. Crowther evokes trials and tribulations of God's soldiers and affirms the fortitude to continue his evangelical work. Two years letter, on February 21, 1854, Crowther is writing again to Venn about silent reading. He characterizes his reading as "feeding" on the scriptures:

> Open a passage of Scriptures for devotion, instead of feeding one's soul with manna from heaven, one's thoughts run to: How should this passage be translated, which is the most suitable word, the most correct rendering? These various thoughts about translation soon take [the] place of meditation upon the

> passage opened. . . . Not thinking of this at first when I was translating the book of Psalms, it happened then I was reading the Psalms in [the] regular course of my morning devotion. But I had not gone through one third . . . of the book when I was obliged to change it for another portion of the Bible because I lost my meditations. My mind was led away from drinking hugely from the fountain of that rich book, and turned upon the rendering of various passages instead, so that sometimes I did not know whether I was reading in English or in Yoruba. (MS CA2/031/29)

The concern he expresses here is that of not being able to concentrate as fully as his calling requires. This is of course a common motif in missionary writing as a genre: the Christian soldier's inability to concentrate on his biblical reading works as temptation or crisis of faith. What is remarkable in this passage is Crowther's explanation of the reason for his straying mind. Quite apart from the bilingualism that the excerpt denotes, it also sheds some light on Crowther's consciousness of his role as mediator, as translator. It further reveals his awareness that translation is a test of imaginative reach and inventiveness.

In these passages, then, Crowther identifies his subject position in terms that are material and linguistic. Superficially, the first passage is about the material (public) arena, while the second has to do with a more private, spiritual space. But both are also interwoven: any strict binary we may assume dissolves when we realize that Crowther's existential angst in both excerpts is resolved in the spiritual realm where, on his terms, repose is made possible by the act of reading. In the first passage, politics in the external world is becalmed by the reassurance of God's will as expressed in scriptural narrative: "we have a hiding place wherein we may quietly retire and commune with the disposer of all things, who has assured us that no weapon which is prepared against us and his cause shall prosper." Likewise, in the second passage, guilt and self-doubt emerge as spiritual agony that happen because of the demands of language and cultural mediation: "My mind was led away from drinking hugely from the fountain of that rich book, and turned upon the rendering of various passages instead, so that sometimes I did not know whether I was reading in English or in Yoruba." Crowther recognizes his task as resting at some level on language, on the inventiveness needed to translate between languages. Might he also be suggesting to Venn that, as a former pagan slave boy, he reads the King James Bible—itself a text of multiple linguistic mediations—in specific ways *because* of his positioning between English and Yoruba?

We cannot know and do not need to know. At the least, it establishes Crowther as an unassuming cosmopolitan subject, liminal in the good sense. His writing is locatable within an order of discursivity where he is not simply an appendage of Anglican Christian history. Likewise, he is not simply a sign of a compromised past that the twentieth-century nationalists had to negate in a clichéd gesture of oedipal immolation. Rather, he participates in a problematic that is ongoing and that takes under its fold later intellectual developments like Pan-Africanism and the institutional category we call African literature. Crowther's case delivers to us an overarching narrative of the formation of a subject. Approached as evangelical discourse would have it, his writings would in their totality constitute a nonfictional, decorous bildungsroman. This bastard bildungsroman would then operate simultaneously as testament to Crowther's industry and the ordained superiority of Christian Europe. I have been exploring, instead, the ways in which, as a nineteenth-century black whiteman, Crowther offers an iteration of a diasporic discursive event. European modernity and its self-understanding offer the enunciatory space within which Crowther conceived and articulated a social role amid the drama of economic exploitation and religious conversion. The pagan native is the other against which members of his class conceived and articulated their subjectivity. Nonetheless, given the weight of nineteenth-century racial discourse, "blackness" emerges as an overarching discursive limit that subtends and threatens, even as it gives civic authority to, their self-construction as enlightened Africans. They become (historical) African patriots because they are interpellated into a subject position opened up by (ahistorical) notions of race and culture. As black patriots, they are obsessed with a vision of future Africa, but they also claim a putatively universal Christian ideal, "the moral landscape and cultural vocabulary of Victorianism," in Simon Gikandi's ("Embarrassment of Victorianism," 180) formulation.

Earlier, I suggested that Peel correctly shows us that in the twentieth-century politics of Nigeria the ethnic category "Yoruba" is meaningless except as distinguished from other Nigerian tribes (Ibibio, Igarra, Igbo, Hausa-Fulani, to name but a few). But Peel underplays the cross-hemispheric, black diasporic dimension of the legacy of the black whitemen whose scriptural translations and language primers contributed to the coalescence of the ethnic identity Yoruba. I argued that recognizing this takes us to the problem of the nation-state, an intractable one that we find in Nigeria and modern Africa in general. Crowther is associated with the narrative of nationhood in Nigeria—so much so that he is often given the credit of being one of the founding fathers. To be sure, he did most of his missionary and translation work in the mid-nineteenth century, before the onset of full-scale Scramble for Africa. He resigned from the CMS in 1890 and died in 1891, just some years after the Berlin Conference (1883–84) that partitioned Africa between the colonial powers. And as we saw earlier, the circumstances of his resignation have to be understood in the context of racialist pseudoscience and the colonial belligerence of European military powers in the late nineteenth century. Crowther's story, then, is closely linked to the story of the state of Nigeria.

On June 11, 1877, Crowther delivered a lecture titled "The River Niger" before the Royal Geographical Society. In his lecture, Crowther, as the Anglican bishop of the Niger Mission pastorate, offers a colonial textualization of black Africa, one that can illuminate such identitarian categories as tribe, nation, and race that continue to impact modern Africa for good or ill. The lecture sets up a textual chain that ranges from the work of Mungo Park to the Lander brothers. Crowther draws on a topos from Park's *Travels in the Interior Districts of Africa* (1799), of native women singing about the heroic missionary:

> The recent explorations, begun by Sir John Glover, and Captain Goldsworthy, and followed by the Revs. Messrs. Maser and Roper of the Church Missionary Society, have made us acquainted with the characteristics of the Western portion of the Niger Delta, and have showed us that as regards the feature of the land there prevails a monotonous uniformity of intricate canal and marsh, villages hidden in the dense growth of reeds, the people partaking of all the characteristics of the dwellers of the African swamps, and all, as far as it was possible to ascertain, speaking, even up to Benin, with slight modification, the Yoruba language, the same as is spoken at Badagry, Abbeokuta, Ilorin, and Ibadan.... One interesting fact these explorers record, that far up in the district of Oke Ondo they heard the women in the songs which accompanied their work, chanting the praise of one who was always a true friend, in every sense, of the African, and the burden of their song was "Gollibar, Gollibar," meaning thereby the late governor of Lagos, Sir John Glover ("River Niger," 5).

The figure about whom the women of Oke-Ondo are supposedly singing is Sir John Hawley Glover (1829–85). Glover was an officer of the Royal Navy and, later, colonial administrator and governor of Lagos colony from 1866 to 1872. As a young naval Lieutenant, Sir Glover served in the capacity of surveyor for the Niger River expedition party of 1857.[15] I indicated earlier that Crowther also traveled with the 1857 expedition; indeed, it was his third voyage up the Niger as CMS agent, and his journal record of the assignment was later published as *The Gospel of the Banks of the Niger* (1859). Addressing the Royal Geographical Society in 1877, then, Crowther pays tribute to the work of a fellow Niger River enthusiast from twenty years earlier who happens, more recently, to have served as governor of the island colony to the west of that river. In so doing Crowther unveils the interconnection of the pursuit of "science" (here, of geographical mapping), the advancement of commerce and religion, and the consolidation of colonial outposts. Crowther's politically astute rhetoric is self-effacing enough to evoke legendary Park in order to underline Glover's, rather than his, place as subject of heroic lore among natives. My own interest here is to recenter Crowther as exemplary of a contradictory location whose ramifications extend into the realm of nationhood and its representation—the province of much of current literary and cultural criticism.

Crowther's lecture traces the progress of the exploration of the Niger River from the vantage point of his own involvement as representative of the CMS in the expeditions of 1841, 1854, and 1857. Midway through the lecture, he describes a series of small communities his party encountered during the expedition of 1854: "About thirty miles further up the river, we came to the town of Zhiru, on the southern bank, and landed; we found this to be another Fulah settlement, as in Gandiko, the conquering *race* reducing to slavery the original inhabitants. These are the Akpoh, or Balni Djukus, who are also met at Fernando Po" ("River Niger," 22, my emphasis). The conquering "race" to which he is referring is the ethnic group variously called Pular, Fulani, Felatah, or Fulah. A short while later, he describes this "race" in the following way:

> Anything like even a vague estimate as to the numerical strength of the *Pulo nation* we have at no time been able to obtain, since we never met with any African traveller far and long enough to undertake a reliable estimation. Suffice it to say that this interesting nation occupies a territory, both irregular and widespread, towards the interior; according to Dr Barth, there is a considerable part of them in Adamawa; they are in power in Sokoto, and there is ample proof of their being largely mixed with the *Hausa nation*.
>
> Ever since the times of Denham and Clapperton, the warlike Fulahs or Filani have continued their hostile and predatory attacks on the *more peaceful tribes*—towns are still destroyed, and it is their frequent attacks which unsettle the tribes, and render them suspicious of the presence of strangers. ("River Niger," 31, my emphases)

The keywords that interest me in the two excerpts quoted here are *tribe, nation*, and *race*. In his text, Crowther deploys them blithely as synonyms that designate the same collective identity. The single category "Fulani" at once designates a purportedly direct and stable referent opposed to the "more peaceful tribes," while also standing in for a larger whole—a "nation" and a "race": "About thirty miles further up the river, we came to the town of Zhiru, on the southern bank, and landed; we found this to be another Fulah settlement, as in Gandiko, the conquering *race* reducing to slavery the original inhabitants" ("River Niger," 22). In this way, Crowther takes up the categories "tribe," "nation," and "race" and foists them on the human beings his expeditionary party encountered on the Niger.

I am not really concerned with the referents of Crowther's geography (i.e., the place names) or ethnography (the tribal or racial groups he claims to be identifying). Crowther's horizon is racial-continental and diasporic, even as it is routed through the language of Christian universal brotherhood. He perceives the natives in the culture areas that became Nigeria as parts of the same unit, metonyms of a racial homogeneity. Crowther also deploys the categories "tribe," "nation," and "race" as preconstituted and unproblematically denominative. More interestingly, he *recognizes* African peoples and places through them, while in fact presuming to delineate, name, and describe. He does this, not immediately for the pressures or desires of the African communities themselves, but for a Western audience—the gathered members of the Royal Geographical Society. The ongoing problems of African states that derive at some level from issues of ethnicity and nationality strike us, then, as a concrete unveiling of the rhetorical sleight of hand that conflates tribe, nation, and race, and imposes them on heterogeneous African communities. We might say that many African countries are today revealing, precisely in the painful conflicts between ethnic groups and regions, the political and epistemic error of the logic of metonymy that masqueraded as documentary representation in Crowther's textualization of Africa.

A similar thought would apply to the teleology of progress at the heart of Crowther's discourse. A range of contemporary work has rejected the historicist-teleological framing of the concept of secularization and its purported imbrication with euromodernity and Enlightenment civic morality (Chakrabarty, *Provincializing*; Connolly). My concern is to emphasize that the concept of secularization as it informs critical thought, together with its conceptual correlates such as nationhood and democracy, take their historical grounding from a Western European philosophical problematic. To graft these concepts undialectically onto the way we talk about African or other non-Western societies is to constrain from the outset the latter's historical particularity and potential for theory. By foisting categories inherited from European discourses of identity and historical time on the African groups among whom he worked, Crowther participates in the textualization of Africa, one where tribe, nation, and race are elided into one another in a metonymic movement and where the proper destiny of whole groups is assumed to be secularization.

In *Citizen and Subject: Contemporary Africa and the Legacy of Late Colonialism* (1996), Mahmood Mamdani has argued that British colonial policy of "indirect rule" generated in black Africa a specific kind of society that persists today. The "Africa of free peasants," he writes, "is trapped in a non-racial version of apartheid" (61). According to Mamdani, what colonial policy in black Africa invented, concretely and in discourse, is properly described as a bifurcated world:

> What we have before us is a bifurcated world, no longer simply racially organized, but a world in which the dividing line between those human and those less human is a line between those who labor on the land and those who do not. This divided world is inhabited by subjects on one side and citizens on the other; their life is regulated by customary law on one side and modern law on the other; their beliefs are dismissed as pagan on this side but bear the status of religion on the other; the stylized moments in their day-to-day lives are considered ritual on this side and culture on the other; their creativity is considered crafts on this side and glorified as the arts on the other . . . in sum, the world of the "savages" barricaded, in deed as in word, from the world of the "civilized." (61)

The major advocate and theorist of the British colonial policy of indirect rule is of course Lord Frederick Lugard. In *The Dual Mandate in British Tropical Africa* (1965),[16] Lugard argues for the necessity of civilizing Africans without "detribalizing" them. Lugard's rhetoric justifies the policy of indirect rule on the premise that it preserves the identity of Africans by preserving native customs and traditions. This idea, whereby natives are supposed to become "modern" by force, even as they preserve their tribal customs and traditions, inaugurates important contradictions. The incursion of colonial modernity into black Africa thus involves a contradictory predication of identity. The educated native, agent of Africa's modernization, is ideally also an "authentic" African subject. The putative subject of change is also supposed to be an unchanging manifestation of racial and cultural essence. As object of discourse and social engineering, Lugard's Africa is the sign of ontological stasis (tribe) as well as, paradoxically, the possibility of change—from savagery to civilization, nature, to culture, tribe to nation.[17]

One crucial observation derives from the accounts of thinkers so different as Mamdani and Lugard sketched above. If in the colonial discourse of Lugard, the terms *African* or *native* contain the inherently contradictory notion of radical difference and the possibility of superseding difference, Mamdani's book elaborates the contemporary repercussions of that contradiction. Following Mamdani, we might say that the notion of tribe, developed in colonial ethnographic discourse and used to define and simplify African life in the private sphere, cuts against the idea of nation in the public domain of state formation and collective identity. Likewise, in the case of Africa, national identity or structure of feeling cannot productively be framed as the end point of a teleological narrative that begins with something called tribe and culminates in something else called nation. This is primarily because the frame whereby society is conceptualized as moving progressively toward secularization and nationhood is historically specific to the West and cannot be universalized to explain the African situation. Put differently, prior to the continent's encounter with European modernity in its colonialist face, there were no "tribes" or "nations" in Africa: none, that is, in the sense in which those terms interpellate individuals and groups today or are deployed in academic and popular discourses. What the terms *tribe* and *nation* encode are historical and linguistic transactions, formerly in colonial discourses and later in African nationalisms, through which modern Africa came to be textualized, brought into the orbit of Eurocentric representations. After the unceasing civil wars and economic stagnation, the experience of Africa's societies should remind us that negotiating statehood in tandem with nationhood is a challenge each society has to address in light of its specific confluence of narratives. "Modernity" is neither inevitable nor prescripted as economic, political, or cultural telos. The paths to it, and within it, are necessarily uncharted.

The Missionary as Race Man

The term *race man* in the title of this section is a nod to Hazel V. Carby's *Race Men* (1998), a critique of the role of masculinity in the construction of African American intellectual and public leadership. The term references culturally sanctioned views of community wherein cohesion, reproduction, and leadership are coded in terms of masculinism. Carby takes up the writings of twentieth-century black internationalists including Du Bois, Paul Robeson, and C. L. R. James. On the surface, the Crowther we have been examining is not a race man. His writing is apolitical, not designed to confront racism or even acknowledge it. But by the end of his life and career, he could not avoid being confronted by the facts of colonialism and racial supremacist logic. His mentor and staunch supporter, Henry Venn, died in 1873, and larger changes were afoot on the wider terrain of European interests in Africa, changes that impacted the politics of religious doctrine and administration within the CMS. In the late-nineteenth-century atmosphere of European imperialism, nationalist belligerence, and racialist ideologies, Crowther lost the confidence of CMS secretaries in London (Ajayi; Ayandele; Loiello). His employers were concerned about his choice of catechists and other staff in the field. There were also concerns about the management and evangelical success of his missionary stations. A younger generation of white missionaries came along who felt that the activities of his staff members, if not his own actions as head of the bishopric, were no longer truly Christian. Sir George Goldie (1846–1925), colonial administrator and head of the Royal Niger Company chartered in 1885, distrusted Crowther's meddling in commercial matters. For Goldie, Crowther and his native crew in the Niger delta dabbled far too much in trade to be trusted in their pastoral duties. In this way, Crowther offends the religious as well as the secular economic instances of the incipient colonial dispensation. For different reasons, the young CMS radical clerics and Goldie—the Cecil Rhodes of modern Nigeria—saw him as a charlatan, a letdown, or an outright threat.

We will be missing something if we reduce Crowther's treatment at the hands of his employers to a moral issue. I want, rather, to pose it as an epistemological gift. Crowther has appropriated the original CMS ideology as codified in Buxton's axiom that Africa's problems should be addressed by the Bible and the plow: that is to say, through Christianization and legitimate trade. That commerce in the full range of its secular-worldly connotations is indissociable from the higher civilization that Christianity was supposed to bring to natives is succinctly captured in Crowther's communication, dated August 17, 1876, where he writes:

> The exploration of the Niger by different travellers, namely Mungo Park, Clapperton, the Landers, Messrs McGregor Laird, Lander, Oldfield, and Lieut. W. Allen, had prepared the way for Trotter's Great Expedition of 1841. Previous and subsequent visits of Mr Beecroft in the little steamer Ethiope, Dr Baikie's

> exploration of the Tshadda branch in 1854, and subsequently the exploration of Dr Baikie and Captain Glover of the Kwara Branch in 1857, when late Mr McGregor Laird made the first attempt to establish trading depots at Abo (Eboe), Onitsha, and at the confluence of the Kwara and Tshadda Rivers determined the CMS at the same time to introduce Christianity on the banks of the Niger and at the confluence. Thus commerce and Christianity began working together to accomplish the same object, the Christian Civilization of the ignorant teeming population of this productive country. (MS CA3/04/554)

This is written in the midst of the Scramble for Africa, seven years before the historic Berlin Conference. Laboriously titled "A Brief Statement of the Advantages Accruing to Protestant Christian Missions through the Benign Operations and Moral Influence of British Government on the West Coast of Africa," Crowther proffers here a summary of early-nineteenth-century British exploratory adventures in West Africa, just as he would do one year later in his address to the Royal Geographical Society. He registers the point that from the onset of European exploratory adventures in West Africa, Christianity and commerce have always been "working together to accomplish the same object." He contaminates religion with commerce and unveils the double discourse all along inherent to Christian missionary rhetoric. Understood this way, Goldie and the CMS are correct to disapprove of, or feel challenged by, the latter Bishop Crowther, for whom Christianization should uplift natives spiritually *and* materially. Crowther reproduces missionary doublespeak by putting it to work at the site of encounter with people and choices, and thereby unmasks it. Capitalist exploitation is revealed to be integral to the stated mission of soul making. It is for similar reasons that Crowther sought to convert the Muslim cultures of the upper Niger in today's northern Nigeria, too. For him, Islam is not the implacable enemy but a potential ally. Thus he writes in *Experiences with Heathens and Mohammedans in West Africa* (1892): "In our dealings with the heathens and Mohammedans we employ the Scriptural examples for their formation and instruction, without rudely and contemptuously attacking their superstitious objects of worship or their erroneous creed" (15). As Peel has shown, in translating biblical text, Crowther borrowed liberally from the Arabic, which had passed into Yoruba through Hausa loan words and direct contact with Muslim itinerant traders from other parts of West Africa. Against the background of literary globalism on one hand, and the reverberations of global jihadism in contemporary Nigeria on the other, the Pan-African, ecumenical black subject envisaged by the black whitemen is an idealist dream—but an inspiring one, nonetheless.

One consequence of the Niger Mission crisis and Crowther's resignation was internal secession of the African clergy who felt insulted by the treatment of their leader. Led by Crowther's son Dandeson, the secession was an opening salvo in what would become broader nationalist agitation in the political sphere.

The autograph and photographs of Samuel Crowther (FIGURES 2.1 and 2.2) and his son Dandeson (FIGURES 2.3 and 2.4) reproduced here may be read as prefiguration of what the elder Crowther's mission would come to mean. Both photographs are in an album that originally belonged to Rev. Henry Charles Binns. The first photograph shows Samuel Crowther and on the opposite page the text of John 10:16: "And other sheep I have, which are not of this fold: them also I must bring, and they shall hear my voice; and there shall be one fold and one shepherd." The verse is copied out in Crowther's handwriting and dated March 5, 1865. The second photograph is that of Crowther's son Dandeson, with the notation: "D. C. Crowther, Son of Bishop Crowther, now Archdeacon of Bonny W. Africa." The facing page similarly holds biblical text written out in Dandeson's hand. This time, the text is taken from Psalm 126:6. Dandeson writes out the text in Yoruba and the English:

> E nniti nsokun lo osi nmu itugbin itebiye, yio pada wa li aisiyemeji, li ayo li yio si mu iti re wa pellu re.
> He that goeth and weepeth, bearing precious seed, shall doubtless come again with rejoicing, bringing his sheaves with him.

It would be productive to dwell at some length on these verses for what they might tell us about the intentions of the two men whose images they adorn in a colleague's album. But this would take us too far afield. Let me therefore restrict myself to two possibilities we may draw from the intertextual commentary that Crowther and his son enact by means of their chosen scriptural texts. Crowther's John 10:16 is about pastoral expansion. It reports that there are "sheep" yet to come within the fold and dedicates itself to bringing them in by means of language and persuasive address: "and they shall hear my voice, and there shall be one fold and one shepherd." Someone, perhaps the album's owner, has glued onto the page an image of a sketch of "Bathurst, Sierra Leone, where Samuel Crowther passed his childhood." The biblical text and the sketch of the settlement where Crowther grew up after his recapture seem designed to underscore his exemplarity as proof of God's work. If the elder Crowther's chosen text is about the notional universality of Christianity, Dandeson's is about a subject who, though suffering, nonetheless holds on to "precious seed." In other words, Dandeson chooses a specific instance of hope in perseverance: "He that goeth and weepeth, bearing precious seed, shall doubtless come again with rejoicing, bringing his sheaves with him." What is most interesting is that Dandeson writes out the text in Yoruba and English. In the passage of time from the elder Crowther to his son, something is happening historically and in language as cultural capital. Crowther's autograph in the album is dated 1865. It is not clear when Dandeson's photograph or his biblical citation found their way into the album. From the notation, we can speculate that it would have been after 1876, when he became

Mission Tide | 91

Fig. 2.1 Bishop Samuel Ajayi Crowther
Church Missionary Society Archive, University of Birmingham

archdeacon in the Niger Mission pastorate. By this time, Henry Venn is dead, the imperialist phase of Europe's African adventure is gaining momentum, and the Niger Mission is under scrutiny by detractors. And yet, by that time also, Dandeson Crowther's chosen text in a colleague's album is able to call up the

92 | *African Literature and Social Change*

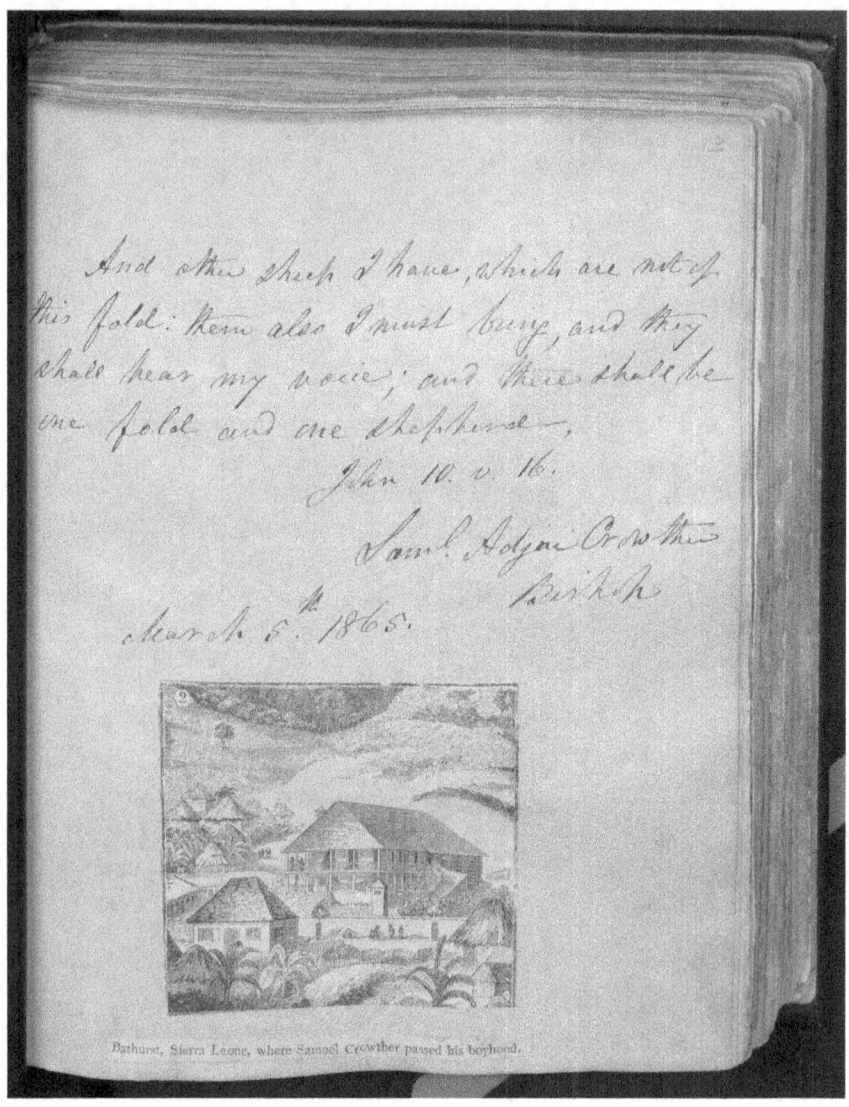

Fig. 2.2 Biblical verse handwritten by Bishop Crowther
Church Missionary Society Archive, University of Birmingham

Yoruba language as vehicle of self-exhibition. The Yoruba is cited alongside the English, exhibited as fait accompli rather than thrilling possibility. The younger Crowther takes for granted what the elder Crowther had to argue for and strategize, here and there, to accomplish.

Mission Tide | 93

Fig. 2.3 Archdeacon Dandeson Crowther
Church Missionary Society Archive, University of Birmingham

I have emphasized Crowther's grasp of his mission as one that straddles religion and commerce, the spiritual and the secular, in order to demonstrate that nineteenth-century black missionaries were race men by default. Another figure whose career exemplified the coalescence of religion, literacy, and race in

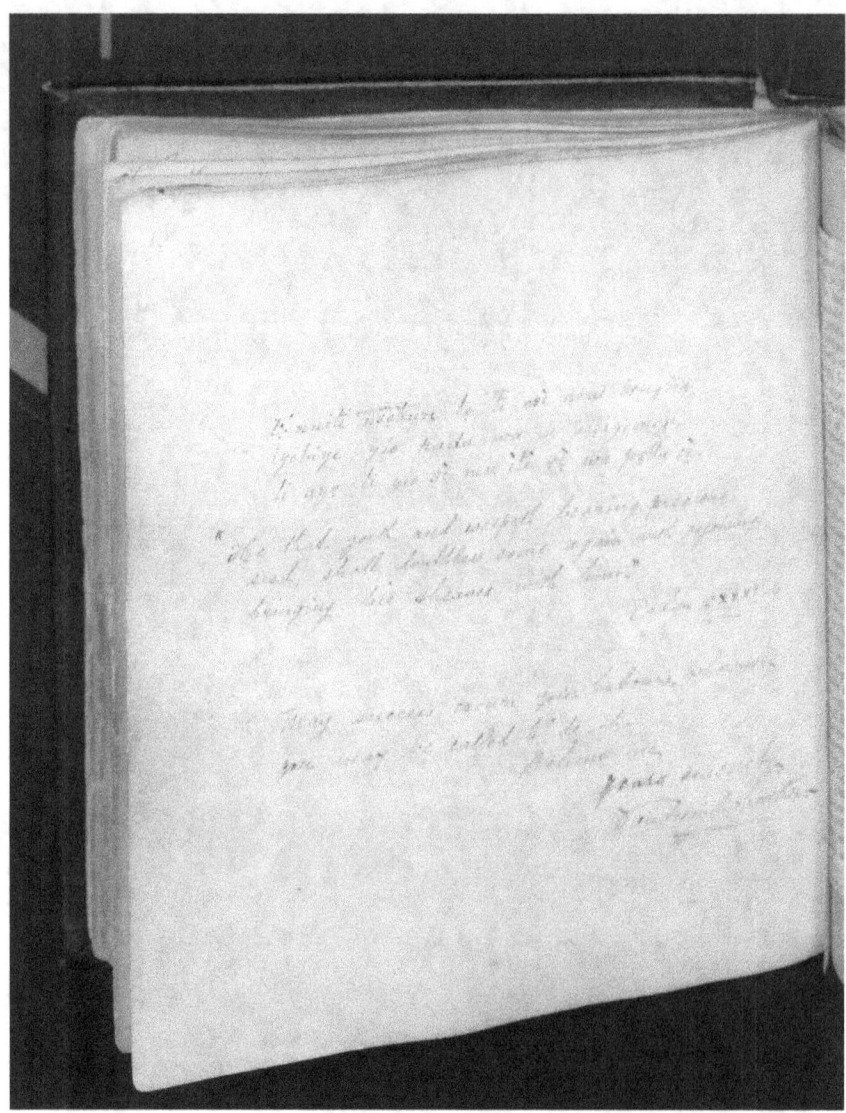

Fig. 2.4 Biblical verse handwritten by Dandeson Crowther
Church Missionary Society Archive, University of Birmingham

the period would be Rev. Thomas Birch Freeman (1809–90), a contemporary and friend of Crowther's. Like Crowther, Freeman's work as Wesleyan missionary in the Gold Coast blurs the divide between the religious and the profane. But unlike Crowther, Freeman was born in England to an English mother and black father.

F. Deaville Walker's biography is titled *Birch Freeman: The Son of an African*, but it is not clear whether his father was a freed slave from Africa or the West Indies. His mother is named Amy Birch, and "Thomas" is the only name with which his father is associated. In his introduction to the 1968 third edition of Freeman's *Journal of Various Visits to the Kingdoms of Ashanti, Aku, and Dahomi in West Africa* (originally published in 1844), Harrison M. Wright follows Walker and suggests that perhaps "both parents worked together as servants in the same household" (xi). Freeman was born in Twyford parish, Hampshire, and went to the Cape Coast in 1838 to work for the Methodist Missionary Society. Thereafter, except for two visits to England in 1840 and 1844, he lived in Africa through to the last decade of the nineteenth century.

Freeman had a checkered career to say the least. He constantly flouted his employers' expectations of pragmatic restraint in the conception and execution of evangelical projects. Having much energy and passion to make an impact, he seems habitually to get into trouble over what was deemed his bureaucratic indiscipline and financial inefficiency. Freeman, it seems, chose to do things when he felt they needed to be done there and then, not necessarily after proper approval has been secured from the authorities back in England. He resigned from the Methodist Missionary Society in 1857 and became a civil commissioner of the "Eastern Regions of the Gold Coast" in Accra, a position he held until 1860. He returned to missionary work in 1873, retired in 1886, and died in Accra in 1890. Freeman's *Journal* was very well known in Christian missionary circles, enough to be cited in Buxton's *The Slave Trade and Its Remedies*. He anonymously published a novel titled *Missionary Enterprise No Fiction* (1871).[18] In addition to his eventful stints as missionary and civil administrator, Freeman holds the distinction of being the first missionary, black or white, to preach a Christian sermon in what is now Nigeria. His arrival in Badagry on September 24, 1842 "marked the effective beginning of missionary enterprise in Nigeria" (Ajayi, *Christian Missions*, 31). Freeman had been asked to establish a mission outpost in Badagry as an extension of the Methodist station that he ran at Cape Coast. In the course of the trip, he traveled to Abeokuta at the request of Sierra Leone recaptives. He met with Sodeke, the chief of the Egba in Abeokuta, and was inspired by what struck him as the latter's readiness to receive the new religion. His visit to Abeokuta and meeting with Sodeke prepared the way for Crowther's and Townsend's arrival in 1846 to establish the Egba Mission.

Freeman's journals contain the usual condescension toward the natives of western Africa, as does the autobiography. The condescending attitude is often complicated by an ambiguous love for the land and its potential, materially and spiritually. His novel *Missionary Enterprise* is a thinly veiled autobiographical narrative of missionary work in Africa. Through the melodrama and purple prose of *Missionary Enterprise*, Freeman combines elements of the cottage

Fig. 2.5 Portrait of Rev. Thomas Birch Freeman
Image from Wesley Historical Society library, courtesy of Oxford Brookes University

narrative, the domestic bourgeois novel, and the outward-bound romance depicting the missionary adventures of his protagonist John Herbert. Heavily laced with Christian hymns, biblical verses, and excerpts from John Bunyan, John Milton, and William Wordsworth, the novel is clumsy in its attempts to impress readers with evidence of the author's piety and erudition. But if *Missionary Enterprise* is dilettantism, it emerges thereby as a transgression of the boundaries of genre and stylistic decorum.

At any rate, it is not for the quality of his prose that Freeman has been interesting to missionary hagiographers; rather, it is for his role as a pioneer of the missionary enterprise in Africa. I want to draw attention to two iconic portraits of Freeman that his contemporaries might have seen, putting the face to the stories, as they say. One appears on the cover and frontispiece of Allen Birtwhistle's *Thomas Birch Freeman: West African Pioneer* (1950). In this portrait, Freeman is a young man attired as any Victorian man of culture (FIGURE 2.5). It has a soft touch: the face reveals no racial coding, no caricature of flat nose and thick lips. But he has woolly hair, and the shading of his features registers a hint of dark skin. On the frontispiece of F. Deaville Walker's *Thomas Birch Freeman: The Son of an African* (1929), Freeman is older, perhaps approaching middle age. The full head of woolly hair is very much in evidence here, too. In this portrait, he seems to be bearing a vague smile but perhaps not. At any rate, in both, he is looking slightly sideways, away from us. His gaze is self-assured, as if his relaxed sight is toward the great evangelical deeds awaiting him in the fabled land of superstition and vice. Despite the number of biographies of him, little is known of his parents other than the fact that the father is black and the mother a widower who had three children before Freeman. Lost to the archive are the stories of the man and woman whose transgression led to his birth: the mother because she is a lowly white woman who must have invited hostility or pity for her dalliance; the father because he is a former slave or offspring of slaves. As in the case of Crowther, countless chapbooks and Sunday school pamphlets were written about Freeman as heroic missionary carrying the light of God to the darkness of Africa.

To the best of my knowledge, it remains unclear whether Freeman's father was born in Africa or in the West Indies. The copy of *Missionary Enterprise* at the School of Oriental and African Studies (SOAS) indicates that it was gifted to Freeman's biographer F. Deaville Walker by one of Freeman's children. In this sense, we might say that Freeman did "go native" or perhaps considered himself a returnee to his "fatherland." In Freeman, it would seem, to be a son of Africa shifts between the literal and the figurative. Ajayi's *Christian Missions in Nigeria* considers the interesting dilemma the Methodist mission faced when Freeman returned to the mission in 1873 and upon his passing in 1890. Having lived in Africa for more than fifty years and marrying a Fanti woman with whom he had children, there were questions about his racial status, an ambiguity that needed to be resolved because his salary depended on it (Ajayi, *Missions*, 257). In a context where whites were paid higher than blacks for the same job, and where the source of funds for staff remuneration depended on the employee's identity ("Native" or "European"), is Freeman to be deemed a white or native missionary in the way his allowance, and later, pension, is paid? It makes sense that the question of Freeman's identity would generate a problem for missionary or colonial organizations whose cluster of suppositions rest on a foundation of racial difference. The circumstance of his race thus becomes the basis of a designation-from-without, a designation that has nothing to do with, at this point, his own will or self-understanding. Living when he did and doing what he undertook to do makes him a race man regardless of his own views on the subject, and thanks only to nineteenth-century racialism.

Freeman's contribution to the establishment of Methodism and its accompanying correlate of Western education can be seen in the fact that the all-male high school I attended in Lagos is named after him. Looking back now, I remember being vaguely aware that the missionary after whom my school is named was "mulatto." The knowledge carried no significance except as recognition of a self-evident tautology. I was aware that Freeman was black because he happened to be black. What carried greater significance was that he represented a moment in Nigeria's history, a moment in the arrival of Western literacy. In this sense, his status was to us students indistinguishable from that of the celebrated white missionaries who brought schools and churches to Africa such as Mary Slessor and Hope Waddell at Calabar in eastern Nigeria, Henry Townsend at Abeokuta, David Hinderer at Ibadan, or Charles Gollmer and Thomas Bowen at Badagry. At one level, this deemphasizing of Freeman's biracial identity is a sign of repression or selective remembering in Nigeria's postindependence educational system. The pretense that race is no longer relevant, whereas nationality and tribe-ethnicity are, is integral to a cultural-nationalist education system that remained colonial—precisely because of its cultural nationalism—after independence. At another level, the deemphasizing of Freeman's racial identity testifies to the historical *objectivity* of his agency. Nineteenth-century confusions about race may have contained the figure of Freeman within a restrictive imaginary, but half a century later, a high school in Nigeria retains the name as sign of objective historical agency, one that escapes the circumscription of racist prejudice and institutional amnesia.

Freeman is thus an early black-Atlantic intellectual and multiply-located subject. What we witness in Freeman's example is the sense in which we benefit from approaching the black missionaries in terms of a cross-hemispheric, black-Atlantic optic. This necessarily involves consideration of the implications of the notions of nationhood and statehood that came with Christian conversion and colonization of the nineteenth century. In his introduction to Freeman's *Journal* mentioned earlier, Wright writes: "Unlike some other missionaries . . . Freeman seemed to view the work of missionary and government officials as being very much the same, as being simply two different methods of achieving the ultimate goal of Christianity and 'civilization' for the Africans" (xxvi). Wright may as well have been writing of Crowther and the nineteenth-century black whitemen in general.

J. E. K Aggrey (1875–1927), the twentieth-century nationalist and educator, is in a direct line of intellectual descent from the likes of Crowther and Freeman. A native of present-day Ghana, a preacher, and a teacher, Aggrey is one of the first generation of Western-educated Africans and nationalists. In the 1960s and

1970s, Aggrey signified African high achievement—many quotable quotes—in Nigerian schools, along with such names as Frederick Douglass, Edward Blyden, Booker T. Washington, and W. E. B. Du Bois from the Americas, or John Mensah Sarbah (1864–1910), J. E. Casely Hayford (1866–1930), and Herbert Heelas Macaulay (1864–1946). His biography has been written over and over again, his life and times a staple in schools and youth organizations across black Africa. He was a member of the Phelps-Stoke research expedition to sub-Saharan Africa in 1920–21 to help design educational policy for the continent. Here is what T. D. Mweli Skota, general secretary of the African National Congress (ANC), had to say in *The African Yearly Register*, which he compiled and edited in 1930: "Dr Aggrey, of Africa, a gentleman, a patriot, a Christian, an educationalist, and a philosopher; one of the greatest luminaries that have lightened the horizons of Africa, and who, by his personal example of self-sacrifice and devotion to duty, has taught the world the distinctive qualities and attributes of the African race, thereby proving the capacity and capability of the African to contribute towards human knowledge and civilization."[19]

In 1928, Georgina Anne Gollock, missionary author and publications editor with the CMS published a collection of biographies titled *Lives of Eminent Africans*. As the title suggests, this is a "who's who" of big people, a collection of inspiring tales. The genre was commonplace in the first half of the twentieth century.[20] The impetus was to record the achievements of illustrious blacks as a way of countering racist accusations of the Negro's intellectual inferiority and moral inadequacies. As Gollock puts it in the preface to *Lives*, "[t]hroughout the world, as in Africa, the new generations are facing changed conditions and paths untrodden before. They need not only good friends beside them, but light from the records of their race.... It is evident from the stories that follow that young Africans have a racial heritage of which they may be justly proud" (v). If Gollock represents a "good friend" for young Africans, Aggrey provides an example of the racial heritage for which those young Africans "can be justly proud." In the section on Aggrey, Gollock recalls a favorite story of Aggrey's that he recounted to schoolchildren in Uganda. It tells of a young eagle that was captured by a man who tries to force it to eat chickens' food. Soon, another character—called a "naturalist"—pays the man a visit. "Passing through the garden, he [the naturalist] said, 'that bird is an eagle, not a chicken.' 'Yes,' said the owner, 'but I have trained it to be a chicken. It is no longer an eagle'" (126). This leads to an argument between the two men until they both agree to find out whether an eagle can actually be domesticated, transformed such that it begins to act like a chicken. Twice, the naturalist attempts to make the eagle fly, and on both occasions, he fails. It is only on the third attempt that his persistence is vindicated. The eagle flies off and is freed.

"The Story of the Eagle and the Chickens" is surely a sermonic parable, pedagogical to the core. The eagle stands for African history and the African subject.

The man who reduces the eagle to the level of ducks and fowls personifies colonialism. Centuries of colonialism and transatlantic slavery have demoralized this affronted eagle, giving the illusion that the eagle has lost its innate capacity to fly. But the eagle rejoins its identity when it leaps up into the skies. In Gollock's account of Aggrey's rendering, language itself seems to take wing as the eagle hesitantly faces the sun, ready to fly, and the image is that of a bright new day: "The sun was just rising, gilding the top of the mountain and making each crag glisten in the glory of the new day" (126–27). In "Moving On Down the Line: Variations on the African-American Sermon," Hortense Spillers has identified the eagle motif to be very common in the tradition of the African American sermon, where the eagle serves as "figurative embodiment of a thematics of liberation" (41). Aggrey's source for the parable is clearly the African American sermonic tradition. Between 1898 and 1918, he lived and worked full time in the United States. He earned an MA and a PhD in divinity from Livingstone College and Hood Theological Seminary in North Carolina, respectively, and was married to Rose Rudolph Douglass, an African American teacher from Virginia. Living his adult life between the United States and sub-Saharan Africa and being intimately connected to the African American church as preacher and educator, Aggrey's address to the young boys in Uganda owes its intellectual background to the African American church.

Spillers's reading of the African American sermonic tradition identifies the epistemic limitations within which their narratives of liberation acquire meaning. Noticing, in particular, the gendered valence of these texts, Spillers stirs heterosexism to the surface, drawing our attention to an epistemic and historical subtext: "We might say that men of their class, of their generation, did the right thing for the wrong reasons, or the wrong thing for reasons that seemed right to them, given the cultural imperatives of high heterosexism under which they operated" (59). Aggrey's performance can be read in a similar light, against a background of the inherited missionary mandate that spurs it on. What is interesting is that the naturalist's benevolence can only be expressed in Aggrey's tale by means of a paradoxical maneuver. If the narcissist is the historical colonialist who knows the eagle's essence but sets out to undermine it, the naturalist is the anticolonialist whose knowledge saves the eagle. As priest, teacher, and "son of Africa," Aggrey and his story bear witness to an intense commitment, that of improving the lot of a downtrodden people, liberating them from racism and colonialism. But the inner logic of the commitment acquires its commensurate power only if Aggrey, like the benevolent naturalist, occupies the same structural and epistemic space as the narcissistic colonizer.

As one of the pioneering agents of the material and subjective infrastructure of modernity in Africa, Aggrey inherits and continues the drama of knowledge and action that figures such as Crowther and Freeman enact. Like Crowther and

Freeman before him, access to Christianity and its educational infrastructure is a means to an end. In this sense, Aggrey's sense of his mission exceeds the restrictive circumscription of religious ideality or simple evangelical hubris. In his foreword to Margaret Musson's pamphlet titled *Aggrey of Achimota* (1944), A. G. Fraser provides a funny anecdote that is relevant here. Fraser, first principal of the Prince of Wales College (later to be known as Achimota School), recalls a dinner conversation involving Aggrey:

> I remember once going with him to dinner and a high ecclesiastic happened to be present. With a desire to test the ecclesiastical atmosphere, I said: "I think, Sir, you might ask Dr Aggrey to speak in your church during Lent." The Churchman immediately turned to Aggrey with a smile and said: "I did not know you were one of us." "Oh, Yes," said Aggrey, "I can preach in your church. I was taught as a Wesleyan, and brought up as one, but when I went to America I wanted to help all my people so I also became an elder in the Presbyterian Church, and then I was confirmed in the Church of England, and I studied dogmatics under a Roman Catholic Professor; so now I can work for all." The ecclesiastic looked grim and did not ask Dr Aggrey to preach during Lent!" (5–6)

Apocryphal or not, this little anecdote speaks to an angle of vision that we have seen in Crowther and Freeman. Here, it would seem, is a Christian soldier whose social vision cannot be contained within the boundaries of Euro-American doctrinal divisions. The African, for Aggrey, needs to be educated to enter the twentieth century, and Christianity merely makes the accession to education and modernization possible.[21]

It is not at all fortuitous, then, that Nnamdi Azikiwe (1904–96), the first president of independent Nigeria, cites Aggrey as a forerunner whose example serves as inspiration for his own sense of mission and possibility. In his autobiography *My Odyssey* (1970), Azikiwe writes of Aggrey's visit to Nigeria in 1921 as part of the Phelps-Stokes Commission. According to Azikiwe, he was particularly privileged to have listened to Aggrey's sermon and later to be presented with the gift of a book by Aggrey during the latter's visit to his school. As Azikiwe recalls, Aggrey had presented him with "a big book entitled *Negro Education: A Study of the Private and Higher Schools for Colored People in the United States*" (38). A year later in 1922, when he was contemplating which school to attend in the United States, Azikiwe consulted this book quite directly as fetish:

> One day early in 1922 I decided that God should guide me in the choice of a university in America. I took out the book given to me by Dr Aggrey. I closed my eyes, prayed for divine guidance and opened one of its pages at random. Behold, it was page 311. I decided to choose by luck the university I would like to attend. So I took a pencil, closed my eyes again, and prayed to God to guide me aright, as I placed the pencil blindly on the page. The point of the pencil stuck at "Howard University, Washington, DC." (45)

As Azikiwe narrates it, Aggrey's gift of a book about the education of African Americans from reconstruction through the early twentieth century is the talismanic fetish that prompts him toward his destiny. Black-Atlantic desire and incipient discursive community is the condition of possibility for Azikiwe's nonfictional bildungsroman, so to speak. Aggrey initiates Azikiwe into black Atlanticism as possibility, as discourse, and as politics. Azikiwe's future as fiery nationalist and first president of independent Nigeria is thereby rendered as dependent on Aggrey's pioneering example, very much as Crowther had linked his sense of mission to the antecedent example of Philip Quaque.

The Pioneers' Solitude

In seeking to understand the epistemic lesson of such figures as Crowther and his cohort of black whitemen, my approach in this chapter has been to concentrate on what is distinctive in their historical location. A necessary question at this point is the risk I invite by stressing the singularity of their difference. Am I not reconstituting a racial—perhaps even racist—perspective by insisting that although they share the discourse of Christian superiority, the black missionaries are to be distinguished from their white counterparts? The answer to this question should be simple. As products and perpetuators of a Victorian ideology of Christian superiority, they are no different from their fellow missionaries who happen to be white. But as subjects positioned in an ambiguous way within the simultaneous ideology of racial hierarchy, they occupy a different subject position. It is this ambiguous position that the oxymoron *black whiteman* captures. This position is sui generis, still in formation, to be stridently rejected only at the onset of anticolonial nationalism in the twentieth century. Crowther is a fitful forerunner of a discourse that articulates social possibilities and collective subjects-in-formation. He participates in a discourse that is at once ethnic, national, and continental/black Atlantic in its possible affiliations. His singularity is to be found in the fact that his writings perform, at one and the same time, a novelization of classic Victorian missionary discourse as well as traditional Yoruba feudal values.

The foregoing is directly relevant to contemporary Anglophone literary and cultural criticism. As I indicated in chapter 1, current discussions of transnationalism and cosmopolitanism often rehearse a rhetoric of crisis. In this, literary globalism enacts a logic that has long characterized the way Africa operates as static signifier of crisis. In the humanities, our anxiety to go with the flow of geopolitical changes on a global scale may turn out to be a gesture of containment, one that silences marginalized cultures in the very attempt to control the present by correcting past errors. Driven by a crisis complex to shepherd diversity into new spurious universalisms, globalism can easily become a chorus of buzzwords—pious harangues that remain tone deaf to the bountiful sounds in the tower of babel. My argument in this chapter is that one way of avoiding this error is to pay attention to what is distinctive in the black whitemen of nineteenth-century West Africa.

If the logic of crisis emerges in world literature theory in relation to methodological and institutional insecurities, it emerges in representations of Africa as a continent of economic woes and failed states. Scholars are called on to become global as a way of dealing with this or that crisis in humanistic scholarship, where humanitarian organizations are invited to save Africans from famine and war. The topos of crisis thus calls up the concept of sacrifice, understood simply as a self-motivating orientation to the world, to action in the world, and to the representational esteem thereby accruing to the self that acts. As we have seen in my analysis of Crowther, the missionaries advanced in their evangelical assault on Africa by using the rhetoric of spiritual crisis of Africans, based on the material crisis brought about by the slave trade. The black evangelists take up and replicate this rhetoric and add additional layers of complication. The most crucial one is the idea that their location as black whitemen is the great work of providence. In this sense, slavery made them possible as worldly actors and agents of God. At a second level, the Christian African subject they seek to bring about will need to sacrifice its particularity in order to become a copy of the West and accede to the status of universal "man." We know now that what their work made possible is not a "Christian" Africa. Rather, they have contributed to a history that predates them and continues on after them. In this unfolding history, "the African" is text: signification, not unmediated being.

The rhetoric of crisis and sacrifice served a purpose for missionary idealism, but it comes with the problem of moral binarisms (good versus evil, past versus present and future). For this reason, it cannot enable a robust understanding of the promise of literature in the era of globalization, still less the unfolding realities of pain and redemption in twenty-first-century Africa. Unlike the missionaries, the secular writers associated with twentieth-century Pan-Africanism cannot inhabit the discourse of sacrifice as unselfconsciously as Crowther and his fellow missionaries do. Likewise, modern African writers such as Achebe and Soyinka are at best contradictory in their deployment of the motif of sacrifice. It is to these twentieth-century iterations that I should now like to turn.

Notes

1. Conversion in its multiple valences has been a leitmotif of Africanist social history for decades now. As such, it is impossible to give any comprehensive list of existing studies on the subject. For a brief sample, see J. F. A. Ajayi, *Christian Missions in Nigeria 1841–1891*; Jean and John Comaroff, *Of Revelation and Revolution: Christianity, Colonialism, and Consciousness in South Africa*; Philip D. Curtin, *The Image of Africa Volume 2: British Ideas and Action*,

1780–1850; Michael J. C. Echeruo; Robert W. July; Lorand J. Matory; J. D. Y. Peel; Derek R. Peterson; Lamin Sanneh; Olufemi Taiwo; Philip S. Zachernuk.

2. See Ajayi, *Christian Missions*; Curtin, *The Image of Africa*; Peel.

3. See Echeruo; Matory; Sanneh. This process, which might appropriately be called "the Freetown experiment," offers a powerful concrete instance of the play of contingency in the making of history as well as its transmission—through literacy—from one generation to another and as official record. The CMS does not appear to have had as much sustained success when it tried to do something similar in eastern Africa by transporting receptives of the Arab slave trade in the Indian Ocean to a British colony named Frere Town. The settlement is named after Sir Bartle Frere, governor of Bombay Presidency, president of the Royal Geographical Society from 1873–74, and British antislavery envoy to Zanzibar (Keen, 15–16). The "Frere Town experiment" does not seem to have drawn the attention of Africanist historians in the same manner that the Freetown experiment did. But here, too, we have a historical event that crosses hemispheres and bridges oceans. Evidently, there is much work to be done in Africanist cultural studies to give appropriate scholarly attention to iterations of diaspora such as was occasioned by the Arab slave trade across the Indian Ocean, different in many ways from the more established tradition of studying the transatlantic Middle Passage but no less important.

4. See Ajayi, *Christian Missions*; Ayandele; Curtin, *The Image of Africa*; Peel; Zachernuk.

5. Fortunately, this situation is changing. For instance, see the special issue of *Research in African Literatures* 40, no. 4 (2009), guest edited by Adeleke Adeeko, Paul Tiyambe Zeleza, and Natasha Barnes, especially the articles by Adeleke Adeeko and Laura Murphy. See also Attwell; de Kock; Taiwo, 98–127.

6. By classic European missionary writing I mean the travel narratives of explorers such as Mungo Park and missionaries such as David Livingstone and Robert Moffat, to name only the most renowned. With regard to Nigeria in particular, we may cite here Mary Slessor and Rev. Hope Waddell of the Presbyterian Church of England, Rev. J. T. Bowen of the American Baptist Church, and Crowther's fellow Anglican missionaries Henry Townsend, Charles A. Gollmer, and David Hinderer, who translated Bunyan's *Pilgrim's Progress* into the Yoruba as *Ilọsíwájú Èrò Mímọ́*. See Gollmer; Park; Townsend.

7. When Martin R. Delany and Robert Campbell toured West Africa on behalf of the Niger Valley Exploring Party in 1859, Delany reported that he was allocated a piece of land "measuring ... Three Hundred and Thirty Feet square," by King Dosunmu of Lagos. The land was in a neighborhood called Okepopo and lies between Popo Aguda and Olowogbowo. In the signed title deed document, it is spelled Okai Po, Po (Delany and Campbell, 68). See Martin Delany and Robert Campbell, *Search for a Place. Black Separatism and Africa, 1860*. The book contains Delany's account titled "Official Report of the Niger Valley Exploring Party" and Campbell's "A Pilgrimage to My Motherland: An Account of a Journey among the Egbas and Yorubas of Central Africa, in 1859–60."

8. See Barber; Gikandi, *Maps of Englishness* and "Introduction"; Hofmeyr, "Reading Debating/Debating Reading"; Jenkins; Lawrance et al.; Mokoena; Newell.

9. See Attwell, *Rewriting Modernity* and de Kock, *Civilizing Barbarians*. Interestingly, Peel finds fault with the poststructuralism of Jean and John Comaroff as well as V. Y. Mudimbe. For Peel (4–9), these scholars are exemplars of the excesses of postmodernism. See Comaroff and Comaroff, *Of Revelation and Revolution, Volume One*; and Mudimbe, *The Invention of Africa*.

10. The classic text of the history of the Yoruba wars that fed so much into the transatlantic slave trade is authored by Rev. Samuel Johnson, himself a product of Sierra Leone and one of the missionaries of the CMS. See Johnson, *The History of the Yorubas*; see also Peel, 27–46; and Ajayi's introduction to Crowther's biography in Curtin, *Africa Remembered*, 289–98.

11. For accounts of Gollmer's and Townsend's missionary work in West Africa, see *Memoir of the Rev. Henry Townsend, Late C.M.S. Missionary, Abeokuta, West Africa*, compiled from his journals by his brother George Townsend and published in 1887; and *Charles Andrew Gollmer, His Life and Missionary Labours in West Africa*, compiled by his son and published in 1889. For Crowther's account of the 1841 expedition, see *Journals of the Rev. James Frederick Schön and Mr Samuel Crowther*, 371–85. Curtin includes Crowther's 1837 account of his capture and rescue, with introduction and notes by Ajayi, in the collection *Africa Remembered*. See Curtin, 298–316.

12. There are countless biographies of Crowther from the nineteenth- and twentieth-century era, most of them devoted to capturing a romantic life of drama and achievement. See Page; Tucker; Macaulay. Crowther's most authoritative academic biographer remains J. F. A. Ajayi. See Ajayi, "Bishop Crowther," *Christian Missions in Nigeria*, and *A Patriot to the Core*.

13. A copy of the Cape Town account can be found in a number of places, including the CMS archive at the University of Birmingham and the Yale Divinity Library.

14. Crowther's papers (letters, quarterly reports, and original manuscripts of published texts) are held in the CMS Archive at the University of Birmingham. The papers are listed in the archive guide as Original Papers CA1/079 (for the period up to 1844), CA2/031 (for his papers from 1844 through 1857), and CA3/04 (from 1857–88). Crowther's journals of his three Niger River expeditions as well as some selected overland travels and lectures are available as print publications. In those cases I cite the published texts and quote from them. In a few other cases I quote directly from the unpublished manuscript. The section of the CMS archive pertaining to the West African missions was published in microfilm by Adam Matthew Publications in 1999. See Keen.

15. Much later, in 1926, Sir John Glover's journal of the 1857 expedition was published by A. C. G. Hastings as *The Voyage of the Dayspring*, with the support of Elizabeth Glover (Glover's spouse) who provided the introduction. See Hastings.

16. *The Dual Mandate in British Tropical Africa* was originally published in 1922; however, the text I have quoted from is the version published by Frank Cass in 1965.

17. On Lugard, see my essay "Postcolonial Reverberations"; see also Taiwo, 128–54.

18. Freeman also wrote an unpublished autobiography that he doesn't appear to have completed. A typescript of this uncompleted biography is in the Wesleyan missionary archive at the School of Oriental and African Studies, London. On Freeman's energy as missionary worker and repeated flouting of the more bureaucratic and managerial strictures of his employers, see Ajayi; Aryee; Ayandele; Wright.

19. Quoted in Tim Couzens, *The New African*, 5.

20. See Gollock, *Lives of Eminent Africans*, 126–27. For examples of other collections within this genre, see Gollock, *Sons of Africa*; Rogers; Perham; Niven.

21. See the foreword to Margaret Musson's *Aggrey of Achimota* by A. G. Fraser. As I've already indicated, Aggrey's story was standard reference in mission schools and, later, public schools in the emerging African countries through the latter half of the twentieth century. Evidence of this is the existence of numerous pamphlets, abridged versions, and ephemeral publications recounting his life and deeds. I did a cursory WorldCat search for translations of these ephemera that may still be extant in African languages. My quick search revealed a translation of *Aggrey of Achimota* into Swahili as *Tai wa Africa* (Anonymous, 1948); into Yoruba as *Aggrey Achimota* (trans. T. T. Solaru, 1958). An abridged text of Kingsley Williams's *Aggrey of Africa* was translated into Xhosa as *U-Aggrey un-Africa* by Samuel Mqhayi.

3 Decolonization Time: Abrahams, James, Wright

IN THE PRECEDING chapter, I concentrated on the work of Samuel Ajayi Crowther as an instructive example of what the black whitemen of nineteenth-century Africa may contribute to our conversations about the black diaspora on the one hand, and literary globalism on the other. This chapter moves to the middle of the twentieth century to take up the case of black diasporic and African intellectuals associated with Pan-Africanism and anticolonial struggle. If nineteenth-century native missionary writing constitutes one iteration of what I am calling missionary moments, the twentieth-century figures associated with Pan-Africanism and anticolonial internationalism constitute another iteration, related but with its own specific nuances. Against a background of generally poststructuralist discussions of globalism in literary studies, such historical discourses as Pan-Africanism or negritude tend mostly to be recalled as conceptual and political dead ends—relics of a Manichean past. The essentialism and particularism of Senghor's negritude or Blyden's and Nkrumah's "African personality" are linked with the racialist phases of European and North American intellectual history, which are then contrasted to the more accommodating politics of cosmopolitanism and transnationalism. While granting the importance of the critique of essentialist thinking, my purpose in this book is to move the conversation to a discursive trajectory that both predates and sublates the moment of negritude (a product, by and large, of the 1930s through the 1960s).[1] Where the previous chapter focused on the nineteenth century, this chapter looks to critical lessons from the work of three intellectuals of African descent who wrote in the middle of the twentieth century.

Strictly speaking, the writings of figures such as Frantz Fanon, Richard Wright, C. L. R. James, Sol T. Plaatje, or Peter Abrahams were not addressed to narrowly academic audiences. Nonetheless, black diasporic writers such as Fanon, Wright, and James have now become influential in academic discussions of decolonization and resistance to racial injustice. By contrast, their African compatriots such as Plaatje and Abrahams have not been given the attention they deserve. This chapter seeks to redress the omission by taking up *Nkrumah and the Ghana Revolution* by C. L. R. James (1977), *Black Power: A Record of Reactions in a Land of Pathos* by Richard Wright (1954), and *A Wreath for Udomo* by Peter Abrahams (1956). On the surface, these texts are generically different; but at a deeper level, all three are in intertextual conversation. Taken together as discursive performances, they replay and exceed the general questioning of stable identities and cultural nationalism in current theory and criticism. James's *Nkrumah and the Ghana Revolution* presents itself as a book of Marxist political commentary, while Wright's *Black Power* perches indeterminately between the nonfiction of travelogue and the poetry—which is to say, the fictionality—of memoir. By contrast, Abrahams's *A Wreath for Udomo* is a work of fiction, at once roman à clef and melodramatic thriller. Yet, these texts share a midcentury perspective on Africa, even as they anticipate the institutional category we have come to call African literature.

Of the three of them, only Abrahams can be said to fit neatly and unreservedly into the label of Pan-Africanist. Relative to Wright, James is closer to Pan-Africanism principally because of his closeness to George Padmore and his work with the International African Service Bureau. As I indicated in chapter 1, my use of the term *Pan-Africanism* refers to the black-Atlantic discursive frame within which their work should compel our attention. Unlike the missionaries, they sought to rescue native traditions from Eurocentric and racist denigration. But their resistance to hegemonic representations of Africa is animated by confidence in the promise of modern nationhood. Their vision for a "revitalized" Africa is of an agglomeration of independent nation-states joining the march of secular modernity. As they saw it, secular Western modernity can become truly universal if purged of racism and other provincialisms. Their insistence on the integrity of precolonial Africa is thus overlaid by a discourse of modernity borrowed from the European Enlightenment. This contradiction is still very much with us, and the concrete political ramifications can be seen everywhere in contemporary Africa where the state fails, teeters on the edge of failure, or lives nominally on, kept in place by despotic violence. In this sense, the passion of writers such as James, Wright, and Abrahams should properly be seen as prefigurations of contemporary investments in literary globalism and intercultural understanding.

If one vision unites the black-Atlantic figures of this chapter, it is to contest the colonialist text and override it in words and material reality. But why use the singular *colonialist text* in reference to writings about a continent of immense cultural, political, and linguistic diversity? The notion of a colonial text of Africa is meant to designate the cluster of inherited ideas that have their roots in the nineteenth century and continue to influence the continent's location within Western European orders of knowledge. For the black-Atlantic intellectuals, the overcoming of the colonial text was not merely a project for the written word; it also had to be accomplished concretely through the building of a new society and a refashioned mode of collective organization. This new social direction is the secular state, founded on rationality and democratic principles. In taking up the legacy of black writing in the 1950s and 1960s, then, we come upon vexed abstractions at the heart of euromodern self-understanding: the big words freedom and nation, and inevitably, their Derridian supplements individuality and responsibility (or obligation). By now, of course, it would be easy to get to work deconstructing and retheorizing these abstractions, too easy to be interesting. Similarly, I don't think it is productive to simply reject them as ideas and material practices. My concern, rather, is to specify why black thinkers and activists found them appealing even while granting that they are historically tainted. I will begin with James writing about Kwame Nkrumah and Ghana, the first sub-Saharan black African country to win independence.

C. L. R. James on Nkrumah's Ghana

In *Nkrumah and the Ghana Revolution*, James demonstrates the difference that an anticolonial black-Atlantic perspective can make to the narration of a narrow slice of African history. What fascinates me about James's text is the novelization in the telling. Socialist, anticolonial activist, and mentor for many of the first generation of Anglophone African statesmen, James's text renders African natives—the denizens of ethnographic tales and objects of missionary altruism—as agents of historical change: active subjects of theory and historical recall. Born in the Caribbean island of Trinidad, C. L. R. James (1901–89) is highly celebrated as one of the preeminent black-Atlantic thinkers of the twentieth century. For figures such as Jomo Kenyatta of Kenya, Nnamdi Azikiwe of Nigeria, Julius Nyerere of Tanzania, and Kwame Nkrumah of Ghana, James served as inspirational thinker who influenced them with his ideas about socialism, about the possibility of a global proletariat, and about the emancipation of black peoples in Africa and the diaspora.

Formerly called the Gold Coast, Ghana is the first black African nation to attain juridical independence from Britain in 1957. At the head of the struggle that led to independence is the figure of Kwame Nkrumah, leader of the People's Convention Party. Nkrumah studied in the United States and then relocated to the United Kingdom. While in the United States, he came under the influence of James, and when he got to England, he became a protégé of fellow West Indian intellectual George Padmore (1902–59), understandably seen by many as another of the "founding fathers" of African nationalism. Nkrumah returned to Ghana in December 1947 and immediately became a leading figure in the struggle against British imperialism in Ghana. In addition to the sheer force of his personality and his early commitment to a Pan-African cultural and political outlook, Nkrumah's mystique derives in part from the rapidity with which he became the leader of the decolonization movement in Ghana within three years of returning, after having been away for twelve years. In James's discussion of the rise and fall of Nkrumah, this phenomenon is explained by Nkrumah's success in galvanizing the teeming masses of rural Ghana. James's approach is to mold the events from 1947 when Nkrumah returned into a kind of picaresque narrative, or perhaps a tragic tale of failed promise.

In considering James's account of Nkrumah's rise to power and subsequent downfall, my concern is to excavate a text of James's that has been neglected in literary and cultural criticism, even in these days of intense discussions about postcoloniality, black Atlanticism, and transnationalism. Compared to James's masterpieces such as *Black Jacobins, Beyond a Boundary*, or *Renegades and Castaways, Nkrumah and the Ghana Revolution* has not, to the best of my knowledge, attracted the attention of scholars in literary criticism or cultural studies. What I wish to do is, first, activate the text for the black-Atlantic archive and, second, demonstrate the sense in which James makes available to us a significant missionary moment and novelization effect. Although James's account operates as political commentary, it can productively be read as a literary text for a number of reasons. The text often works as picaresque account and intellectual biography of a moment in the adventure of black Atlanticism. James approaches Nkrumah's career as a critic might approach a literary text: that is, as a narrative of sheer human desire. Such an approach is consistent with James's tendency to conceptualize historical events in poetic terms.[2] The dimension of social and historical processes that makes them thinkable in literary terms is their inevitable human core. And to reach for the human core of the event is to set one's sights at its particularity. For James, the further we go into what is particular in a given literary or social text, the more we stand to encounter human dimensions therein that carry universal implications. It is particularity that gives content to universality: the latter opens up as graspable potential, only in the wake of the former. This ability to see the universal *in* and *as* the particular informs James's reading of the independence struggle of Nkrumah's Ghana. At the present time, when Anglo-American literary and cultural criticism is preoccupied with the challenge of productive intercultural or comparative analysis, the mode of thinking dramatized in *Nkrumah and the Ghana Revolution* is quite suggestive.

Kwame Nkrumah (1909–72) was the first prime minister of Ghana when the country became independent in March 1957. He saw himself as a revolutionary thinker and activist, dedicated to Pan-Africanism and African socialism. His rule was truncated in February 1966 in a military coup, and he died in exile in Guinea. He has been accused of descending into corruption and dictatorial rule soon after the euphoria of independence.[3] The degeneration of Nkrumah's tenure into dictatorship has led the Africanist political theorist Ali Mazrui to refer to him as a "Leninist czar." It is the background to the Ghanaian novelist Ayi Kwei Armah's (1968) *The Beautiful Ones Are Not Yet Born*, an excruciating critique of corruption and misrule in independent Ghana. And Nkrumah might as well be the figure satirized as the uninspired dictator Kongi in Wole Soyinka's play titled

Kongi's Harvest (1967). The story of Nkrumah and Ghana exemplifies a phenomenon that played out in many other African countries since the independence era of the 1960s. By the time James published the essays in *Nkrumah and the Ghana Revolution* together in 1977, Nkrumah was more a figure of failed opportunity than of heroic mastery. In line with his tendency to reach for poetic truth in order to articulate political truths, James's rendering of Nkrumah casts him as a flawed protagonist who happened to be the right person, in the right place, at the right time.

James uses his preface to the 1982 reprint of the book as occasion to reiterate, with the benefit of hindsight, the poetic truth of the story told in the book. The fact of hindsight is also evident in the book's structure. The heart of the narrative of Ghana's decolonization is in part I, and part II consists of five short pieces that James wrote after Nkrumah had become president of independent Ghana. As James indicates in the introduction, the articles included in part II serve to document his continued engagement with Nkrumah's activities after the initial euphoria of independence. In the third article titled "Slippery Descent," James announces his disassociation with what Nkrumah had by then become. In *African and Caribbean Politics*, Manning Marable suggested that James idealized Nkrumah's achievement from the outset. Similarly, Kent Worcester remarks that James invested too much in an inflated image of "Nkrumah's importance as a world historic individual" (198). My concern here is not the accuracy or otherwise of James's interpretation of Nkrumah and Ghana at the moment of independence from colonial rule. I do not discount the importance of arguing about accuracy or inaccuracy in historical reconstruction, but my interest in James's narrative comes from a different direction. Worcester's conclusion rests on a presupposition of the self-evidence of what counts as world historical. I am suggesting that James does idealize the meaning of Nkrumah's historical agency through poetic personification, but this is not because Ghana's decolonization is not a bona fide revolution. Rather, it is because revolutions and world historical figures are matters for interpretation. In other words, revolutions and revolutionaries do not come to us outside the phenomenological orbit of apprehension; that is to say, outside of the texts that name them as such. Understood this way, James's rhetorical inflation of Nkrumah is most appropriately read as a representational and philosophical challenge. James is challenging his contemporary left radicals to elevate their thinking to that zone where a local event in Africa can illuminate an understanding of shared global history, instead of being subsumed under it at the level of interpretation and cultural memory.

In his book, James offers a narrative of historical becoming and social change in an African society, one that can enrich ongoing discussions in postcolonial as well as African studies. Like any twentieth-century cultural nationalist, Nkrumah's language has ample room for the myth of prediscursive or transhistorical racial belonging. Marable rightly suggests that Nkrumah is in many respects more drawn to Marcus Garvey's Pan-Africanism than to James's class approach to nations and cultures. James undertakes to explain how Nkrumah's rhetoric and organizing strategies succeeded in galvanizing the masses of Ghana in a way that no other figure before him could. The most crucial issue for James is why Nkrumah's message moved people to action, not the abstract limitations of his rhetoric. In literary terms, James's approach to Nkrumah's legacy may be posed as a move beyond intrinsic analysis, toward a meditation on the dynamics of reception. According to James, four factors contributed to Nkrumah's success in galvanizing the people. First, the existence of large numbers of urban youths who felt disenfranchised and disoriented in the colonial city. These youths still retained ties to their ethnic villages. When Nkrumah came into the picture, it was possible to rally this constituency within cities such as Accra while also using them as a link between the urban and the rural countryside with which they still retained active contact. Second is the place of the traditional African social organization that places emphasis on collective social functioning in religious and secular domains. This basic factor offers tremendous potential for organization and the forging of a united front. James does not mystify this factor into some sort of tribal unanimism or a priori political efficacy. Like Frantz Fanon, he emphasizes the ultimately secular ground of the phenomenon. If the traditional system of social organization made it easier for Nkrumah to forge a united front, the galvanizing principle of that unity resides, as James puts it, "not in its black skins," but in "the conditions under which it is lived" (53). The third factor is related to the second: it is the importance of the market in the traditional society and the centrality of women in this domain: "In Accra there are thousands of women in action in the market, meeting tens of thousands of their fellow citizens every day. European visitors and officials up to 1947 saw in these markets a primitive and quaint survival in the modern town. In reality here was, ready formed, a social organization of immense power, radiating from the center into every corner and room of the town" (55). The final factor is the ferment of ongoing black struggles in the New World, and the social and epistemological consequences of this and World War II. If the first three factors derive from the internal dynamics of Ghanaian life and society, the fourth derives from the contact of that society with events from the outside world. With black struggles in the diaspora and the achievement of independence by India, a specific subjective state became available.

The implication of James's account is that the entity that became Ghana was being forged in the period after World War II, even as that forging was made possible by conditions already present within the heterogeneous ethnic groups that constitute modern Ghana. The traditional mode of life of these groups turns out, somewhat paradoxically, to provide a ready anchor for Nkrumah's rhetorical and organizational skills in articulating a vision of modernizing Ghana. The tendency to see tradition as being limited to local ethnic politics is here rewritten by James, such that a local, ethnic configuration becomes the enabling mechanism for a transethnic (that is to say, nationalist) movement. This mode of analysis enables James to sketch collective identity in terms that avoid the trap of ethnic essentialism. In describing "the people" of Ghana, what James does is to narrate how they became a collective at a specific point in time and how that dialectic of becoming led to a juridical entity and a subjective image that came to be known as Ghana.

In this regard, the pivotal chapter is the third chapter, titled "The People in 1947." Seeking to "form an estimate of the people in 1947," James begins with a meditation on the problems as well as necessity of the task:

> Let us try to form some estimate of the people in 1947. It is a necessary task even if at best it can only be an approximate one. The fundamental difficulty is that only after a revolution or at a definite stage in it, as for example in the 1951 elections in the Gold Coast, is one able to estimate what the people were like before the revolution began. The people themselves do not know. The process of the revolution is essentially the process of the people finding themselves. As they scale one height, that girds them to attempt another. It is sufficient to say that this rapid movement is contained in them before they move a step, though it may be only in vague aspirations and thoughts which they do not think through to the end. (50)

James does not ascribe priority to any of the factors he identifies as contributory to the Ghana revolution and the contingent, datable identity that accompanied it. In his account, all four factors coalesced at the moment of the struggle. On James's terms, it is in the nature of social upheavals that each of the factors be indispensable without being solely determinant. In *Hegemony and Socialist Strategy*, Ernesto Laclau and Chantal Mouffe (1985) redeployed the psychoanalytical concept of overdetermination to argue that economic factors alone cannot account for social change. Their critique of economism in cultural analysis is of course entirely legitimate. And yet, as Stuart Hall puts it in his complaint about Anglo-American postcolonial theory, what has resulted from the critique of economism in literary and cultural studies is often a disavowal of economics altogether. It is as though "since the economic in its broadest sense, definitively does *not*, as it was once supposed to do, 'determine' the real movement of history in the last instance,' it does not exist at all!" (Hall, "When Was 'the Post-Colonial'?," 258). James identifies multiple factors to explain Nkrumah's success in interpellating people. He grounds these factors as much in the people's preexisting modes of life as in global developments around them; and all the while, the economic dimension inheres in each of the factors. The centrality of the market in its traditional as well as modulated modern version testifies to this economic dimension, as does the factor of the urban youths, who are of course in the cities for material reasons. In this way, in telling the story of a successful elaboration of collectivity by an African nationalist, C. L. R. James articulates a vision, not of simple plenitude of African being, but of a datable instance of change.

It is very instructive that James's procedure is retroactive-explanatory, not normative-prescriptive. He explicitly drives this point home in the chapter titled "The Revolution in Theory." "What is written here," he notes, "does not embrace all that is involved [in Ghana's decolonization struggle] and it is certain that it could not have been written at the time nor was there any need to do so" (74). The simple self-circumscription revealed in this passage is remarkable in light of the easy certainty with which notions of resistance sometimes emerge in Anglo-American cultural criticism influenced by poststructuralism. As I argued in my discussion of Alain Badiou and Hardt and Negri's *Empire*, it is taken for granted that because cultural-nationalist discourses rely on notions of prediscursive identities, those discourses are *necessarily* doomed to political inefficacy. In this, such theorizing reenacts familiar leftist theoretical condescension toward every major black Marxist of the twentieth century.[4] In James's account, one can apprehend Nkrumah's conjunctural agency while at the same time retaining the qualifying force of historical hindsight. In other words, the fact that Nkrumah and his compatriots did not establish an equitable society that would be free of colonial structures does not negate the significance of decolonization as a watershed moment. By proceeding with a substantive demarcation between the preindependence (anticolonial) movement and the postindependence Nkrumah, James makes it possible to assess both as distinct moments, albeit in an ultimately single narrative of Ghanaian modernity.

Based on colonial documents and Nkrumah's life story, *Nkrumah and the Ghana Revolution* is a work of interpretation, but what is being "read" is rich with complications. James makes no qualms about the fact that he is telling Nkrumah's story as much for its intrinsic interest as for its theoretical value for global politics at the moment of his writing. With James, we are not in the realm of claims made solely on the authority of individual experience. By this I mean a procedure where thought responds to external causal factors by misrecognizing linguistic representation as capacious, totalizing objectivity. Very much to the contrary, we are in the realm of experience (understood as affective partisan involvement) nourished by interpretive distance, by the labor of reflection. The opening paragraph of the preface gestures in the direction of knowledge and its production and representation: "Few people whom I meet," he writes, "even learned and scholarly ones, have any idea of the tremendous event—the historical miracle—which has taken place during the last twenty-five years. I am fairly well read and I know nothing like it" (7). By emphasizing that his account is a labor of love as well as of intellectual exertion, James positions Nkrumah's Ghana as an object of knowledge in addition to whatever else it happens to be. An important theme in *Nkrumah and the Ghana Revolution* is therefore the theoretical value that Ghana's independence struggle might have for the telling of transnational history in the mid-twentieth century. For James, Africa's decolonization is not a secondary event in a global history that illuminates it or directs its unfolding:

> Myth-making conceals [a] virulent poison for the myth-makers. It insists that they see themselves always as the givers, and Africans as the takers, themselves as teachers and Africans as the taught. In the thousands of reports, articles, speeches, that I have read about events in Ghana, I have never seen a single word, the slightest hint that anything which took place there could instruct or inspire the peoples of the advanced countries in their own management of their own affairs, and this is as true of friends of Ghana as of its enemies. Yet I doubt if, with the single exception of the Hungarian revolution, any event since the end of the Second World War has been so charged with symbolic significance for the future of Europe and America as what took place in the Gold Coast between November 1947 and February 1951. (38–39)

In this passage, James positions Ghana at the center of a discourse on global culture. On these terms, Nkrumah's story is universal precisely because it happened in Ghana and could only have happened there at that time. Writing of Shakespeare's universality, James once quipped that Shakespeare is universal, not because he transcends his time and place as they say, but because "he was so much of an age."[5] In a similar vein, James demonstrates by means of his reading of Nkrumah's career that every creative act owes whatever universal meaning it has to the depth of its immersion in its local and particular determinations. In this way, James overcomes the covert tendency to disguise metropolitan concerns as paradigmatically global and universal.

So far, I have approached James's account as record of an intellectual journey into a culture he doesn't live but with which he aligns himself politically. Posed this way, *Nkrumah and the Ghana Revolution* could equally well be read as an intellectual autobiography, a text of black Atlanticism that does not evacuate continental Africans of agency. In James's hands, Ghana emerges as the occasion and center of a discourse on the global adventure of modernity. As a black diasporic subject, James precedes current cultural criticism in his recognition of the immanence of black-Atlantic discourse within modernity, even if only on its abjected margins. The epistemological potential he discerns within otherwise disparate social processes gives his thinking an immanent cosmopolitan design. Since James's active working years with Pan-Africanism, a lot has changed in the way Africa is written about. If, in colonialist and old-style ethnographic writing, Africa designated static ontological difference against which normative Western discourses articulated the conditions of modernity, many Africanist scholars and writers have since worked to undermine the notion that Africa holds some opaque unitary metaphysics. To preempt a claim I will develop in the next chapter, creative writers such as Chinua Achebe and Wole Soyinka of Nigeria have also contributed in many ways to the critique of the discursive construction of Africa as static signifier of the primordial and the premodern. Although many African writers replicate ideologies of modernization and the nation-state that are open to criticism, they also meditate on the historicity of the yearning for nation and the modern. And they do so with a humane charge that imaginative literature distinctively makes possible. They thereby make visible the paradoxes of the social engineering that began in black Africa with nineteenth-century Christian conversion, formal colonialism, and anticolonial nationalism. James precedes them in this vision and practice. Read like a literary text, an act of language and gesture of will, James's *Nkrumah and the Ghana Revolution* instantiates an early decolonizing current in the understanding of African modernity.

James's discussion of Nkrumah's career raises a set of questions that become especially pertinent to current literary and cultural criticism. In a context where paradigms of globalism—understood as conceptual progress beyond nationalist particularisms—have now become the new hegemonic value, what is the place of peripheral nations in the recent embrace of the transnational? What are we to make of the continued impact of nationalisms and the ongoing currency of various aggressive constructions of identity? If nations are not organic units despite the tendency of nationalist rhetoric to figure them as such, is it possible to endorse this insight and also give conceptual space to the historicity of specific nationalisms? In *Writing Ghana, Imagining Africa*, Kwaku Larbi Korang (2004) examines the beginnings of nationalist self-understanding in Ghana. He shows how successive generations of the westernized elite contributed to the shaping of a national identity in and through rhetoric. Korang demonstrates the black-Atlantic reach of this ferment of ideas from the nineteenth century through the twentieth, placing well-known figures such as Blyden, Horton, Casely-Hayford, and Nkrumah next to their less studied compatriots such as Rev. C. C. Reindorf, Attoh Ahuma, J. Mensah Sarbah, and Kobina Sekyi. He identifies two ideological currents in the writings of these intellectuals. The first, which he labels Orphean, seeks to retain the past and posits westernization as capitulation to the colonizer. The second current, which he calls Promethean, fixates on the challenge of the present and the possibilities of the future. For Korang, this second ideological current sees what is required of middle-class Africans in terms of a daring act of creative appropriation and visionary pragmatism. In his account, this ideological current begins with Horton, "becomes relatively muted under colonial rule, but [is] rekindled in post–World War II African anticolonialism . . . embodied centrally by Kwame Nkrumah" (17). According to Korang, "Orphean and Promethean alike . . . were confronted . . . by the problem—into which the imagining of nation, as a problematic, will come to be folded—of African modernity.

The sum of their navigations and negotiations of problem and problematic has been a projection of a modernity that would be African, an African modernity centered in the modernist given of nationality" (19). Korang makes his account of Ghana's decolonization conduce into a meditation on the present challenges facing the continent and the writers who represent it, as well as the intellectuals who study it. Addressing the issue of Nkrumah's self-presentation on the public stage, Korang suggests that James "goes completely overboard" in presenting Nkrumah as solely a product of Western modernity. For him, we should take seriously Nkrumah's claim in his philosophical treatise, *Consciencism*, that modern Africa is a site of heterogeneous entanglements: the West (Christianity), the East (Islam), and traditional African values (Korang, 316). Korang is correct to contest James's tendency to read the first generation of African intellectuals unambiguously as products of Western formation, primarily because the lexicon of their modern aspirations derives from missionary schools and the tradition of Shakespeare and Hobbes. In this respect, James's Eurocentric exuberance might be construed as a symptomatic unthought, one that he shares with Wright and Abrahams, as we shall see.

However, there is more to be said about James's emphasis on the Western sources of Nkrumah's style. I suggest that James does underplay dimensions of Nkrumah that derive from an African cultural formation, but he thereby instantiates an approach that is attentive to change rather than the stasis of inheritance and the given. Academic and popular discussion of things African has dwelt for too long on the trope of traditional culture in conflict with modernity. Likewise, discussion of African literature too often takes for granted the stability of things European and things African. And yet, the everyday reality of postcolonial Africa reveals more complicated realities. Take for instance the ubiquity of Pentecostal Christianity in contemporary Africa. This international million-dollar industry deploys all the transmedial resources of the digital age. From Lagos to Nairobi to Johannesburg, Pentecostal organizations are engaged in hybridizing traditional cultural elements (music, oral performative styles, etc.) with a belief system imported from the West. These organizations and their followers put into fluid motion traditional performance forms alongside biblical narratives and the metaphysics of Christian redemption.

Yet, what is at stake here is more fraught than merely academic recognition of hybridity and syncretism. The vibrancy of religious practices in Africa, as elsewhere, also comes with unpredictability and danger. As we know, the rise of Pentecostalism in African countries is coeval with the rise of militant Islamic groups such as Boko Haram. It is here that the potential of such materialist Pan-Africanism as James's should strike us with especial relevance. I am reminded of the case of Umar Farouk AbdulMutallab, the young man who tried to detonate a bomb on a Northwest Airline flight in December 2009. This privileged young man, twenty-three years old at the time, comes from a wealthy family background. His father had served as a major bank chairman and was former federal minister for economic development in Nigeria. While discussing the case with a colleague of mine at an academic conference some years ago, my colleague remarked that if the young man had been a student in the early twentieth century, he might have had the option of socialism or Pan-Africanism rather than religious militancy. As an undergraduate at University College, the young man could be said to be following in the footsteps of the African elite before him. We may randomly mention some examples. Although it was not published until 1930, Sol T. Plaatje probably wrote some of his novel *Mhudi* in London between 1914 and 1917, during his visit as member of a delegation of African National Congress leaders to protest the South African Natives Land Act of 1913. In the course of his stay in London, he was associated with University College through his collaboration with linguistics scholar Daniel Jones on the phonetics of Tswana. During another visit in 1922–23, Plaatje recorded an early version of "Nkosi Sikelele i'Africa" to piano accompaniment by Sylvia Colenso. Plaatje's recording in October 1923 immortalizes a song that later serves the anti-apartheid resistance and becomes the opening movement of post-apartheid South Africa's national anthem.[6] Jomo Kenyatta (1938) wrote *Facing Mount Kenya* while studying with Malinowski at London School of Economics and helped to organize the Manchester fifth Pan-African conference in 1945 in the company of Du Bois, Padmore, James, and of course, Nkrumah. In Wole Soyinka's *Death and the King's Horseman*, colonial district officer Simon Pilkings is exasperated that Olunde, the African student in wartime England, may be spending too much time with "commies and anarchists over there" (66). Pilkings is speaking of a character type from a previous era: the Pan-African cultural nationalists. In the first half of the twentieth century, a colonial student in London would have intellectual options to learn from other than sacrifice (of self or others) in anticipation of the afterlife. In this sense, AbdulMutallab's turn to religious militancy, in the form it came to take for him, is a sobering regression from the vision of the Pan-Africanists who congregated in European capitals in the mid-twentieth century. Nkrumah may indeed not be a world historical figure as Kent Worcester suggested, and the decolonization era certainly has its limitations. But inherently contradictory as it was, its intermingling of nationalist idealism with cosmopolitan internationalism is, by all measures, more generative. James's reading of Nkrumah illuminates a moment of possibility from that era. He presents us with a vision from the mid-twentieth century, oriented toward a future that is now ours but also more than ours.

James discerns in Ghana's independence struggle a drama of human desire—individual and collective. He thereby confers on the African decolonization movement a poetic aspect. But his narrative consistently maintains a theoretical alertness. James disentangles Nkrumah's rhetoric of black essentialism from the actual pragmatics of his maneuvers during the decolonization struggle. If these aspects of Nkrumah and the Ghana Revolution constitute its pluses, they are yet accompanied by a blind spot. In Benedict Anderson and many other commentators, the rhetoric of nationhood arose to fill a lack occasioned by the death of God in the public sphere; in James, Nkrumah's rhetoric of nationhood served to enclose and sublate the polytheism of the ideational universe of natives. The many deities of the native are sublated, canceled, and raised up into the single god of the secular state. My metaphor of the single god is meant to draw attention to the way in which James brings together the interrelated ideas of secularism, rationality, and the state. For the metaphor betrays a *slippage* that James does not recognize: the single god of the rational state is as well the "nonrational" God of Christianity—the religious ground upon which its logic of emergence rests and from which its contemporary ramifications can never be delinked. This slippage emerges even more strongly, and indeed becomes abrasive, in Richard Wright's critique of Africa's colonial modernity. I will develop this point in the next section by focusing on Black Power, Wright's travel memoir about Ghana at the moment of independence.

Richard Wright and the Terror of Gods

Black Power: A Record of Reactions in a Land of Pathos was published in 1954—in the United States by Harper and in Britain by Dennis Dobson. The American edition begins with two photographs of Nkrumah. In 2008, HarperCollins released an edition of *Black Power* in an omnibus package that includes *The Color Curtain* and *White Man, Listen*. This edition comes with an introduction written by Cornel West but omits the photographs of Nkrumah. The British edition published in London in 1954 also omits the images but reproduces photographs of people and sites taken by Wright himself in the course of his visit to the Gold Coast. In "Nation Time: Richard Wright, *Black Power*, and Photographic Modernism," Sara Blair has examined Wright's travel memoir in terms of modernism's complicated attachment to the photographic image. Commenting on the difference between the American and British editions, Blair writes:

> During the ten weeks in 1953 Wright spent living, traveling, and writing in Gold Coast, he shot over 1,500 photographs with his own professional-grade camera (an apparatus with which he was intimately familiar ...). The making and use of photographs during his travels was of such a high order of priority that Wright went to great lengths—not only in port towns or larger villages and the capital, but in far more remote areas in the bush country—to obtain chemicals and supplies for developing and printing his negatives as he traveled. Only thirty-four of these images were ever published as part of Wright's text, and only then outside the United States (they appeared in the British edition of the text). (131)

Blair shows the ways in which Wright's self-positioning as critical observer and camera-wielding artist reveal the tense interaction of Eurocentric forms (in this case, modernism and its mid-twentieth-century afterlife) and temporalities (here, tribal as opposed to decolonized, modernizing Africa) in the memoir. It is interesting that the Dennis Dobson edition does not include the Nkrumah photographs but reproduces images reflecting Wright's photographic gaze on everyday Ghanaians (curbside food sellers, young girls at play, tribal elders, slave castle). It is no less interesting that the American edition does not use the photographs but begins instead with images of Nkrumah himself. For my purposes, what is of most interest is that the issue of temporality and subjectivity identified by Blair emerges also in the photographs of Nkrumah in the first American edition.

I would like to begin my discussion of *Black Power* with the two images of Nkrumah on the frontispiece of the first American edition.[7] In the first photograph, he is wearing the iconic Akan traditional kente fabric. Nkrumah faces the camera directly, and the low-angle shot frames his broad upper body such that his broad grin reaches outward and slightly downward at us. This is a big man who is sure he knows his worth; the statesman out on a political campaign, expansive with his crowd. In the second photograph, he is wearing a dark-colored suit. The shot here is perhaps eye level, but the subject is positioned sideways relative to the camera. The result is that Nkrumah's gaze is directed away from us, staring enigmatically into the distance. He is also smiling in this picture, but the smile is far less expansive. The eyes are haunting, penetrating; the smile might be rueful or devious, but in their boyish freeze, they could just as well suggest basic inwardness. In this second photograph, Nkrumah's gaze suggests neither timidity nor confidence, neither studied affability nor indifference. The calm gaze focuses on something other than present audience or company—indeed, something other than the present altogether. Where the first photograph offers a confident, affable extrovert, the second gives us a somber, less readable thinker.

It is fair to say that the frontispiece places the image of extrovert next to that of enigmatic thinker; in doing so, it evokes the cliché of inherent difference between the politician (read extrovert) and the intellectual (read enigmatic thinker). It is doubly interesting, then, that Nkrumah of the second photograph (i.e., Nkrumah the intellectual) is in a Western suit. The immediate desire is inward, away from the camera's intrusion, and more introspectively toward the void of space that thereby becomes also a void of time. The photographs are positioned so that the intellectual Nkrumah is bottom right inset of the politician. It is as though the insertion of the intellectual figure within the political figure subordinates one to the other. Let me push this idea as far as it would go: the subordination of the intellectual to the politician in the frontispiece of the first American edition of *Black Power* might be read as a caution. The caution here would be that the emerging nation-state that then went by the name of Gold

Coast (and indeed, Nkrumah) should be aware of a difference between the intellectual's brooding reticence and the politician's capacious charm. The fact that the figure of Nkrumah as intellectual is in a Western suit while the politician is in an iconic traditional fabric points up some ideological assumptions. The traditional dress becomes code for grassroots popularity even though its wearer is supposedly leader of a secular liberal state on the Western model. By means of the kente and the expansive self-presentation of this Nkrumah, the extroverted is equated with the popular, and both are dressed in the indexical garb of "tradition." It is as though traditional Africa could not have produced the insecure, solitude-loving introvert.

The juxtaposed images arrest me as reader and initiate the complication of temporalities in Wright's *Black Power*. Much more than James, Wright is obsessed with the explosive interactions of religion with science and rationality. He visited the Gold Coast from June 2, 1953 to September 2, 1953, and *Black Power* is the book that resulted from the trip. This book has not been given much attention in the critical discussions of transnationalism and diaspora. In the 1970s, Michel Fabre attributed its relative obscurity to the fact that audiences were not very interested in Africa. Several critics who have examined *Black Power* rightly remark Wright's obvious condescension toward the culture and people he is describing.[8] For my concerns in this study, *Black Power* is significant as much for Wright's contentious representation of Africans as for his recommendation for the path forward. In relentless prose that sometimes becomes repetitive, Wright describes the practices and rituals of the people he is visiting as childlike and unreflecting. The people are simply victims of their own primitive beliefs, their inability to become *individuals* as opposed to members of a tribal collectivity. In the letter to Nkrumah that closes the book, Wright concludes, "African culture has not developed the personalities of the people to a degree that their egos are stout, hard, sharply defined; there is too much cloudiness in the African's mentality, a kind of sodden vagueness that makes for lack of confidence, an absence of focus that renders that mentality incapable of grasping the workaday world" (343). I will have occasion to return to this passage.

Recently, Henry Louis Gates Jr. has offered an engaging critique of Wright's essay "Tradition and Industrialization: The Plight of the Tragic Elite in Africa," delivered at the International Conference of Negro Writers and Artists held in 1956, two years after *Black Power* appeared. In that essay, Wright reiterates his point about the antinomy between tradition and industrialization, an antinomy that for him implies that the tribal world needs to be superseded, mythic thinking needs to disappear to make room for the demands of modernization. In Gates's reading, Wright's disdain for the Africans who are his subjects betrays a tendency to see Africa as the negative antithesis of the West. Equally troubling for Gates is Wright's error of seeing the West as symbol of rationality. For in such an equation, the only way Africa can survive is to become a belated copy of the West. Gates rejects Wright's exhorbitation of science as a new kind of missionary zeal, where Science replaces God, but the imperious mystification of self and other remains untroubled. Gates positions Wright's heroic protectiveness toward the colonized culture as a version of Thomas Babington Macaulay's attitude to India under the East India Trading Company. In this sense, his critique of Wright is as much about the limitations of Wright's black Atlanticism as it is about postcolonial and transnational studies at the present time. His rejection of Wright's heroic rationalism operates as a cautionary tale for paradigms of transnationalism and global theory in their diverse manifestations. Gates is correct on many levels; however, my aim here is to elicit what Wright's text makes available to us right alongside its undeniable limitations. What lessons, I want to ask, might Wright's account of Ghana and Africa in the 1950s have in store for literary globalism and African studies at the present time?

For starters, consider the subtitle of Wright's lecture: "The Plight of the Tragic Elite in Africa." The notion of a tragic elite invokes the category of "tragic mulatto" in African American letters, and it is difficult not to suspect that Wright is deliberately being provocative here. As is well known, the so-called tragic mulatto in American literature is a figure of liminality belonging neither to the black nor the white world. The liminality, which generates confusion and tragedy, is also a position of privilege in the hierarchy of racist colorism. Approached from this perspective, Wright yields the historical particularity of his language and conceptual infrastructure. In *Black Power*, Wright expresses strong antipathy toward any approach to the world that is not grounded in secular-scientific reason. For him, Christianity is as irrational as African animism. His *Pagan Spain* (1957) sees the rigid Catholicism of Franco's Spain as a pagan manifestation. Likewise, racism is for him a premodern disposition because it operates at a prelogical level and projects fears upon a fetishized other. Wright's injunction, then, is that Africa should get rid of its irrationalities in order to catch up with modernity.

Wright's problem in *Black Power* might be posed as one of genre, for the book presents itself as a memoir, a work of nonfiction. It is supposed to document an experience in language, to reflect on that experience and, on the strength of the reflections, suggest a direction for the future. Taken on his own terms, Wright's nonfictional mode undertakes to articulate problems and formulate possibilities for solving them. The book invites these expectations in its subtitle: "A Record of Reactions in a Land of Pathos." To take the text on the generic expectation it sets up, then, is to expect political or philosophical clarity. The sort of reading that takes the text on its own terms has its justification, but it is helpful to set aside Wright's intention and the terms of its formulation. I suggest, rather, that much can be learned from reading *Black Power* as a productive provocation, a novelization of the discourses of savage Africa inherited from the nineteenth century.

A first clue is the anthropomorphism of Africa mobilized in the phrase "land of pathos." As a geographical category, a space in time on a map, "Africa" cannot be the subject of the pathos. That is, land uninscribed with human intention cannot elicit pathos. If the land evokes a sentiment of pathos, then, the subject of the sentiment is not the mute incandescence of space in time but rather, the human affect that grasps it as such. To ask what the subject of the pathos is—is it the author or his readers?—is to stir up one of the contradictions at the heart of *Black Power*. Wright's journey follows a familiar pattern of nineteenth-century travel narratives about Africa. The progression is of the Western cognitive subject traveling from the coast into the interior, penetrating the unknown. In this way, we would do well to register the novelistic dimension of Wright's narrative. His journey takes him from Paris to Liverpool. He disembarks at Takoradi and moves from there to Accra, still on the coast. From Accra he travels inland to Kumasi, capital of the Ashanti Empire. Ashanti is one of the most powerful conquest states of nineteenth-century Africa, alongside other kingdoms such as Oyo, Benin, and the Zulu Empire. It is the Kumasi that fascinated missionaries and Christian chapbooks enormously. In 1941, just over a decade before Wright arrived on the Gold Coast in 1953, M. R. Bielby published one such pamphlet in homage to the heroism of Thomas Birch Freeman and saw fit to title it *Alone to the City of Blood*.

Being the fabled center of superstition and sheer blood lust, Kumasi works in Wright's text to reinvigorate colonial discourse about African despotism. But Wright's journey is circular in that he retraces his steps, from Kumasi back to Cape Coast. Wright's account therefore resonates with clichéd colonial accounts of the African hinterland but nuances it with the specter of the Middle Passage: the intimacy of the sea and its coast. He suffers from the oppressive heat, the lack of sanitation and conveniences of urban life. In other words, he suffers physically from the fact that Accra is not Paris, London, or New York. However, his antipathy to the people and the environment is at every point complicated by a curious identification, or at least ambivalent recognition, of what others might have expected to be "natural" racial bonding. Constantly, Wright remarks and simultaneously disavows racial kinship. The book begins with a dedication to "the unknown African" who, "because of his primal and poetic humanity, was regarded by white men as a 'thing' to be bought, sold, and used as an instrument of production; and who, alone in the forests of West Africa, created a vision of life so simple as to be terrifying, yet a vision that was irreducibly human." This invocation makes the Africa of Wright's text discursive: that is, a representation that holds meaning, first and foremost, within the language of modernity that Wright has inherited. And so, Wright the existentialist novelist is able to universalize the irrational beliefs of his Africans as evidence of the "wild and dark poetry of the human heart" (293).

Wright is disdainful of the so-called African and the so-called "average American Negro." According to him, both suffer from backwardness and absence of reflection. By contrast, he locates himself at an abstract point of epistemic transcendence. On one occasion, he informs an informant named Nana that Africans should not expect to learn anything from African Americans: "The American Negro has done no reflective thinking about the value of the world into which he fought so hard to enter. He just panted to get into that world and be an American, that's all. The average American Negro is perhaps the least qualified person on earth to guide you in matters of this sort" (288). He tells his interlocutor: "I'm black, Nana, but I'm Western, and you must never forget that we of the West brought you to this pass" (288). The "we" in this sentence is as much an abstraction as the unknown African that Wright references in the excerpt we examined earlier. Wright claims to be part of that "we," to be "of the West" even as he acknowledges that the belonging is uneasy.

What I have been indicating is that Wright's "African" should be thought of as both object and product of the discursive field of modernism in literature, art history, sociology, and psychology. The text dramatizes this quite powerfully in a passage that occurs at the beginning of Wright's travel. The ship taking him to the Gold Coast has just left Freetown (Sierra Leone), and "as we sailed . . . I saw my first real tropical sunset" (20). The new experience prompts him to reflect on religion: "As I watched the sea and the sky I knew that it was from feelings such as these floating in me now that man has got his sense of God" (21). Wright continues:

> These feelings I do not deny, and I've not been the first to feel them. I do not know why they are such as they are, what they really mean, but I stand before them with the same attention that I stand before this sea and this sky. I refuse to make a religion out of that which I do not know. I too can feel the limit of my reactions, can feel where my puny self ends, *can savor the terror of it*; but it does not make me want to impose that sense of my terror on others, or rear it into a compulsive system. Detached, I contain my terror, look at it and wonder about it in the same way that I marvel about this sea and sky. (21, emphasis added)

The passage casts the African landscape as a kind of art object to be contemplated, approached alternately in the mode of the abject or the wounded that demands patronizing solidarity. The passage displaces the author's anxieties about the numinous cosmos into an object of pure thought confronting him. Wright transforms his feelings as he approaches Takoradi in the tropical heat ("the echoing declarations . . . roused in me") into language about the fear of the unknown. The author engages this challenge through an ekphrastic logic that transmutes his fear into art and contemplates this art/fear as aesthetic experience. He contemplates it without any optimistic hope that he can fully understand or assuage the terror. The sensation of terror in fact becomes something he means to "savor," somewhat like the audience savors bloodbath when Elizabethan tragedy unfolds on stage.

It is crucial to the text's design that this reflection occurs as the author approaches Ghana, home of the Ashanti. It is crucial also that the immediate setting is a ship in the Atlantic. The sea, the sky, and the transatlantic ship taking Wright to the old Ashanti Empire become the backdrop against which Wright's narrative unfolds. The defeated remains of an old empire and the Gold Coast as colonized "man" on the verge of freedom: these combine to offer Wright a glimpse of modern history and primal humanity. But the cognitive subject places himself squarely within the frame of the canvas, in the middle of action, so to speak. Wright references his limitations as cognitive subject and narrating self: he can "feel where [his] puny self ends." He is there not just as "man" but as a man of African ancestry and recognizes it at many points. Upon seeing what he calls a "kind of queer shuffling dance" among a crowd of cheering women of Nkrumah's People's Convention Party, he recalls seeing exactly that kind of dance "in store-front churches, in Holy Roller Tabernacles . . . in unpainted wooden prayer-meeting houses on the plantations of the Deep South" (56). The recognition prompts him to consider the question, then animating the discipline of cultural anthropology, of African survivals within African American culture. Even though he rejects any explanation that would see in such survivals evidence of racial affinity beyond history and culture, the very fact that he has to recognize the issue and seek to sort it out makes his point of view specific. In this way, Wright's imperious text enacts a distinctive struggle marked by diasporic questioning about cultural heritage and racial belonging.

Later, Wright considers the enormity of the challenge facing Nkrumah in light of the fact that there would not be enough Ghanaians with the professional (Western) training to manage the country's affairs initially upon independence. After positing that what Nkrumah has unleashed in the people is "liquid emotion," he continues: "But could this liquid emotion be harnessed to modern techniques? . . . And from where would come the men to handle the work of administration when self-government came?" (65–66). The image of liquid emotion carries the implication of latent energy that could be dangerous, if for no other reason than that it can be driven in *any* direction by the appropriate force. The liquid is not static; it moves and is moved. A demonstration of this occurs in the section where Wright has a conversation with one chief. The chief claims that his subjects are not as energetic and progressive in their pursuit of modernity as he would like. Wright cautions the chief not to be too sanguine in his valuation of modernity as an ideal. The section concludes with the following passage:

> The pathos that arose from my talking to Africans about their problems was that their minds were uninformed—thanks to the contribution of British education—about the bodies of knowledge relevant to their situation, bodies of knowledge which other peoples had erected at a great cost of suffering, toil, and sacrifice. Hence, I felt that almost any decision that the Africans would make, perhaps for some time to come, would be a hit-or-miss proposition, that they would have to tread ground already laboriously trampled by others. But there was no turning back; historic events had committed the Africans to change.... For good or ill, the die was cast. The game was up. What had been done, could not now be undone. Africa was moving.... (289)

This passage does a number of things. The phrase "bodies of knowledge" implies modern science, philosophies of secularism, and the superseding of premodern hierarchies based on station. Wright is indirectly echoing Marx's infamous claim that British colonialism and capitalist incursion into India would bring that benighted society into the march of progress. This is why, in his closing letter to Nkrumah, he asserts that the problem of Africa is that Africans need to be "hard" in order to be ready for modernity. In his words:

> I found only one intangible but vitally important element in the heritage of tribal culture that militated against cohesiveness of action: African culture has not developed the personalities of the people to a degree that their egos are stout, hard, sharply defined; there is too much cloudiness in the African mentality, a kind of sodden vagueness that makes for lack of confidence, an absence of focus that renders that mentality incapable of grasping the workaday world. And until confidence is established at the center of African personality, until there is an inner reorganization of that personality, there can be no question of marching from the tribal order to the twentieth century.... At the moment, this subjective task is more important than economics! (343)

We note the language of empirical discovery with which Wright opens the passage ("I found . . ."). And yet what he finds is "one intangible but vitally important element." Testifying to this intangible element, according to Wright, is the prevalence among Africans of "sodden vagueness" and "absence of focus." These arise because "egos" are not "stout, hard, sharply defined." The remedy Wright suggests is no less intangible: an "inner reorganization of . . . personality"—a task that supposedly rests in the realm of the subjective as opposed to the economic. Wright complicates the language of inwardness and subjective "intangibles" with that of military efficiency. In order to "march from the tribal order to the twentieth century," it is necessary to be hard and stout from the inside out. The soldier who marches, it would seem, does not stop to think about questions that have not been asked or cannot be answered. In this way, Wright's letter yokes together the language of interiority and that of external instrumentality. The force of the yoking should direct us to the moment and purpose of his Eurocentric vision. His sense of history is paradoxically Eurocentric and anticolonial, precisely because he imagines the non-West as static prior to Europe's arrival on African shores. History, in other words, commences only because the West came upon these societies and colonized them by violence.

Here, we come upon the theme of sacrifice, one that Wright brings up consistently as he reflects on his biases in the face of Africa's epistemological challenge. Whether in the guise of colonial violence, the violence of certain traditional African practices, or the violence of the slave trade, the problem of violence enters into Wright's meditation under the metaphorics of sacrifice. Let us consider his notion of "hardness," for example. In "Richard Wright as a Specular Border Intellectual," Abdul JanMohamed has argued that the notion of hardness in Wright should be seen as a trope that doesn't just surface in his reflections on Africa but rather, runs through all of his work. For JanMohamed, the mask of "hard" unsentimentality is a sort of coping mechanism, as psychic as it is consciously thematized, through which Wright seeks to negotiate the trauma of American racism and the specific challenges that black people had to face in the twentieth century. For his part, Manthia Diawara's *In Search of Africa* defends Wright's claim that Africa needs to be "militarized" by showing that such a notion was very common in the 1950s. Diawara reminds us that these are, after all, the years soon after World War II. Africans who had been conscripted to fight in the war had returned to their home countries, and militarization was a term that meant discipline and comradeship in pursuit of a common goal. Diawara writes of a conversation he once had with Dr. Abdoulaye Ly, "a retired history professor and former minister in Senghor's government in Senegal." According to Diawara,

> When I told him that I had some problems with Wright's use of the term to "militarize," Professor Ly, who is a veteran of the Second World War, explained to me how commonly the word was used in the Forties and Fifties—not only in the communist sense of creating a proletarian army, but also in the sense of educating the African people, creating fraternal bonds beyond tribal groups, and forming disciplined militants for the Pan-African cause of decolonization and modernization in Africa. He reminded me that in French the words *militaire* and *militant* had the same root, the Latin *militis*, which means disciplined and committed to an ideal, ready to fight for a cause. (69)

Diawara's reading is convincing. Yet, the dream of "fraternal bonds beyond tribal groups" evokes the logic of sacrifice; in Wright's terms, what needs to be given up along with tradition is the collectivism (as opposed to individualism) that has been rendered inoperative by modern technologized life. But sacrifice is also the primary metaphor through which Wright connects the African past—the belief systems based on social hierarchy, the lust for power and lust for money—to the Middle Passage. Everywhere he goes, Wright finds evidence of human choices or accidents that he interprets in terms of sacrifice.

His exploration of interrelated tropes of religion and sacrifice reveal the ways in which his rhetoric is informed by modernist discourses of primitivism ranging from Freud's *Totem and Taboo*, T. S. Eliot's "The Wasteland," Joyce's *Ulysses*, to Waugh's *Black Mischief*. Yet, the nature of Wright's debt carries the specific intonation of black Atlanticism. Outside the train window at Euston Station, the landscape, he tells us, was as bleak as any described by D. H. Lawrence, Arnold Bennett, or George Moore. And Liverpool brings the reminder that "it was here that most of the slavers had been organized, fitted out, financed, and dispatched with high hopes on their infamous and lucrative voyages" (7). Wright ends his journey to Ghana with a visit to a former slave castle in Cape Coast. In the haunting passage that closes the memoir, Wright links economics and greed to suffering and sacrifice. The passage bears quoting in its entirety:

> Rumor among the natives has it that there is a vast treasure trove buried somewhere in the depths of the castle fortress. I don't think there is; but the native, remembering the horrible tales of what went on within these walls, likes to think that there is gold dust here, thousands of tons of it. If there is any treasure hidden in these vast walls, I'm sure that it has a sheen that outshines gold—a tiny, pear-shaped tear that formed on the cheek of some black woman torn away from her children, a tear that gleams here still, caught in the feeble rays of the dungeon's light—a shy tear that vanishes at the sound of approaching footsteps, but reappears when all is quiet, hanging there on that black cheek, unredeemed, unappeased—a tear that was hastily brushed off when her arm was grabbed and she was led toward those narrow, dank steps that guided her to the tunnel that directed her feet to the waiting ship that would bear her across the heaving, mist-shrouded Atlantic. (341–42)

These are the very last words of Wright's narrative as a record of travel. Immediately after the passage is his letter to Nkrumah. The closing image of Wright's travel account, then, is the enslaved woman and the tears historically caused by capitalist greed. The passage invites us to reconstitute in our proverbial mind's eye the enslaved black woman as a subject in a dark-toned painting. The closing sentence is charged, as though the author's fallible self is getting breathless even as the words spill out on the page. We are, after all, not gathering information but reading an accomplished novelist. The force of the passage resides in the fact that the diagetic mode is interrupted, even as it is ornamented and intensified, by the literariness of the mimetic. Wright thereby calls attention to the memoir as rhetorical performance, and the register is directly religious. The paratactic "unredeemed, unappeased" suggests Christianity's poetry of the Messiah's passion on

Calvary. But if Christ's suffering is understood to be in the service of redemption and appeasement, the enslaved woman's is the very opposite. Her tears hang in suspension, in Wright's severe parenthesis: "unredeemed, unappeased."

Wright gives character to the image even in the fleeting moment that it flares up at the end of his text. The woman he imagines is self-effacing, wiping her tears for fear of her returning captors. It is the image of a pear-shaped tear that remains as the woman is dragged away to confront the horror of the Atlantic passage. Wright writes of "the heaving, mist-shrouded Atlantic" to reference the waves and the wind but also the pain and uncertainty of the enforced journey. The suffering of the enslaved—the tears of the heaving heart—is tied to the unpredictability of the future, the shroud of mist over the sea. And Wright speaks of the enslaved woman's tears as the real "hidden treasure" in the "vast walls" of the slave dungeon. Opposed to voice and self-ownership, the "tiny, pear-shaped tear" has a "sheen that outshines gold." At this point, an important question emerges: is Wright suggesting through this metaphor that suffering yields greater life-affirming meaning than material comfort? If not, then what are we to make of his elevation of the woman's suffering over and above the glitter of gold—the lure of capitalism and modernity? These questions become especially crucial in light of Wright's caution to Nkrumah, as we saw earlier, that subjective intangibles might be more important than economics. Here again is the excerpt: "until confidence is established at the center of African personality, until there is an inner reorganization of that personality, there can be no question of marching from the tribal order to the twentieth century. . . . At the moment, this subjective task is more important than economics!" (343). On the logic of this injunction, the African cannot enter modernity until there is an "inner reorganization of . . . personality" that would prepare him for military focus and efficiency. Yet, this personality would be the product of a reorganized dispensation that is said to be specifically modern. In this non sequitur, Wright unveils the epistemic order governing his vision of modern rationality as the antithesis of premodern metaphysics.

By now, of course, Wright has rejected international communism (see Fabre, JanMohamed). But if he has denounced communism, he retains an internationalist optic on society and collectivity. For him, an economic approach to the telling of the history of colonialism is useful: "If anyone should object to my employment of Marxist methods to make meaningful the ebb and flow of commodities, human and otherwise, in the modern society, to make comprehensible the alignment of social classes in modern society, I have but to say that I'll willingly accept any other method of interpreting the facts; but I insist that any other method *must not exclude the facts*" (xiii, emphasis in original). The reliance on an economic account is accompanied by Wright's stress on psychology in his attempts to understand his African interlocutors and what he takes to be their collective dispositions. The very idea of something called "the African" takes us into the domain of interiority. Wright claims that whatever interior life there is among Africans exists at the level of material sustenance and a self-paralyzing fear of the supernatural. In his attempts to understand the psychology of human sacrifice, both of the powerful who practice it and the subjects who accept it as part of their culture, Wright draws uncritically on anthropological accounts of the primitive mentality.

Black Power is as much about Wright's ethical-political investment in the future of Africa as it is a staging of his desire for collectivity, defined in terms that are neither racial nor national. Wright doesn't make clear what this collectivity might involve, and that is where the gap as well as promise of Wright's struggle can be located. Abdul JanMohamed gets at how this elusive community might be construed in his essay on *Black Power*, where he describes Wright's location as that of a specular border intellectual. According to JanMohamed,

> A writer such as Wright ... is a border intellectual, in that he is caught between two groups, that is, between the racialized construction of white and black groups, with neither of which he could fully identify or disidentify: he felt simultaneously included and excluded by both groups. Rather than passively suffering his fate, Wright ended up dedicating his life to an investigation of the border space between the two, and in so doing he in effect became an archaeologist of the site of his own formation, devoting most of his fiction to deconstructing the formation of the black (male) subject on the racial border and hence reforming his own subjectivity-as-a-writer around his project of archaeological excavation. In other words, Wright's identity as a *constituting* subject comes to be formed around his commitment to deconstructing the black male subject (the "Black Boy" of his autobiography) as a *constituted* pseudo-subject. (232)

In the view I have been developing so far, it is by means of the enabling excavation that JanMohamed theorizes here that Wright participates in the black-Atlantic detour of his moment. That moment is constitutively international, emblematized in the best Pan-Africanist thinkers and writers of the immediate post–World War II era—the era of the nonaligned movement and the Bandung Conference, a record of which Wright (1956) gives us in *The Color Curtain: A Report on the Bandung Conference*.

In the middle of the nineteenth century, Crowther and the black whitemen invited their Victorian audience—church benefactors and laity—to be properly universal in rhetoric and practice by recognizing humanity as singular. In the middle of the twentieth century, Wright argued in defense of modernization as much for the potential material benefits as for the interior self-improvement of individuals. Africa is the immediate subject of this condescension, but it would as well apply to Wright's reading of the nonaligned new states at Bandung and African American aspirations in the middle of the twentieth century. If in racist ethnography not much of historical worth existed in Africa prior to the incursion of outside forces through Christianity and commerce, James and Wright respect the integrity of the African past while insisting on its obsolescence. The movement toward decolonization is in their sense a movement toward putatively Western models of selfhood and social organization. It is also a move away from tribe, construed as relic of a past that has been rendered obsolete by modernity's one-dimensional efficiency. Upon arriving in the village of Nkawkaw, "some sixty-six miles from Kumasi" (261), Wright retires to his room to reflect on his day:

> Arriving at Nkawkaw at midday, I ate, rested, went out upon the narrow verandah of the resthouse.... Emotionally detached, I feel the spell of this land. Those still, stagnant clouds snared in the tops of those tree-clad mountains—must not that have been an ominous sign in the old days? And that blood-red sun at sunset, what does it mean? That crawling line of ants, was it not pointing the way to a guilty man? Was not the veering flight of that bird the gesture of an unseen ancestor trying to communicate something? ... And that child dying so young? Who did that ... ? What punishment was being visited and for whose sins?
>
> Night comes suddenly, like wet black velvet. The air, charged with too much oxygen, drugs the blood. The scream of some wild birds cuts through the dark and stops abruptly, leaving a suspenseful void. A foul smell rises from somewhere. A distant drumming is heard and dies, as though ashamed of itself.... The sound of a lorry whose motor is whining as it strains to climb the steep hill brings back to me the world I know. (263)

These paragraphs indicate Wright's questioning of the material environment facing him and the discursive infrastructure—the prejudice, in phenomenological terms—that equips him to inhabit and understand that environment by projecting his obsessions upon it. And as we might expect, the crucial themes recall those that preoccupy Wright throughout the book. To cite a couple of examples, one would be ancestors and memory, as when Wright wonders: "Those still, stagnant clouds snared in the tops of those tree-clad mountains—must not that have been an ominous sign in the old days?" Another would be the theme of individuality within a necessary collective, as in this line, where he imagines a column of ants in search of a renegade: "That crawling line of ants, was it not pointing the way to a guilty man?" Finally, the overarching problem of sacrificial violence, indexed in the image of a dying child: "that child dying so young? Who did that? What punishment was being visited and for whose sins?"

At the end of the passage, he is brought back to reality so to speak, away from his intense self-absorption. What brings him back to reality is the sound of a vehicle struggling to go uphill: "The sound of a lorry whose motor is whining as it strains to climb the steep hill brings back to me the world I know." It doesn't take

Fig. 3.1 Nigeria, Lagos 2002. By Stuart Franklin
Stuart Franklin and Magnum Photos

much to conclude that the lorry is a commercial vehicle transporting some raw material (timber or a cash crop like cocoa) from the hinterland to the city. In the contemporary context of globalization and multilayered violence, Wright's text is thereby challenging cultural criticism to enrich theoretical engagements by listening for the recalcitrance of the world as it is—gruesome and unpredictable, but lived nonetheless.

In an image by British photographer Stuart Franklin [FIGURE 3.1], we are taken to a ferry terminal in Apapa in the city of Lagos. This is a contemporary photograph from 2002, but key signs of the Atlantic slave trade might be read therein: the hull section of a ship that covers roughly half of the image, sitting on the wavy expanse of the lagoon. But the photograph does not restrict itself to the water and the vessel anchored on it. We see in the background the skyline of urban Lagos: tall boxlike buildings against a horizon of overcast sky. Against the sky and next to the ship's metallic overhang, the buildings are gray miniature toys. Into this tableau the photograph places five adults (four male, one female) stepping off the dock. All are looking downward, focused on the floor of the dock and their stride. They are intently focused and seemingly oblivious to everything else. One wrong step could mean falling and breaking a bone or drowning. And so, the photograph catches them in midstride. Having grown up in Lagos, I recognize this scene and the human story it tells. The subjects in this photograph are black and African, but they are so much more as well. These are working people, probably boarding a ferry from Apapa wharf to sell their labor or engage in petty trading in the center of the city. There, they will work in the boxlike buildings or sell their tidbits to the workers in the boxlike buildings. Or perhaps they have just disembarked from the ferry after a day's work. The symbol of the past is in evidence and so are the skyscrapers of a contemporary outpost of globalization—the soon-to-be megacity of Lagos. Amid these signs of the past and present we encounter individuals in motion, stepping onto a ferry or disembarking from one. My argument is that alongside its rhetorical problems and despite whatever Wright himself may have intended, *Black Power* directs us beyond itself to a reminder contained in this photograph: a reminder of the present being lived.

Peter Abrahams in the Province of Fiction

Let me now turn to Peter Abrahams's (1956) *A Wreath for Udomo*, a text that covers ground very similar to those we have been considering so far. Born to an Ethiopian father and South African mother classified as "colored" in South Africa's biopolitical system, Abrahams was active in the Pan-Africanist ferment of the mid-twentieth century. In his autobiography published in Jamaica in 2000 under the title *The Coyaba Chronicles: Reflections on the Black Experience in the Twentieth Century*, Abrahams recounts in exquisite detail his experiences with the black-Atlantic intellectuals of the mid-twentieth century. *A Wreath of Udomo* is especially illuminating because it is about the African elite as students in London. The novel follows its major characters from their activist days in London to their return to Africa, as they try to merge theory with praxis. Needless to say, the challenges are different and altogether insurmountable, at least within the novel's time-span and the future it can reasonably project or imagine.

Rendered principally in the idiom of melodrama, *A Wreath for Udomo* also operates as a kind of roman à clef, and we shall soon see why. It is set in a fictional country called Panafrica and follows a group of students from the initial utopic moment of anticolonial organization to the aftermath of juridical independence. In the novel, the moment of independence is haunted by a constitutive contradiction, whereby the emerging nation-state is caught between the demands of nationalist self-preservation on one hand and supranational Pan-Africanism on the other hand. So the main character, Michael Udomo, becomes leader of the independent state of Panafrica and promptly betrays his friend and comrade Mhendi. In turn, Udomo is abandoned by his former allies Adebhoy and Selina for what they perceive as his pernicious assault on tradition and embrace of modernization. Left to his enemies, Udomo is subsequently assassinated in what the novel depicts as a ritualistic dance of death.

Neither Abrahams nor his novel occupy a significant place in discussions of canonical African novels. To speak only of the Anglophone sphere, the critical practice has been to associate the institutional category we call African literature with names like Achebe, Soyinka, Ngugi, Aidoo, Armah, and more recently, Farah, Dangarembga, or, say, Adichie. This is because the institutionalization of modern African literature followed the model of national literatures that continues to govern literary studies in the academy. The reason *A Wreath for Udomo* is not a well-known text of African literature might perhaps be that critics have not known what to do with it. In terms of artistic craft, it is not as accomplished as some of Abrahams's other works. Ideologically, it doesn't profitably lend itself to an ethnographic reading. Indeed, to the extent that such a reading might be developed, what *A Wreath for Udomo* offers is an unsympathetic, thoroughgoing deconstruction of such ideological categories as "African tradition" or tribal organization. My claim is that Abrahams's novel cannot comprehensively be understood within the conceptual or institutional rubrics under which African literary texts are most often discussed: specifically, such rubrics as area studies (in anthropology or history), world literature (in current literary studies), or even African literature as cultural capital.

My approach in what follows is to read *A Wreath for Udomo* as a performance of diaspora in the domain of literary representation. Like James and Wright, Abrahams's text allows us to resituate the discourse of Pan-Africanism, together with the cultural-nationalism of African literature, in terms of a constitutive internationalism. To read both discourses in this way goes against the grain of conventional accounts of African literature in its coarticulation with postcoloniality and globalism. But that, precisely, is where *A Wreath for Udomo* shows itself to be a theoretically suggestive text. Roger Field has written that when Abrahams's novel first appeared, it "was regarded as a reactionary and pessimistic account of postcolonial African politics, but it is now seen as a prophetic work on postcolonial Ghana and Kwame Nkrumah" (5). There are indeed similarities between the broad outline of Nkrumah's career and the figure of Michael Udomo in Abrahams's novel. But the novel appeared before Ghana's independence in 1957, so it's not helpful to stress the question of whether Udomo is based on Nkrumah or, indeed, whether the characters are based on real historical figures.[9] I will focus on the novel's ambiguous and, for many, troubling textualization of Africa. But rather than simply criticize or reject (on a simple moral register) the Africa we encounter in Abrahams's text, I want to explore the sense in which the novel squarely anticipates the canonical texts of African literature. The novel's contradictions are in this sense not very different conceptually from what we can see in the more celebrated texts of African literature.

The Pan-Africanism of the novel's historical moment and intellectual context accounts for its juxtaposition of racial identity politics with a trenchant critique of any reification of collectivity, understood in terms of race, ethnicity, or class. For instance, we see an illustration of essentialist cliché in the section where Udomo returns to Panafrica after his stay in England. Selina (the leader of the market women) characterizes Udomo's return to lead the independence movement as a kind of cosmic-metaphysical event, one that the irredeemably "westernized" academic Tom Lanwood simply cannot replicate. In its depiction of Lanwood, the text resorts to a version of what, in a different context, Svetlana Boym has theorized as "restorative nostalgia."[10] Lanwood is a Creole returnee from Britain. But his specific historical and cultural location is presented in the novel as a lack—one that becomes a political liability for the otherwise patriotic diasporic subject. In Abrahams's rendering, Lanwood's relationship to the Africa he loves is purely intellectual, and although he is able to overcome this cultural alienation at the conscious level of epistemic filiation, he cannot inhabit the culture at the visceral, phenomenal level.

Based in England, he writes books theorizing African decolonization and organizes to bring it about, but faced with the culture itself as real place rather than an abstract object of activism or intellectual investment, he becomes a burden to the revolutionaries. Eventually, he has to leave for England, defeated and heartbroken. On his way to the shipping office, "he passed a group of women selling their wares on the sidewalk on the other side of the open gutter. Their laughing voices were raised in a language he couldn't understand. They gestured to him, inviting him to buy their fly-ridden wares. He knew suddenly that he would always be an outsider here. For all his dark skin, the barrier between him and this world was too great, he was too old to make the crossing successfully. He belonged too firmly, had lived too long in the Western world to be any good in any other" (294). The novel here reifies cultural difference such that Lanwood is not just incapable of returning to the Africa of his ancestors, but his age and temperament have made him too "intellectual" and "rational" beyond the possibility of return. Rationality is here surreptitiously posed as a facet of culture that is at once historical and ontological. On the novel's terms, Lanwood is intellectual and rational because he is irredeemably westernized, whereas what a rapidly decolonizing Africa needs is the passion, poetry, and ritual—that is to say, the irrationality—of primal man.

In its geography of Africa, the novel takes leave of any semblance of historical realism. Panafrica is reachable through a jungle that separates it from Pluralia, and the two countries are very different in their experience of European colonial presence. In David Mhendi's Pluralia, what we have is settler colonialism, while Udomo's Panafrica is indirect rule. Likewise, Panafrica's anticolonial struggle is to bring about a negotiated end to colonial rule, whereas Pluralia is engaged in armed guerrilla warfare. Abrahams here points to a crucial difference between the specificity of the decolonization struggle of West African countries as opposed to southern Africa or Kenya. Udomo's betrayal of Mhendi later in the novel allows Abrahams to explore how the moment of independence is haunted by a contradiction, whereby the emerging nation-state of Panafrica is caught between nationalist self-preservation and continental loyalty.

The passage that describes Queenstown, the capital of Panafrica, presents the African section of the town as static and unchanging from time immemorial:

> First there is the sea. Then there is the white sand at the edge of the sea. Behind the white sand, on rising land, standing like sentinels against the sea, palm trees are dotted all along the coastal edge. Behind the palms the land rises gently to the crest of a low rolling hill, then falls away into a wide flat-bottomed valley. All this valley is taken up by Queenstown, the capital and first seaport of Panafrica.
>
> Really, Queenstown is no more than an overgrown African village with an immense European façade. Along the docks it is all European; the cranes and huge storage houses, the immigration and port police offices, and the big buildings of the great Pan-Africa Company, which controls practically all Panafrica's trade and is one of the five biggest monopolies in the world. But just to the left of all this, spilling over the rolling hill and down into the basin of the low valley, is the old African town, much as it was before the coming of the Europeans. . . . Once away from the main centers, the houses huddle on top of one another any way you like. Mud and wattle jostle with timber or corrugated iron. And the people, here, live communally. Doors are always open. Anyone can always enter. There is no privacy, no need for it. Here, away from the port and the centre of the city, life goes on much as it might have done one, two, three thousand years ago. (150–51)

In this way, traditional Africa is rendered as static and unchanging in time, reminding us of the ideological discourses, concurrent with the novel, of negritude and African personality. The history of the conquest states of the Ashanti, the Oyo, or the Mande Empire in West Africa or, in southern Africa, the Zulu and Ndebele Empires offer historical evidence of the inaccuracy of this idealization of Africa outside the ruptures of human struggle. The Queenstown of *A Wreath for Udomo* could be based on Jamestown in Accra, but its image of traditional Africa is romantic and undialectical. In this vein, we are to see the photograph by Stuart Franklin that we examined earlier as an update, an immanent contestation, of the novel's image of the African port city in the capitalist era.

At the novel's end, Udomo's assassination is represented in distinctly Conradian language. The sequence comments on itself, so to speak, such that the intensity of the moment is mimicked by the diegetic insistence on the volume and tempo of frenzied drumming. As the guards hack away at Udomo, their brutish physicality is placed squarely in the fact of their black skins and the opacity of night. In murdering Udomo, the agents of Selina's and Adebhoy's tribalism take us back to what the text poses as primordial tribal frenzy:

> He became aware, suddenly, of a steady, regular throb in the silent night. Drumbeats, soft and subdued and just outside his window. No. All about him.

Everywhere. Drumbeats everywhere. Low and insistent. And as he listened, the drumbeats increased in tempo but not in volume. Then he recognized them. Talking drums; and they said:
Udomo traitor Udomo die.
. . . .

A split second before he switched on the light he knew he was not alone. There were two men in the room with him; one at the window, one at the door.
Udomo traitor Udomo die.
. . . .

Udomo fought down a wave of terror. They had long knives in their hands. They watched him with glazed, unrecognizing eyes. Nothing hostile about those eyes. Just glazed. Heads cocked, listening to the drums. Breathing attuned to the beat of the drums.
Udomo traitor Udomo die. (350–51)

The essentialism and freezing of Africa into a static past that I have been tracing is a consequence of the Hegelian notion of history as linear movement of spirit. Abrahams shares this vision of history with the Pan-Africanists of his era, and we are yet to do away with this view and Africa's place in it. But I also want to draw attention to the logic of sacrifice that governs the novel's representation of Udomo's assassination. Approached as an evocation of the social logic of sacrifice, the regressive Conradian tenor of the assassination scene is profitably countered by the possibility of an allegorical reading. On this reading, Udomo is to be understood as the sacrificial victim of a costly but seductive ideology of modernization and development. The interesting thing is that thus positing Udomo as sacrificial victim makes him at once a villain and a hero, the sacred and the accursed.

Let me develop this last point a little bit more. Udomo is rejected as villain by Adheboy and Selina for the very same reason that Mabi considers him a hero. Such ambivalence, as theorists of sacrifice from Bataille to Girard and Agamben have shown, is built into the logic of sacrificial thinking. In the particular case of modernization and sovereignty, one man's heroic sacrifice is another's memory of loss, one man's epic protagonist, another's blood-stained villain of conquest. One man's hard advocate of modernization is another's soft contamination of so-called tradition. The novel unfolds this ambivalence from another direction as well. Clearly, Udomo is a dynamic and well-meaning leader. But his sense of mission as liberator leads him to attract and then betray liberal English women who sympathize with the anticolonial cause. He shows disloyalty to Lois Barlow, his girlfriend in England, by having sexual intercourse with her friend Jo Furse. Insisting that Jo Furse terminate the pregnancy that results from the affair, Udomo explains his selfishness as necessary to Africa's liberation. His destiny is to return to Panafrica as anticolonial liberator, and any personal ties need to be sacrificed in the service of that historic obligation. Later, he betrays his friend Mhendi in order to secure the economic support of white settlers who see Mhendi's activism to free Pluralia as a threat. In this way, Udomo betrays a political compatriot and explains his choice as necessary to ensure infrastructural development for his new nation. Udomo sacrifices Mhendi and his political aspirations, not to talk of friendship, in order to pursue his vision for modernizing his new nation.

It is in this treatment of the motif of sacrifice in relation to modernization that Abrahams powerfully presages African literature. Abrahams's choice to figure Udomo's assassination as sacrificial violence anticipates a trope that re-emerges in the work of later African writers. By narrating Udomo's career and demise in terms of the ambiguities of sacrifice, Abrahams strives to position the artist figure Mabi as the one whose humanist vision outlasts the ideologues, even though he is the least self-assured of them all. There is a deep insecurity in Mabi's sense of himself, an acknowledgment of vulnerability in the midst of nation building, where modernization has to confront the precedent hegemony of tradition. Yet, it is to Mabi that the novel gives the final word, so to speak. In the last section, Mabi pens a letter to Lois Barlow, the former lover whom Udomo had betrayed in order to take up the tasks of decolonization and nation building. To Lois Barlow, Mabi writes: "You can guess the reason for his murder. They wanted to go back to the days of tribal glory. You know there are people all over the world, white as well as black, who are attracted to tribalism. Among other things, it has security, color, and emotional outlets that the bleak, standardized, monotonous chromium and neon benefits of mass-production civilization lack.... I can't tell you why I have this impulse to defend his memory now. But the impulse is strong" (355–56). Mabi feels the "impulse to defend" the memory of Udomo precisely because he shares the latter's commitment to modernization, construed as antithesis to tradition. This commitment is thus accompanied by a simplification of the preceding hegemonic formations—that is, the various ethnic formations to be sublated under the desired nation-state form. And yet, Mabi himself had earlier rejected Udomo's tactics and felt himself temperamentally unsuited to the pragmatism required in the realm of politics and governance. Like the English woman Lois, Mabi is the liberal cognitive subject, the artist figure whose ethos relegates him to the status of outsider in the field of power and social engineering. So, Mabi retreats to his studio, there to lament the failure of a utopic dream. Abrahams seems to place his own agency as artist in Mabi's sphere: to work through the contradictions of collective existence by means of artistic form.

We should of course quibble with the familiar idealization of art and artists in this aspect of *A Wreath for Udomo*—or, at least, I do. Abrahams not only idealizes the figure of the artist, but he also locates the power of art in powerlessness. In so doing, he privileges Mabi's critical distance over the intensities and betrayals of the political field, where the engaged characters Udomo, Mhendi, Selina, and Adebhoy dwell. What interests me most is that Abrahams's empowerment of critical distance—coded as a distinctly artistic ethos—is a recurrent topos in the work of many African writers who come after him. In this direction, Abrahams anticipates key topoi that the most accomplished African writers explore quite obsessively: namely, change, social identities, and the role artistic representation might play. In the next chapter, I will anatomize one way in which the work of Achebe and Soyinka might be read to unpack the logic of metonymy whereby tribe (or ethnicity) transfigures into nation/state, and both at once operate as indexical signifiers of race in the cloyed spectacle of the Euro-American gaze—no less in the public sphere than in literary studies. This metonymic movement is overdetermined and can serve good as well as bad causes. For now, I am suggesting that Abrahams's novel had already pointed in the direction of this insight, although we miss the insight because of his figure of tribal drums and frenzied Africans hacking at one another. Operating as it does at the level of imaginative literature, Abrahams's novel is able to dramatize and reflect on the problem of modernization and African identities with which, as we saw earlier, James and Wright were also grappling. In the register of imaginative literature, Abrahams thematizes the possible tension between nation-statehood and Pan-Africanist identification. And through Mabi's loneliness and self-doubt, Abrahams explores as well the ambiguous location of the idealistic westernized artist—arguably, alter ego for the novelist himself. In this way, *A Wreath for Udomo* is able to meditate on its own anxieties and condition of possibility.

Labors in the Vineyard

Students of the New Testament will recognize the source of this subtitle in Christ's parable of vineyard workers that appears in Matthew 20:1–16 and subsequently becomes a favored metaphor for missionary evangelism. Students of Richard Wright might also recognize it as the metaphor he uses in the opening sentence of his controversial letter to Nkrumah at the end of *Black Power: A Record of Reactions in a Land of Pathos*. "Dear Kwame Nkrumah," he writes, "My journey's done. My labors in your vineyard are over" (342). Wright is of course parodying white missionaries, but he thereby figures his role, and that of anticolonial intellectuals of his moment, as a secular recomposition. In this opening gesture, Wright underscores a view he had pursued all through *Black Power*. For him, as for James and Abrahams, the modern world will be a better place if Science displaces the God of scriptural texts as well as the many Gods of traditional animism. My concern in this chapter has been to consider the consequences of this view for their representation of Africa in the middle of the twentieth century. I position their texts of Africa within a black-Atlantic frame, one that is not focused on national literary history, still less on global theory.

I am claiming that the Pan-Africanists share a Eurocentric angle of vision, but we benefit from attending to the nuance they bring to the table. James celebrates modernization and debunks superstition, even as he recognizes that so-called superstition can resurface through the very same pressure of modernization. Wright shows condescension toward Africa in tones that one would find in other modernists and twentieth-century critics of Western modernity, from Graham Greene or Evelyn Waugh, to Saul Bellow, V. S. Naipaul, not to talk of Conrad. Wright abjures "sacrifice" and casts the cruelty of the Middle Passage as immolation of innocent individuals by traditional power on both sides of the Atlantic. Meanwhile, he looks to Nkrumah as herald of a different sort of sacrifice, one that is secular, scientific, and therefore properly modern—even if only in the sense of potentiality. For his part, Abrahams brings the logic of sacrifice to the very heart of his narrative of modernization. In different ways, then, the texts I have been discussing offer iterations of detour as theorized by Édouard Glissant. Their perspectives are circumscribed by modernity's signal categories: racial emancipation, nationhood, and progress. In their writing, race is elided with nation, and tribe is depicted as relic of a past that can only hinder the present. I am suggesting, however, that from out of these limitations we can elicit a more far-reaching set of lessons. My readings so far are meant to elicit one way in which we can present these black Atlantic modernists to our students—that is, the collective to whom I referred in chapter 1 as "readers on the ground." As Ernesto Laclau and Stuart Hall have argued, we inherit significations that cannot be totalized and are therefore open to resignification in the struggle for hegemony.

The issue of inherited representations takes us to a text that has proven to be durable in its divisiveness. I refer to Joseph Conrad's *Heart of Darkness*, together with the controversy that emerged around it in the 1970s. Of course, the shadow of Conrad's novella has been stalking this chapter all along, indexed in the image of drums, old deities, and sacrificial violence such as we encountered in Wright and Abrahams. After the appearance of Chinua Achebe's 1975 essay "An Image of Africa: Racism in Conrad's *Heart of Darkness*," critics came up with various positions on the merits or otherwise of Achebe's charge that Conrad is a racist. The accusation of racism prompted theoretical reflections about representation and the extent to which a text might be said to reflect collective values or predispositions. It should be entirely significant that Achebe's essay was delivered and published in the 1970s—the era of civil rights, anti-apartheid armed resistance, and academic debates about theory in literary studies. To that turbulent era, Achebe was able to say his piece, annoy many literary critics, and invigorate countless others.

In light of the argument I have been developing in this chapter, we can approach Achebe's critique from a refreshingly different perspective. Here is something worth thinking about: the debate that surrounded Achebe's essay too often takes him at his word in order to argue for or against him, which is to say, for or against Conrad. Whether one accepts his reading of *Heart of Darkness*, pursuing the argument on Achebe's terms is at this point terribly limiting, if for no other reason than the distance between the moment Achebe first read the novella and the time I did as a student, or the time our students will have read it. Remaining within the terms of Achebe's critique hypostatizes both Conrad and his antagonist and reduces the lesson of Achebe's critique to his reaction to a canonical European text. In this way, the problematic continues to be about *Heart of Darkness* and something called Western literature, rather than about the canonical text's multiple meanings and how it might be teased to mean differently. In this framing, Achebe is the antagonist who is thereby *tethered* to what is being antagonized—belated in relation to the European requisite particular. Forty odd years after "An Image of Africa: Racism in Conrad's *Heart of Darkness*," my argument is that it is urgently necessary to position Achebe in a different frame, that of postcoloniality and black Atlanticism. If Conrad is a modernist avatar, responding to the crisis of European man at the end of the nineteenth century, Achebe's essay, and the problematic to which it testifies, is the postcolonial event that rejects the conflation of "European man" with something called "man."[11]

In concluding this chapter, I want to foreground two further issues that Abrahams, James, and Wright raise for us. First, by positioning African agency (positive or negative) at the center of their engagement with modernization as discourse and social organization, they provide dramas of existence that exceed the narrow confines of "literature" as cultural capital. Beyond his idealization of modernization, James's narrative frame restores the agency of Nkrumah and Ghana, together with all the fissures and missteps. And for all his arrogance, Wright memorably marks the limits of his own perspectives. In doing so, he thematizes his vulnerability as cognitive subject. For his part, Abrahams glimpses the dangers waiting ahead for newly decolonizing Africa. From our vantage point, we do well to look back at *A Wreath for Udomo* as a foreshadowing of Fanon's critique of the African elite in *The Wretched of the Earth*. Equally so is the novel a foreshadowing of classics of modern African fiction: from Achebe's *A Man of the People* and Ngugi's *Devil on the Cross*, to Soyinka's *Season of Anomy*, Armah's *The Beautiful Ones Are Not Yet Born*, Marechera's *House of Hunger*, and every novel Farah has published since his tentative debut, *From a Crooked Rib*.

On this level, we are not dealing with the Fanonian yearning for the dawn of a "new man" after the stormy night of anticolonial resistance, still less the merits or otherwise of what has come to be called posthumanism. Such questions have yielded much productive discussion and debate since the moment of literary and cultural theory in the 1970s. But as we saw in chapter 1, these conversations do not always thematize their own particularity or positionality in relation to cultural difference and the pressures of self-definition. The fact that the problem of "man" continues to exercise us now, about a century after it became a pressing preoccupation in various disciplines of the humanities, suggests that it cannot be resolved at the level of theory. The search for something beyond the ideology of "man" inevitably returns us to the sovereignty of modern man in his self-parody and self-flagellation. More crucially from my perspective, the back and forth over dissolving or reconstituting man, of rejecting mastery and instead celebrating constraint, presupposes an antecedent historical trajectory where "man" has self-evident signification. The history of pseudo-scientific racism tells us that the black and the African were once posited as not-man or less than man—however contradictorily so. By contrast, in the black-Atlantic texts we have been examining, "man" is the sign of a historic exclusion and struggle.

The final issue I want to foreground has to do with genre. The texts of Abrahams, James, and Wright that I have been exploring blur generic boundaries. In terms of literary value as a simple question of style, they are neither the best examples of their kind nor the best work to come from all three. *Nkrumah and the Ghana Revolution* is not of the quality of *Black Jacobins* or *Beyond a Boundary*, although it is impossible to read James's way of accounting for Nkrumah without thinking of his immortalization of the Haitian revolution. The sheer repetitiveness of some of Wright's observations often works to the detriment of *Black Power*. Similarly, *A Wreath for Udomo* moves from realist melodrama to ritual and allegory and does not convey the same level of stylistic finesse as, say, *Tell Freedom*, *Mineboy*, or *Wild Conquest*. My argument, however, is that these texts equip us to exceed the narrow question of form without leaving it behind altogether. The direction I want to pursue next proposes a similar question in relation to two highly canonical Nigerians: Chinua Achebe and Wole Soyinka. Here, then, are three questions to set the scene and lead us on. How might these globally credentialed "spokesmen" of Africa be defamiliarized so that they yield a different kind of knowledge, one that undoes the myth of prediscursive community in order to consider the making and remaking of collectivity?[12] How might we reframe Achebe and Soyinka in a way that approaches their texts according to Glissant's terms, as detour rather than return? How might African literature be teased to resonate in ways that avoid a familiar overvaluation of literature as cultural capital?

Notes

1. See Abiola Irele, *The African Experience of Literature and Ideology*, 67–124; *The African Imagination*, 39–81; Paulin Hountondji, 79–157; Jones; July; Kesteloot; Miller, *Nationalists and Nomads*; and Mudimbe, *The Invention of Africa*, 135–86.
2. See Nielsen, Scott, and Surin.
3. For accounts of Nkrumah's career, see Korang, Marable, and Rooney. See also Nkrumah's (1957) self-portrait up until the moment of Ghana's independence, *Ghana*.

4. In chapter 1, I called this tendency the race-or-class delirium. For a striking example of this, see the intemperate critique of James's attitude to Nkrumah launched by the South African historian and anticolonial activist Baruch Hirson (1990). Rightly suspicious of "charisma" and populism in political leadership and theory, Hirson buries the passion of black-Atlantic and African intellectuals insofar as they don't align properly with dialectical materialism. He writes: "The problems of the 1960s, when James played a central role in Pan African politics, are of more than historic interest. The theoretical confusion of the left when confronted with class struggles in backward societies goes back to the polemics in Russia before the revolution of 1917: an issue resolved in practice, but leaving a legacy of theoretical confusion. The struggles for colonial independence were denied the insights that Marxism should have offered. Instead, mysticism prevailed and populist theories replaced scientific analysis" (72). For more measured accounts of the multiple disciplinary spaces and theoretical ramifications of James's oeuvre, see the following: Brennan, *At Home in the World*, chapter 5; Henry, chapter 2; Lazarus, chapter 3; Nielsen; San Juan, chapter 7; Scott; and Worcester.

5. See James's essay "Notes on Hamlet," 243–46.

6. On Plaatje's *Mhudi*, see Couzens, "Introduction"; on the background to Plaatje's recording of "Nkosi Sikelele i'Africa," see Willan, 290.

7. *Black Power*, Harper and Brothers, 1954. All quotations from the book will be taken from this edition. Greenwood Press reprinted the American edition in 1974, retaining the Nkrumah images. All the editions include a partial map of Africa captioned "Northwestern Africa and the Gold Coast" and a letter from Nkrumah writing in his official capacity as prime minister. The letter certifies that Wright is visiting as guest of the prime minister to research "the social and historical aspects of the country."

8. For instance, see Gates and Shanker. For less disapproving readings of Wright's depiction of Africa, see Diawara, Goyal, JanMohamed, Olaniyan, and Pratt. In *Romance, Diaspora, and Black Atlantic Literature*, Goyal charts the ways in which a range of black diasporic and continental African writers have drawn upon subgeneric codes of either romance or realism—and sometimes both in generative tension—in contemplating and representing Africa and black modernity. Her discussion of *Black Power* approaches Wright's travel narrative as a text that dramatizes with particular force the conceptual links and tensions that connect black Atlanticism with varieties of cultural nationalism and anticolonial internationalism. Olaniyan concentrates on Wright's essay "Tradition and Industrialization" and argues that Wright exemplifies black-Atlantic thinkers of his generation who tended to locate decolonization and racial struggle in the political domain. It is not until later, in the post–civil rights, postcolonial era (roughly dated by Olaniyan to the 1970s) that the realm of culture came to be recognized as an important site of struggle.

9. See Field. See also Ogungbesan, Rathbone, and Chiwengo. For Abrahams's reflection on the Pan-Africanist movement, see his conversation with Dunn.

10. See Boym, esp. 3–55.

11. See Achebe, "An Image of Africa." For a sampling of the arguments that Achebe's essay has generated, see Graff; Harris; H. Miller; Said, 4–31; Sarvan; Spivak, *Death of a Discipline*, 69–101; and Torgovnick.

12. Kwame Anthony Appiah famously characterized Achebe as "archetypal African writer." See *In My Father's House*.

4 Globalization Time: Achebe, Soyinka, and Beyond

IT IS COMMON in academic and popular discussions of black Africa's problems to stress the colonial underlay of the different countries that today claim sovereignty on the continent. Now perhaps more than ever, it is useful to be reminded that the boundaries of the nation-states of contemporary black Africa were drawn by European powers at the Berlin Conference of 1884–85. This act of mapping and naming was in line, by and large, with the interests of the main European powers themselves. The geographical and juridical authoring of many sub-Saharan African nations derives, then, not from historical or political logics internal to the continent itself but rather, from late-nineteenth-century Western European exigencies. In this sense, the project of nation building advocated by Pan-African nationalists since the decolonization struggle of the 1950s might be thought of as one of engineering African versions of a preconstituted Western model. Black African nationalism of the mid-twentieth century was all along an attempt to translate a Western category of the nation-state by re-creating it in African political space.

Current work in postcolonial studies has shown the problem with rhetorics of nationalism and modernization. The critiques of the elisions of nationalist rhetoric yield useful insights into the situation in black Africa. Taking up one of the insights of postcolonial theory and cultural criticism, we may use the idea of translation to resituate the lofty colonial categories underpinning the continent's modernity. To talk of re-creating or translating a "Western" form in a non-Western space is to adopt a questionable understanding of the dynamic of cultural encounter and historical change. Briefly, this understanding grasps the encounter between the colonized and the colonizer fundamentally as one of "transfer." The transfer would straddle both the realms of thought as well as action, mind as well as social structure. The process would be passive, and the translation would be successful or not, depending on the extent to which it mimics a stable original. By first rejecting essentialist notions of originality that serve Eurocentric representations of formerly colonized societies, we begin to approach the actively deconstructive sense of translation that can productively inform the way we frame the contemporary problems of black Africa.

Another reason why the notion of translation needs to be rejected when it comes to the aspiration to nationhood and citizenship/democracy in the Western sense is that it allows us to evade the risk of the teleology that follows from uncritical acceptance of Eurocentric temporality. In the last chapter, I looked at the examples of James, Wright, and Abrahams as black diasporic figures whose rhetoric of development unveils a set of blindnesses that we can only appreciate from the vantage point of our present. This Eurocentric temporality is the source of the historicism and teleology for which the ideology of progress has been taken to task in a range of disciplines in the humanities and social sciences. If understood simply as a project of replicating the nation-state form inherited—through colonial imposition—from Western Europe, the nationalist project was doomed from the outset. For our purposes, what is most interesting is that this doomed project was simultaneously endorsed and criticized in literary treatments of African societies since the decolonization era of the 1960s. My concern in this chapter is to argue that the achievement of the best of modern African novelists should not be located in the success with which they translate Eurocentric ideologemes about nationhood and the proper destiny for African societies. Rather, the achievement should be located in the depth with which they reveal the problems in the nationalists' undertaking. In turning to two of the most globally renowned African writers, I want to open up a way of conceiving and representing collective life in Africa such that the continent's failures appear, not just as a catalog of woes but, very specifically, as temporal flashes in an uncanny continuum, where a different future can neither be foreclosed nor guaranteed. Here, what we have is a representational mood that stresses notional possibility (what is and can be), rather than relational calibration based on a spurious norm and a nonexistent model.

In what follows, I construe the challenge of globalism and cosmopolitanism as a version of the familiar, and interminably relevant, issue of particularism and how it may relate to universalism. I proceed by means of a close reading of two texts by each author: *Arrow of God* (1964) and *Anthills of the Savannah* (1987) by Achebe; *The Interpreters* (1965) and *Aké: The Years of Childhood* (1981) by Soyinka. Between the early 1960s and the 1980s when these texts appeared, many African countries had been plagued with civil wars, dictatorships, and failing states. I show the ways in which *Arrow of God* narrates the reconstitution of Umuaro tradition and society in spiritual as well as secular domains. But properly grasped, the conversion is not rendered as unproblematically linear; rather, it is occasioned by a messy historical transaction, a juncture of crisis that nonetheless dares us to contemplate the possibility of change. I argue that the emergence of the educated elite is presented as no more than a moment in the life of a fully rational social order. In other words, enforced (colonial) conversion is not the transcendence of something called tradition—read primitive, prerational— toward Eurocentric modernity. In *Arrow*, it is precisely the intersubjective, intercultural conflicts that signal the traditional society's rationality and dynamism. *Anthills of the Savannah* propels us to the future that is, of course, our present: in it, the foresight coded into the earlier novel is redoubled and elaborated upon, with the hindsight of twenty-odd years. Turning to Soyinka, I tease out what *The Interpreters* and *Aké* may tell us about nationhood and nationalism in an African context. I read both novels in terms of their inflections of categories of identity and subject position, such as class, race, tribe, and nation, in the Nigerian context. The interplay of race, nation, and ethnicity in Soyinka derives from a dual impulse that is at once nationalist and internationalist. Soyinka's rhetoric reveals itself caught between both impulses, thereby complicating the familiar binarism that much of current criticism tends to set up between the national and the transnational. In this way, Achebe and Soyinka anticipate contemporary anxieties about globalism by foregrounding Africa in terms of desire and agency, rather than mere epiphenomenon of Western modernity. Finally, against a background of global terrorism and destructive assertions of ethnic or religious exclusivity, the novelists offer a way of thinking about present challenges and future prospects in terms of change, as opposed to crisis and sacrifice.

The Nation and the Tribe

It is helpful to begin by considering the specificity of the nation-state form and its incarnation in black Africa. We might briefly touch on what is at stake in postcolonial nationalism by revisiting Frantz Fanon's account, set out in *The Wretched of the Earth*. As is well known, for Fanon, nationalism in the third world is precisely what makes it possible to break out of a mythical ethnic purity and reach instead for a national identity. This national identity joins universal humanity by virtue of its worldly and datable particularity. Fanon permitted his rhetoric to speculate that the tribal organization and worldview within which the Algerian peasants got their sustenance prepared them well for a central role in the fight for independence. This participation depends on and will, in turn, foster a broadening out of the peasant's world from the domain of the clan to that of the nation, posited as the realm of freedom and self-identity in modernity. In Fanon's account, the nation denotes desire, one whose predication and consequence is a realignment of selves and the superseding of tribe. If, in the discourses of traditionalists and colonialists alike, the tribe is frozen as ahistorical identity, this lie ideally fractures under the pressure of decolonization and nationhood. The fracturing becomes, through the intensity of its agony and danger, the narrative of the nation in secular history. And that narrative, according to Fanon, is as well the phenomenological, cultural, and political content of the nation in its unpredictable spasms of emergence.

Fanon is often romantic and idealistic in his evocation of the nation and the multitude it calls into a new identity and a new freedom. However, in the case of black Africa, the idea that the nation could be productive of a new identity that explodes and reconfigures ethnic particularities remains interesting. It could be shown that much of African literature in the European languages supports Fanon's account of nationalism in terms of cosmopolitan possibility—a gesturing outward, rather than a nativist inwardness. For instance, writing of the era of bourgeois cultivation that led to the struggle for decolonization, the Senegalese novelist Mariama Bâ (1979) touches on the promise of transethnic cosmopolitanism in *So Long a Letter*. Her protagonist Ramatoulaye reminisces on the continental African cosmopolitanism that the white headmistress of her student days inculcated:

> Let us hear the walls of our school come to life with the intensity of our study. Let us relive its intoxicating atmosphere at night, while the evening song, our joint prayer, rang out, full of hope. The admission policy, which was based on an entrance examination for the whole of former West Africa, now broken up into autonomous republics, made possible a fruitful blend of different intellects, characters, manners and customs. Nothing differentiated us, apart from specific racial features, the Fon girl from Dahomey and the Malinke one from Guinea. Friendships were made that have endured the test of time and distance. We were true sisters, destined for the same mission of emancipation. (15)

The students are interpellated into a cosmopolitan *continental* identity, one that the consolidation of "autonomous republics" later mitigates. But even this mitigation, consequent upon the consolidation of nation-states and the comprador elite, are actually tense sublations of distinct tribes, ethnic configurations, and castes. As Ramatoulaye's friend Aissatou's experience shows, the reason for the breakup of her marriage is directly linked to traditional caste snobbery. We are told that Mawdo Bâ, the man she marries, is of royal Toucouleur background, whereas she is a goldsmith's daughter. In this sense, Aissatou's Western education proves incapable of completely escaping entrenched (traditional) social hierarchies.

We do well, of course, to remark Ramatoulaye's wistful invocation of a "mission of emancipation." But to remark this is to tell only half of the story. For the ideological grid that sponsors her rhetoric of enlightenment also underpins the racialization that would enable any transethnic cosmopolitanism. Looked at this way, as bearers of a continental African or sovereign national identity, Ramatoulaye's generation of educated (and, in this case, female) Africans enter euromodernity's liberal-juridical structures as citizens of a nation, a continent, and a race. This transtribal or transethnic subject position is thus posed as being more compatible with modernity, insofar as the nation, the regional-continental (French West Africa), or the wholly continental (black and African) become available to the subject's consciousness and social location as a consequence of euromodern interpellation.

This is where an important complication at the heart of contemporary African nation-states might be located. As I noted in chapter 2, Mahmood Mamdani's

Citizen and Subject: Contemporary Africa and the Legacy of Late Colonialism identifies a crucial source of the problems of African nation-states in a basic antinomy that characterizes the formation of these states. This antinomy derives from the fact that, much more importantly than the issue of the arbitrariness of geographical and cultural boundaries, the administrative structures of postcolonial African states were "bifurcated" from the outset. By this Mamdani means that theoretically, the countries operate at once on the model of modern civil societies and as adaptations of putatively traditional structures. Where the former presupposes euromodern technologies of statehood, the latter is posed as deriving from primordial tribal identity. But so-called tribe is bound to filial kinship: static, genetic, and inherited. By extension, the social organization it implies cannot entirely be characterized by rational choice. In other words, so-called tribal society can only be the antithesis of what we have come to value as the social contract in its post-Enlightenment construal. One consequence of this legacy is that modern African countries are structured on multiple cultural and juridical spheres that are posed as simultaneously viable, yet coded in colonial discourse as mutually exclusive. European colonialism in black Africa simplified the profusion of precolonial narratives, generating instead bifurcated states and epistemic orders: the "traditional" and the "modern," the tribe and the nation, and so on. In one sphere of this bifurcation, you have the educated elite who replaced the colonial powers and assumed the task of engineering the new, modern nations. In the other, you have the teeming millions whose mode of incorporation into the bureaucratic structures of the state is defined by tribal identity. Where the first sphere takes signal European constructs of the state, history, and progress as normative narrative streams into which the new nation flows to join global humanity, the second is couched in discourse as radically different from that same narrative.

In this way, the colonial imaginary represents its structural impositions as necessary to the secular-historical progress of the native and yet destructive of "his" metaphysics and sociological being. Posed differently, the native's world needs to be transformed and at the same time protected from the corruption of westernizing transformation. We risk underplaying this foundational contradiction if we see black Africa's experiment with the form of the nation-state as so much failed translation of a stable Western model. We are today bombarded by media images of racial/ethnic conflicts and terrible suffering in various parts of Africa. Judging by what we read and the images we see, everyday life in Africa is one expansive scroll of disease and political turmoil. We are called on to accept that in these sites people do little that is genuinely productive of a prosperous collective existence. It is as though nothing but genocide, coups d'etat, and underdevelopment happens in black Africa: people don't fall in love, children don't rebel against parents, fast merchants don't seek to make higher profits off their equally eagle-eyed customers. We will be evading the issues to claim that these images, and the story they tell of Africa's modernity, are not based on some filtered version of reality. Likewise, the issue here should not be reduced to the unfruitful (yet intermittent) argument over whether Africa's problems should be blamed on colonialism and the West, or on the continent's own leaders. I am suggesting, rather, that it is more productive to pose the story of black Africa's modernity in terms of the logic of its unfolding rather than what it fails to be. The story of contemporary black Africa can be told in a way that does not underplay the crises but rather highlights in them disparate undercurrents of struggle. This way of telling Africa's story places the crises within an ongoing narrative of global modernity but puts the emphasis on the specific modalities of the continent's incorporation into the global narrative. In this way, the present reveals a genealogy and an immanent density, one that may turn out to yield a realm of freedom that is neither traditional nor Western humanist.

In the next section, I explore the ways in which Achebe dramatizes the African situation in terms of the complexities of conversion and translation, both understood as motions of becoming. Achebe's works have for long been recognized as meditations on the adventures of the nation-state in Nigeria in particular and black Africa in general. Achebe explores the issue of conversion by repeatedly staging scenes of translation, even as the novels themselves embody, thematically and stylistically, the problematic of translation and conversion. As I use it, conversion does not simply refer to the phenomenon of religion and faith. It also points to the social and political domain, to the encounter between traditional society and what we will continue to call modernity. The notion of translation as I use it also refers beyond the basic level of linguistic transfer. In addition to this conventional meaning, the term connotes traffic between one idiom and another or one conceptual scheme and another.[1] The traffic here would involve processes of translation from the traditional folktale to the modern novel, the oral to the written, or the pagan to the secular. In this way, Achebe posits the issue of nation building in particular, and sociohistorical change in general, in terms of translation and its tensions and epiphanies.

Historical Entanglement, Linguistic Transaction

Let us begin with *Arrow of God*. Set in fictional Umuaro in southeastern Nigeria in the first two decades of the twentieth century, the novel tells of an intersection of circumstances and interests that leads to the conversion to, or at least a more favorable disposition toward, Christianity in Umuaro.[2] Prior to this change, the god Ulu had been the most important deity for the people of Umuaro. In the words of Robert M. Wren, "Ulu's roles [within the community] are protector of the people, cleanser of society, and governor of the ecological cycle" (122–23). The chief priest of Ulu ministers to this god and watches the ecological cycle by keeping the community's agricultural calendar. His is the life-replenishing task of ceremonially announcing when crops are to be planted, when harvested. His announcement carries the dual force of the constative and the performative, a naturalized correlation of utterance, meaning, and practical consequence that has never been strained in the life of the society. Ezeulu muses to himself at the beginning of the novel:

> Whenever Ezeulu considered the immensity of his power over the year and the crops and, therefore, over the people he wondered if it was real. It was true he named the day for the feast . . . but he did not choose it. He was merely a watchman. His power was no more than the power of a child over a goat said to be his. As long as the goat was alive it could be his; he would find it food and take care of it. But the day it was slaughtered he would know soon enough who the real owner was. No! the Chief Priest of Ulu was more than that, must be more than that. If he should refuse to name the day there would be no festival—no planting and no reaping. But could he refuse? No Chief Priest had ever refused. (3)

Arrow of God is about just such a situation, where Ezeulu refuses to announce the time for the harvesting of crops. Whether his refusal is willful and deliberate (as some of his fellow villagers think) or due to sincere obedience to the will of his god, the result is that he puts the people in a life-threatening dilemma: either they disobey Ezeulu and harvest their crops, thereby incurring the god's wrath, or they endure the priest's recalcitrance and starve. Seizing the opportunity offered by this impasse, missionary agents step in to promise the protection of the Christian God for those who are willing to take the risk and harvest their crops. With the ecological cycle and their livelihood threatened, the people of Umuaro defect to the Christian church. The Umuaro people see their choice in simple but altogether revolutionary terms: they have pragmatically accepted the offer of one spiritual force to protect them from the wrath of another. The power of gods to guide the affairs of human beings is here affirmed by the people of Umuaro, precisely at the moment that they subordinate two such gods—one pagan, the other Christian—to the contingencies of secular human interests. Subordinating the gods to the will of man, the pagans of Umuaro affirm what we have to call secular desire and the immanence of being.

The idea of immanence of being invoked here comes from Michael Hardt and Antonio Negri's (2000) *Empire*. According to Hardt and Negri, "The origins of European modernity are often characterized as springing from a secularizing process that denied divine and transcendent authority over worldly affairs. That process was certainly important, but in our view really only a symptom of the primary event of modernity; the affirmation of the powers of *this* world, the discovery of the plane of immanence" (71). My concern is not the revolution in thought and action that, in their account, unfolded in Europe between 1200 and

1600, only to be contained and rechanneled in a counterrevolutionary direction in the centuries of the Enlightenment. Rather, I am interested in their reading of twentieth-century antihumanism (precisely in its Althusserian and Foucauldian versions) as a project that "can be linked effectively to a battle that Spinoza fought three hundred years earlier" (91). For Hardt and Negri, Spinoza's philosophy of immanence succeeds in "putting humanity and nature in the position of God, [thereby] transforming the world into a territory of practice" (77). The Deleuzian concept of plane of immanence, then, designates this "territory of practice": the material horizon of knowledge and action, where all meaning is made, where meaning lives and dies.

Whether one agrees with the details of Hardt and Negri's reconstruction of European modernity, their materialist stress on the divinity of nature—and on man-as-nature—comes close to Achebe's depiction of the pagans of Umuaro as producers. Achebe represents the people of Umuaro as pious iconoclasts who make serial apostasy an important advantage of the polytheistic, as against monotheistic, worldview. As a matter of principle and historical memory, Umuaro pagans claim the power to discard old gods and create new ones to grapple with worldly contingencies. Looked at this way, Achebe's pagans do not require imperialist Europe's guidance in the practice of subordinating the gods to man and nature or integrating such a worldview into what Hardt and Negri call "a new consciousness of reason and potentiality" (71). For instance, according to Anichebe Udeozo, one of the village elders who visits Ezeulu to persuade him to eat the ritual yams and name the day of the harvest: "These are not the times we used to know and we must meet them as they come or be rolled in the dust" (208). Speaking for and as "Umuaro"—that is, the entire village as one laboring collective—Anichebe Udeozo informs the recalcitrant chief priest,

> "Umuaro is now asking you to go and eat those remaining yams today and name the day of the next harvest. Do you hear me well? I said go and eat those yams today, not tomorrow; and if Ulu says we have committed an abomination let it be on the heads of the ten of us here. You will be free because we have set you to it, and the person who sets a child to catch a shrew should also find him water to wash the odour from his hand. We shall find you the water." (208)

The novel does not quite settle the question of the actual motivation behind Ezeulu's refusal to declare the harvest: indeed, the chief priest is not in conscious grasp of his motivations. At the background of the conflict over the power to control the agricultural cycle are two worldly factors that Ezeulu perceives as threats: one is the British colonial presence, the other the rivalry of another deity and its devotees. Ezeulu tries to contain the threat of the encroaching colonial power by sending one of his children to the Christian school. This decision is clearly motivated by a desire to position himself to the best advantage by having one of his own acquire whatever new power comes with Christian schooling and modern administrative structures. It is also motivated by a desire to outmaneuver his two local rivals Ezidemili and Nwaka. The former is the chief priest of Idemili, an important deity within the community, and the latter is his wealthy friend and accomplice.

Ezeulu and his rivals understand their contest in terms of a struggle for supremacy between the two most important deities in Umuaro, Ulu and Idemili. The battle between Ezeulu and his rivals is understood by both parties, and by the entire community, as being at once spiritual and secular-political. Their understanding of what is at stake operates on a spiritual-metaphysical level (which god is primary and supreme), as well as a political one (who, on behalf of either of the deities, should have more power in the community's affairs). But *Arrow of God* also suggests that Ezeulu's decision to send Oduche to the Christian school might be based on another motivation, one that has to do with male succession. The office of chief priest of Ulu (Eze ulu) is hereditary, and the options for the protagonist's successor are restricted to his four male children. The eldest, Edogo, is a carver. The text presents him as introverted, socially awkward, and sullen. He is most comfortable in the confines of a small hut built for the carving of ancestral masks. There, he relishes solitude and the thrill of artistic accomplishment, as in the following passage, which describes him at work on the carving of a mask for an annual ritual: "Edogo had always found the atmosphere of this hut right for carving masks. All around him were older masks and other regalia of ancestral spirits, some of them older than even his father. They produced a certain ambience which gave power and cunning to his fingers. . . . Now and again he heard people talking as they passed through the market place from one village of Umuaro to another. But when his carving finally got hold of him he heard no more voices" (51).

By contrast, Obika, Edogo's younger brother, most resembles Ezeulu in physical appearance and temperament. A leader among his peers, Obika is physically prepossessing, generous, but stubborn and volatile. Although the father prefers him to Edogo, he remains deeply worried by Obika's tendency to violence and self-destructive choices. The two siblings therefore appear not to be suitable candidates for the role of chief priest after their father. And of course, Obika's death at the end of the novel rules him out definitively.

At any rate, given Edogo's retiring nature and seeming lack of leadership qualities, and given Obika's character flaws and seeming disinterest in the office of chief priest, the choice seems to be left to the two younger sons, Oduche and Nwafo. The text suggests that the youngest, Nwafo, is the father's favorite, thereby raising the possibility that Ezeulu sacrifices Oduche to the Christian school in order to leave the field clear for Nwafo. The eldest son Edogo articulates this possibility in the following passage, rendered in a combination of omniscient narration and interior monologue:

> Edogo remembered how much his father had liked him when he was a boy and how with the passage of years he had transferred his affection first to Obika and then to Oduche and Nwafo. Thinking of it now Edogo could not actually remember that their father had ever shown much affection for Oduche. He seemed to have lingered too long on Obika (who of all his sons resembled him most in appearance) and then by-passed Oduche for Nwafo. . . . A strange thought seized Edogo now. Could it be that their father had deliberately sent Oduche to the religion of the white man so as to disqualify him for the priesthood of Ulu? (92)

This possibility is raised more strongly in the scene where Ezeulu tries to explain his reasons for befriending Tom Winterbottom, the British district officer. In the heat of an argument with his best friend Akuebue, Ezeulu links the origin of Ulu to sacrifice, made in the past by the people of Umuaro to protect themselves from a powerful intruder. As he puts it:

> Our fathers have told us that it may even happen to an unfortunate generation that they are pushed beyond the end of things, and their back is broken and hung over a fire. When this happens they may sacrifice their own blood. This is what our sages meant when they said that a man who has nowhere else to put his hand for support puts it on his knee. That was why our ancestors when they were pushed beyond the end of things by the warriors of Abam sacrificed not a stranger but one of themselves and made the great medicine which they called Ulu. (133)

In addition to the struggle for supremacy between Ezeulu, on the one hand, and Ezidemili and Nwaka, on the other hand, the text poses domestic and familial competition as a second possible source of Ezeulu's calculations. The tragedy at the novel's end is that Ezeulu is defeated politically and in the domestic sphere. He has a falling-out with the British colonial administrator he had befriended, and the death of Obika deals him a devastating blow that results in his insanity. Circumstances thus conspire to weaken Ezeulu's position to such an extent that the people of Umuaro not only turn to the Christian God but also interpret his misfortune as a reprimand from the deity: "To them the issue was simple. Their god had taken sides with them against his headstrong and ambitious priest and thus upheld the wisdom of their ancestors—that no man however great was greater than his people" (230). Like King Lear, the overbearing patriarch is reduced to a fragile figure who loses touch with the history he sought to control and direct.

It is possible to read further the interlayering of public and domestic, secular and spiritual dramas that I have only sketched here. What interests me most is the sense in which the public conflict is complicated by the undercurrent of family tension in Ezeulu's polygamous household. It is in this domestic sphere that Achebe figures a level of change and social realignment that none of the main actors recognize. In a scene that depicts Oduche studying his alphabet primer surrounded by his mother and sister, Achebe figures a ferment of conversion and translation, where orality cohabits with literacy in the unassuming shelter of a maternal hut. The scene is a cozy one, toned in the ethnographic hue that Achebe's fiction patented. The three children of Ugoye (one of the two living wives of Ezeulu) have just completed supper and pester their mother to tell them a folktale. After some thought, the mother chooses the story of "Eneke Ntulukpa" (190) to tell the children. I should like to quote this moment at some length:

> Once upon a time there was a man who had two wives. The senior wife had many children but the younger one had only one son. But the senior wife was wicked and envious. One day the man and his family went to work on their farm. This farm was at the boundary between the land of men and the land of spirits. . . . Ugoye, Nwafo and Obiageli sat in a close group near the cooking place. Oduche sat apart near the entrance to the one sleeping-room holding his new book, *Azu Ndu*, to the yellow light of the taper. His lips moved silently as he spelt out and formed the first words of the reader. . . .
> Meanwhile Ezeulu had pursued again his thoughts on the coming struggle and began to probe with the sensitiveness of a snail's horns the possibility of reconciliation or, if that was too much, of narrowing down the area of conflict. Behind his thinking was of course the knowledge that the fight would not begin until the time of harvest, after three moons more. (190)

In this scene, Ugoye's oral folktale is placed alongside Oduche's learning of the alphabet.[3] Where the oral story is being told under the natural illumination of moonlight, Oduche's silent reading proceeds against this background and the added light of a taper. The boy's reading is thus in a context that is at once solitary and communal. That is, Oduche's engagement with the letters of his Igbo language in the Roman script is figured as an occasion of solitude at the moment of community. Separated from the communal oral setting of the family storytelling session, his reading nonetheless takes place within that text, as its interface. Achebe thus places orality and literacy in coeval time, and recasts their relationship as a supple dialectic rather than a deterministic teleology. Moreover, the mother's folktale resembles the plot unfolding in the novel itself. Ugoye's tale— of a man at a boundary between two worlds, married to two warring wives— parallels the central conflict of the novel, which is after all about a patriarch at the crossroads, confronted by an alien power. In this way, Achebe gives the scene of oral storytelling an allegorical moment and reach, such that the folktale enfolds the novel that contains it.

The 1964 first edition of the novel contains the full version of the folktale that Ugoye tells her children. This section was removed from the revised edition that was published in 1974. In his preface to this second (revised) edition, Achebe indicates that the changes and revisions were made in order to address "certain structural weaknesses" in the first edition. In the full version, Ugoye's folktale is about a polygamous household and incorporates archetypal characters of the domestic moral fable: the wicked, scheming wife and her superficial son, contrasted to the good wife and her thoughtful son. Where the thoughtful son and his mother are rewarded with wealth at the tale's end, the wicked wife and her spoiled son bring disaster upon themselves and the world. In this extended version, the tale ends on a tragic note, with "diseases and abominations," let loose upon the world because of the wicked wife's scheming. Cutting the folktale from the revised edition does tighten the narrative by eliminating the awkwardness of the folktale form as it was inserted within the novelistic structure of the 1964 edition. It also allows the 1974 edition more sharply to underscore Ezeulu's delicate location at that point in the narrative: at a crossroads of cultures and political future. If we set aside the sexual politics of the archetype of wicked wives and good wives, the folktale is about a patriarch at a crossroads, confronted by alien spirits. Removing it in the revised edition eliminates the folktale's moral lesson that human choices go a long way toward advancing, if not determining, whether the collective attains prosperity or devastation. The revised edition came out in 1974, that is, after the Nigerian civil war. Although the tale is cut in the 1974 edition, the fact that the original 1964 edition contained a figurative lesson about catastrophe let loose by human machinations is instructive in the distinctive way of folktales and imaginative literature.

In *Achebe's World*, Robert M. Wren suggests that Oduche can arguably be said to be Ulu's choice as the next chief priest after Ezeulu's demise. According to Wren,

> the remarkable thing about such a choice is that it would transcend the gulf between the traditional religion and Christianity. Ulu must recognize that the good of the clan depends upon a peaceful and orderly transition. As the agent of transcendence, Oduche need not be aware that in serving the Christian God he serves Ulu as well. Indeed, the transfer of spiritual power must require the god's acceptance of being forgotten by the priest and the clan he served and cherished. The god himself becomes a kind of sacrifice, the climax to the series of sacrifices the god required of his unwitting priest. (124)

Wren's reading is persuasive, although I would not locate the passage from Ulu to the Christian God simply on a spiritual level, or, indeed, formulate it as a transfer. The transition, such as it is, is played out on social, economic, and political levels from which the spiritual dimension is indissociable. It is also not quite "peaceful and orderly," and the family catastrophe that befalls Ezeulu's household points to the cost of the transition. Obika is the central symbol of this cost. In the scene where he is whipped by the British public engineer Mr. Wright, he "only shivered as a sacrificial ram which must take in silence the blows of funeral dancers before its throat is cut" (82). And in the climactic sequence leading up to his death, he enters the frenzied state of a speeding masquerade named Ogbazulobodo, "at once blind and full of sight" (226). The text continues: "A fire began to rage inside his chest and to push a dry bitterness up his mouth. But he tasted it from a distance or from a mouth within his mouth. He felt like two separate persons, one running above the other" (226). The tempo of this passage intensifies its insistence on bodily dysfunction and, even more interestingly for our purposes, bifurcation. The Igbo epithet Ogbazulobodo may be translated as "the one who runs for the village," or, "the one who runs as protection for the village."[4] Engaged in a communal ritual of energetically circling the village to cleanse and replenish it, Obika-as-Ogbazulobodo symbolically becomes the spirit and life-force of communal historicity itself. He embodies the very motion of history that the Umuaro community is shown enacting in the novel.

Another mask called Agaba, commissioned to celebrate the coming-of-age of Obika's age group, is carved by his older brother. Edogo is the artist figure who records in wood the itinerary of the community's history as embodied by Obika's generation. By extension, Obika is the scapegoat or sacrificial lamb for his generation. Looked at this way, Oduche's acquisition of Western literacy singles him out for more than just the role of chief priest for the new generation. As we have seen, his nascent literacy settles willy-nilly into a vintage ethnographic scene of traditional orality. In doing so, he implicitly offers a new manner of witnessing to and ordering experience. The sounds of his language in an alien script take their place alongside the sounds of the language in the voices of his mother and siblings. The novel thus figures a dynamic of cultural traffic taking place in the midst, but beyond the recognition, of the characters on the political stage. If Ezeulu wanted to get Oduche out of the line of succession by sending him to school, the scene points to something the ebullient chief priest does not clearly grasp. In seeking to manipulate his succession by sending Oduche to school, Ezeulu seeks to master history. In that direction, he fails, for the defection of Umuaro to the Christian God implies a conversion toward the culture of literacy, the very culture into which Oduche had been "sacrificed." It is as though the chief priest of Ulu is enacting the Christian narrative of the Father sacrificing the Son for the continuity of society. Pagan and Christian—or savage and civilized—therefore appear in a serene light of inner compatibility, defined in human and historical terms, beyond the logic of radical otherness. Moreover, because *Arrow of God* is a novel—a literate form unlike poetry or the traditional epic—it has served to encode the mother's folktale in a new idiom, a new linguistic transaction. In other words, the cultural process that Oduche embodies in the scene we have been discussing actualizes itself in Achebe's craft.

In *Time and the Other*, Johannes Fabian (1983) writes of the different notions of time that emerged in Western Europe from about the Renaissance era.

Adapting his account, we might say that missionaries engaged in converting natives to Christianity and euromodern institutions conflated the "sacred time" of Christian teleology with the "secular time" of social Darwinism and progress. Conceptually, African nationalists took up this modernist secular time (with its teleology of progress and development), and complicated it with a strategic vindication of traditional African worldviews. V. Y. Mudimbe touches on the implications of this in *The Invention of Africa*: "since most African leaders and thinkers have received a Western education, their thought is at the crossroads of Western epistemological filiation and African ethnocentrism. Moreover, many concepts and categories underpinning this ethnocentrism are inventions of the West. When prominent leaders such as Senghor or Nyerere propose to synthetize liberalism and socialism, idealism and materialism, they know that they are transplanting Western intellectual Manicheism" (*The Invention of Africa*, 185). This situation has significant conceptual as well as historical consequences. As Fabian indicates, many traditional African communities believe that a dead ancestor may coexist with the living in the same material dimension. To believe that an ancestor or spiritual entity can, for instance, inhabit a human being, as the mask Ogbazulobodo takes temporary residence in Obika, is to deploy a narrative of existence that cannot have a unitary teleological direction or intending agent.

This is in part what Achebe implies in the famous passage from his essay "Chi in Igbo Cosmology." As he puts it, "Wherever Something stands, Something Else will stand beside it. Nothing is absolute. *I am the truth, the way, and the life* would be called blasphemous or simply absurd, for is it not well known that a man may worship Ogwugwu to perfection and yet be killed by Udo?" (161).[5] In this passage, Ogwugwu and Udo refer to distinct metaphysical entities that are also grasped as material intending agents. What Achebe articulates in the passage is the polytheistic logic of existence and becoming as it pertains to Igbo culture. On the logic of Achebe's formulation, ancestor worship and polytheism suggest views of temporal unfolding that are, at the least, less unidirectional than Christian teleology and the ideology of progress that marked euromodernity at its core. I am not suggesting that the contemporary failure of many African nation-states is linked, in a simplistic relation of causality, to a collision of different construals of temporality. I am arguing, however, that the conflation might be thought of as one of the specific ways in which contemporary black Africa bears, and is borne by, the postcolonial modernity we presently live.

Our discussion so far has pointed up a contradictory aspect of the nation-state form in Africa, whereby tribe and nation were posed as (culturally) mutually exclusive, on the one hand, and (politically) coextensive, on the other hand. The modalities of ethnicity and national identity in Africa have a good part of their sources in the contradictions of colonial rule and the nation-states that are its legacy. We have also seen that Achebe's *Arrow of God* imaginatively represents the story of a black African village in a way that draws out the dynamism of traditional cultures and insists on their immanent integrity. This narrative project does not conduce to simplistic relativism of the kind that some contemporary cultural critics love to invent and refute. Naoki Sakai has drawn attention to the sense in which the opposition of universalism (of the bad sort) to particularism (also of the bad kind) actually turns on a complicity between both sides. For Sakai, "Contrary to what has been advertised by both sides, universalism and particularism reinforce and supplement each other; they are never in real conflict.... In this respect, a particularism such as nationalism can never be a serious critique of universalism, for it is an accomplice thereof" (163). My point with respect to Achebe is that he undoes the false opposition between the universal and the particular upon which critics of what is called cultural relativism often depend. In Achebe's fiction, the particular contains within it lessons of universal amplitude; and the universal lives up to its naming, precisely to the extent that it devolves around an intimate particularity.

Achebe's relativism is designed to underscore what we share that defines our humanity, the claim to truth that each society, in its own hubristic way, makes. Achebe is an artist figure, a literate incarnation of Edogo the carver. As creative writer, his ancestor in the intellectual history of modern black Africa is Oduche. We may at this point ask: where in the new order does the novel locate Oduche's younger brother Nwafo or, indeed, his female siblings like Obiageli and Ojuigo? To pose this question is to come upon the limit of Achebe's narrative labor in *Arrow of God*. The novel's horizon is circumscribed by the patriarchy of Ezeulu's household. Its immediate concern is the drama of elite male succession. But we get a glimpse of Nwafo and his sister Obiageli initiating the retreat of the royal python—a pagan symbol of reverence and authority in Umuaro—at the recitation of a newly devised song: "Python, run! There is a Christian here" (205). In this way, the text leaves us with two younger siblings taking on the role of agents, albeit in the innocence of childhood play, of a new song to render a new reality.

When Ezeulu asks about the royal python's response to the children's song, Nwafo's reply bears no hint of nostalgia: "It ran away *fiam* like an ordinary snake" (205). Nwafo's characterization of the python as just an ordinary snake completes the progressive demythologization it undergoes in the novel. The onomatopoeic *"fiam"* connotes speed and flexibility, such as one would not otherwise associate with the stately python. A similar stress on speed occurs in the incantation by which Obika is transformed into the masquerade Ogbazulobodo: "The speed of the deer / Is seen on the hill" (225). The couplet initiates Obika's possession by the spirit of communal regeneration and history. It also recognizes the force of that spirit, names it as energy-in-motion. The energy unravels on a plane of immanence that can best be appreciated with historical hindsight or, pursuing the novel's metaphor, from an elevated distance. Writing in the 1960s, Achebe may not have clearly foreseen the problems that would beset Africa's postcolonial history. But the keenness of his vision of Umuaro's conversion allows him, as far back as 1964 when *Arrow of God* first appeared, to cast it in terms of sheer human choices and movement.[6]

At the beginning of the twenty-first century, we are positioned on that metaphorical hill, witnessing the human cost of Africa's postcolonial energy-in-motion. But we are also implicated in the motion, for the narrative of Africa's conversion, its complications and revelations, are unfolding right before our eyes. The translation that European colonialists and African nationalists sought to effectuate, whereby traditional societies become modern by approximating a European model, turns out to contain a costly error: no translation re-creates an original in a simple motion of either adequate or infelicitous transfer. Indeed, the notion of a stable original to be replicated is itself the foundational myth. Looked at this way, the contemporary situation in black Africa testifies to the true complexity of cultural encounters and historical transitions. To represent Africa's problems simply as the consequence of failed translation/conversion, or unrelenting tragedy, is to miss an important lesson that should rise, ever so cautiously, over and beyond the continent's woes. Because we cannot go back in history, every moment of disaster in the present carries the immanent possibility of change, of movement into a notionally different future. This notional future is uncertain and terrifyingly unpredictable, but it remains a possibility nonetheless.

Where *Arrow* meditated implicitly on the future, that future confronts us as the present in *Anthills*. The earlier novel, set in the beginning of the twentieth century, thematized the emergence of a Western educated class in a small village. Coming later, *Anthills* is set in a troubled African country in the late twentieth century. The novel anatomizes the legacy of British colonialism as well as the cultural nationalism of the educated class, the inheritors of Oduche's mantle. A range of studies in poststructuralist literary and cultural criticism, and especially the postcolonial vector within it, have had many things to say about natives who willingly participated in the epistemic capture of their own cultures: the colonial translators, the schoolmasters, the Christian converts. The theory of hybridity is by now so ubiquitous in cultural criticism that it has had to face a backlash. I maintain, nonetheless, that it does equip us to understand the psychic and social drama underneath the native collaborator's choice. To take a couple of influential examples, Homi Bhabha's theory of hybridity, Paul Gilroy's account of the black Atlantic, and Kwame Anthony Appiah's account of the cosmopolitan patriot all share a common strain. In all three accounts, the agency of the non-Western subject is to be located in the subject's participation in and reconfiguration of Eurocentric modes of seeing. The reconfiguration proceeds from within Western modernity, thereby dissolving facile binary oppositions of West and non-West. The theoretical developments that first flourished in the 1980s have enriched discussions about the varied legacies of colonial modernity such as racial terror, willed migrations and forced displacements, or biopolitical economic reproduction. But such theories (of hybridity, liminality, and so forth) often undercut their own promise by not giving proper conceptual weight to the materiality and inflections of particular social and psychic processes. Hybridity and its related constellation of concepts remain relevant as the twenty-first century lumbers on and old enmities are rekindled on the global stage. In this vein, postcolonial theory would do well to dig deeper than the generalizing claim. That is, we should assume that the literary-theoretical argument for hybridity (as against essentialist notions of identity and culture) has been won. It would be useful, then, to press the discussion deeper, beyond the generalities, and toward particular instantiations of postcolonial hybridization. There, I believe, some rich questions may begin to invite attention: what actually gets hybridized in particular contexts, and what cluster of discursive and material effects arise as consequences?

In "Signs Taken for Wonders," Homi Bhabha discusses a scenario, "played out in the wild and wordless wastes of colonial India, Africa, the Caribbean, of the sudden, fortuitous discovery of the English book" (*The Location of Culture*, 145). In Bhabha's theory, the imposition or willful acceptance of the European book cannot but encounter a moment of translation: "The discovery of the book installs the sign of appropriate representation: the word of God, truth, art creates the conditions for a beginning, a practice of history and narrative. But the institution of the Word in the wilds is also an *Enstellung*, a process of displacement, distortion, dislocation, repetition" (149). We might say that Achebe carries forward the black whitemen's confidence in the written word, and Pan-Africanism's confidence in the modern state. In carrying forward the confidence and the passion, the fictionality of Achebe's fiction allows him to interrogate hegemonic representations of natives and their peculiar ways. To adapt Bhabha, "the institution of the Word in the wilds" becomes in Achebe's craft an implicit process of repetition by interrogation and displacement. Here, the missionary's ethnography is contested by the novelist's imaginative performance. Achebe has the historical advantage of witnessing, deep into the twentieth century, the adventure of a modernity that came with Victorian mercantile interests, Christian missionary condescension, and later colonial imposition. Between 1958 when *Things Fall Apart* appeared, 1964 when *Arrow of God* appeared, and 1987 when *Anthills of the Savannah* was published, Nigeria had been plagued with a civil war and a succession of military interventions in state governance. From this vantage point, Achebe reconsiders the forms Western modernity was taking in the young African states. *Anthills of the Savannah* thus mounts a sustained reassessment of his previous texts. In so doing, the novelist comments in fiction upon his other fictions. Pressed by the historicity of the real, however construed, Achebe's own representational truth turns to contemplating itself.

The character Beatrice Okoh is one of the narrators of *Anthills*. She is at various points in the novel referred to as a goddess figure, a secular reincarnation of the deity Idemili.[7] She is also university educated, armed with a first-class degree in English literature. And she has read her inventor's *Things Fall Apart*: as she tells a friend at one point in the narrative, she sometimes feels like Chielo, a priestess from the earlier novel (*Anthills*, 105). In this way, Beatrice serves as Achebe's device to look back at his own earlier novels, as well as the narrativization of Igbo mythology undertaken in those novels. She also serves to question the authority of the other narrators in the novel, all of them Western-educated and male. She warns them not to mistake their narrow and specific story for the story of the Nigerian nation itself: "who am I," she wonders, "that I should inflict my story on the world?" (80). The novel also takes up the issue of the pagan past of Igbo culture in particular, and precolonial Africa in general. The language of chapter 8 of this novel is remarkable for its oracular cadence, one that temporarily arrests the flow of the narrative. The chapter's lyricism calls attention to itself as poetic inspiration, an oral ancestral speech whose superior cadence momentarily interrupts the prosaic ordinariness by which it is surrounded. Whatever else it does, chapter 8 dialogizes the language of the narrative action that led up to and follows after it. It begins with an omniscient, collective voice: "In the beginning Power rampaged through our world, naked. So the Almighty, looking at his creation through the round undying eye of the Sun, saw and pondered and finally decided to send his daughter, Idemili, to bear witness to the moral nature of authority by wrapping around Power's rude waist a loincloth of peace and modesty" (93). A little later, after Beatrice has been identified as a modern incarnation of the goddess Idemili, we encounter the following: "knowing or not knowing does not save us from being known or even put to work. For, as a newly-minted proverb among her people has it, baptism (translated in their language as Water of God) is no antidote against possession by Agwu the capricious god of diviners and artists" (96). The shift between the first-person plural ("our world," "us") and the third person ("her people," "their language") indexes an inevitable perspectival distance between narrator and characters.[8]

But what does the novel do with the myth of origins and dispersion that is elaborated in chapter 8? In "Onitsha, Gift of the Niger," an essay from the 1970s, Achebe had given a literal portrait of the River Niger that spoke directly to its historical fate as object of European fascination and profane, unmetaphorical appropriation:

> In its 2,600-mile journey from the Futa Jalon Mountains through savannahs, scrublands, and desert and then southward through tropical forests, finally losing itself in a thousand digressions in the Bight of Biafra, the River Niger sees many lands and diverse human settlements, old and new, picturesque and ordinary: Goa and Timbuktu of medieval fame; Lokoja created by British

zealots of "legitimate commerce" [i.e., the 1841 expedition] one hundred years ago and ridiculed by a skeptical Charles Dickens as so much "Borrio-boola-Gha"; Bussa, passive witness to an explorer's disaster in 1805 [Mungo Park], now itself sunk beneath the waters of a gargantuan hydroelectric lake. By the time the River Niger gets to Onitsha, it has answered many names, seen a multitude of sights; it is now big, experienced, and unhurried. Its name is simply *Orimili* or plenitude of waters." (*Morning Yet on Creation Day*, 154, emphasis in original)

Chapter 8 of *Anthills* takes up the majesty of the river again, this time as metaphor and critique. Achebe deploys the figure of the river to elaborate the myth of Idemili ("pillar of water") whose lake flows into the Niger itself (Orimili, "plenitude of waters"). The chapter stresses the mutations that Idemili's significance for the Igbo community has undergone. In Achebe's telling, Idemili's worshippers dispersed over time and space, spreading from their original location to reach the area where contact with European interests became possible: "As it happened, good land was more plentiful than good water and before long some hamlets too far from streams and springs were relieving their burning thirst with the juice of banana stems in the worst years of dry weather. Idemili, travelling though the country disguised as a hunter, saw this and on her return sent a stream from her lake to snake through the parched settlements all the way to Orimili, the great river which in generations to come strange foreigners would search out and rename the Niger" (94). Here, naming itself is at stake. Where in colonial discourse, the Niger is primarily a means to an end, a signifier of spiritual darkness and superstition, in *Anthills* the river becomes a familiar source of subsistence and meaning for the pagans on its banks. In this way, Achebe inscribes a mythological understanding of the permutations and significance of the river and its tributaries, one that is posed from a pagan perspective. The river is thereby associated with a fully comprehensible temporality, one that subsumes the hegemonic Eurocentric narrative of history and progress.[9]

Anthills comments critically on yet another difference in perspective, this one between traditional worldview and the secular-scientific option offered by "strange foreigners" who turn Orimili into River Niger in print. On the terms of the novel, the worshippers of the goddess whose lake flows into the Niger have no illusions that their representational tools can render the deity in her full significance. The spiritual import of the deity is precisely its status beyond the containment of human representational agency: "Man's best artifice to snare and hold the grandeur of divinity is always crumbling in his hands, and the more ardently he strives the more paltry and incongruous the result. So it were better he did not try at all; far better to ritualize that incongruity and by invoking the mystery of metaphor to hint at the most unattainable glory by its very opposite, the most mundane starkness—a mere stream, a tree, a stone, a mound of earth, a little clay bowl containing fingers of chalk" (94). In this passage, the pagan fetish worshiped "in numberless homes" (94) becomes in Achebe's hands a representation of pagan insight regarding representational adequation. "Divinity" is Achebe's code word for deity and (lower-case) history, what he elsewhere calls "powers of event" in *Arrow of God* (230). By suggesting that traditional Igbo discourse makes no claims to representational mastery in relation to nature and human agency, Achebe raises to the surface of his text the very status of his own novels as representation of Africa. *Anthills of the Savannah* thereby thematizes its own limitation as representation of reality and site of ideational reckoning.

By the self-reflexive move, Achebe registers a caution that should be of interest to literary and cultural criticism in the moment of globalism. At this moment in the adventure of modernity that all societies share, masses of people struggle voicelessly under economic deprivation. In the desire to create a good life for themselves, restless masses try to assert themselves using the language of prelapsarian plenitude. The belief system might be different, but the structure of thought is easily shown to be similar. Against this background, Achebe is in fact exploring a universal human drama that criticism can elicit only by attention to historical particularity. I will return to this point later on in this chapter. For now, I want to take up the case of Wole Soyinka.

The National and the Transnational

Soyinka is globally renowned as a writer and political activist. His contributions to modern African literature provide an exemplary combination of aesthetic pleasure and cultural critique. But he has also been a tireless activist, often at real physical risk.[10] As an engaged intellectual devoted as much to words as to action, Soyinka humbles me in the warmth of my study. He is of course more widely known as poet and dramatist, but here I am interested in two of his prose writings. *The Interpreters* is generally considered a text that draws on modernist formal techniques, whereas *Aké*'s idiom is the realist coming-of-age narrative. *The Interpreters* is his first novel, and by the time of its publication in 1965, he had established himself as perhaps the leading dramatist from the continent to use the English language. The novel was a controversial departure from the tradition of realist fiction that had been the norm in African literature when it appeared. It deals with the adventures and neuroses of a group of male intellectuals in the urban environment of Lagos in postindependence Nigeria. The central characters, Bandele, Egbo, Kola, Sagoe, and Sekoni, are presented in a milieu populated by tourists and visiting European and American artists and academics. But the world of the novel also includes corrupt politicians and the teeming underclass, inhabitants of the slums of the capital city. The main characters thus represent specific ideational dispositions and temperaments, allowing the novelist to explore the excesses and growing disillusionment of the educated elite in postcolonial Nigeria.

Interpreters also explores the social and intellectual context within which the main characters have been formed and which they idealistically hope to further. Although they are the text's multiple sites of consciousness, they are also subjected to the novelist's satire. Their limitations can be seen in the depiction of Egbo's narcissistic mystification of sex, Sekoni's shortsightedness and comical stammering, or Sagoe's bouts of drunken hallucination and phony philosophizing. The novel elaborates a symbolic system over and beyond the bleak comedy that surrounds the characters' lives. It does this by means of Kola's painting of a pantheon of Yoruba gods, using the principal characters as models. The novel thus poses the farcical reality of its characters' lives against the ideality of the world of pagan gods rendered in Kola's painting. In this way, by means of Kola's painting, the novel comments on its own creative effort immanently.

The mythological system upon which Soyinka draws is that of the Yoruba of western Nigeria. As critics have shown, Soyinka's use of Yoruba mythology is heavily mediated. He draws on aspects of Yoruba mythology precisely to elaborate his own personal artistic and sociopolitical vision. The novelistic world of *Interpreters* is for this reason recognizable in Soyinka's other works, linked as they are by figural allusion and rhetorical cross-referencing. The famous opening paragraph of part II, which describes the car accident in which Sekoni is killed, offers a striking instance of this intertextual linkage:

> The rains of May become in July slit arteries of the sacrificial bull, a million bleeding punctures of the sky-bull hidden in convulsive cloud humps, black, overfed for this one event, nourished on horizon tops of endless choice grazing, distant beyond giraffe reach. Some competition there is below, as bridges yield right of way to lorries packed to the running-board, and the wet tar spins mirages of unspeed-limits to heroic cars and their cargoes find a haven below the precipice. The blood of earth-dwellers mingles with blanched streams of the mocking bull, and flows into currents eternally below earth. The Dome cracked above Sekoni's short-sighted head one messy night. Too late he saw the insanity of a lorry parked right in his path, a swerve turned into a skid and cruel arabesques of tyres. A futile heap of metal, and Sekoni's body lay surprised across the open door, showers of laminated glass around him, his beard one fastness of blood and wet earth. (155)

There is of course a modernist echo here of the fragile human body broken by the efficiency of technological progress, even as nature glowers relentlessly on the landscape. Soyinka burdens this modernist trope with allusions that are recognizable staples of his myth-based vision. Sekoni's car accident is presided over by the sky itself: active nature, imaged as a sacrificed bull, destructively agential at the very moment of its ongoing immolation. The dead man is himself a sacrificial victim, claimed by modernizing technology and its lethal potential. Soyinka's early poems "Death in the Dawn," "In Memory of Segun Awolowo," and the long poem "Idanre" (1967) all take up this theme, as do his plays *A Dance of the Forests* (1960) and *The Road* (1965).[11] As in these other works, the destructive moment is not necessarily the end of the story; it may well be the occasion for a productive reorientation. And so the final image of Sekoni's corpse is of his beard mingled with "blood and wet earth," an image that can at once signal waste and fertility, death and life.

The motif of sacrifice also emerges in the text's treatment of Kola's painting, "The Pantheon." In the painting, Kola uses the novel's main characters as models for his representation of the pantheon of Yoruba gods. For Kola, Egbo is a model for Ogun, the Yoruba god of war and metal artisanship, destruction, and regeneration. This makes a lot of sense, for Egbo is the one figure from among the group of friends who is most volatile and impulsive. We are told that his communal roots are in Osa, a rural village crisscrossed by a network of creeks. His parentage reveals a dual heritage of the traditional and the modern. Where his grandfather is a war chieftain and his mother a princess of Osa, his father is a local cleric of the Christian church. Egbo flees the hereditary role expected of him as child of royalty and chooses instead a life in the city as civil servant. He rejects also the morality of his Christian background, choosing to celebrate his freedom from secondary school by seeking fulfillment in the phantasmatic sexuality of a courtesan Simi.

For Egbo, sex is a religious experience, but his vision of transcendence is bound to heteronormative masculinity. Upon discovering that Joe Golder, the biracial American friend of Kola's, is gay, Egbo's reaction is one of disgust, as if Golder were "some noxious insect" (236). The intensity of his phobic recoil is surprising even to Bandele and Kola, who "stared at him, isolated from this hatred they had not known in Egbo, and the sudden angry spasms that seemed to overtake each motion of his body" (236–37). His idealization of solitude and heteronormative physicality comes up later when he impregnates an undergraduate student of Bandele's. Egbo's sexual encounter with the female student, a "shy girl ... perhaps nineteen" (127), is ambiguously rendered in the text. Quite apart from the power differential involved in this ostensibly consensual encounter, or the age difference between him and the girl, the episode unfolds entirely from Egbo's perspective. The student's voice is reduced to that of pragmatic reaction only after the consequential act: "Egbo drew her to him. The hardness was only an outside crust, only the stubborn skin on her self-preservation and it gave in his eager hands. The centre pure ran raw red blood, spilling on the toes of the god, and afterwards he washed this for her, protesting shamefacedly, in the river. And Egbo confessed, not since that night of Simi, have I been so nervous, so fearful of the venturing. She said, "My exams are next month. You must not try to see me again" (134).

Here, Egbo is the virile figure of impulse and action: he "drew her to him," and the "crust" of her virginity submits to what we have to interpret as the force of his will. The passage depicts a physical encounter between two individuals, but the language—of "hardness," "eager hands," "self-preservation"—suggests a deeper metaphorical reach. In the register of Fredric Jameson's materialism, we would say that the text's figuring of Egbo as desiring subject takes us in the direction of a libidinal economy that is inherently masculinist.

Neville Hoad has developed an astute reading of the novel that draws out its treatments of sexuality and its black-Atlantic discursive frame. In *African Intimacies: Race, Homosexuality, and Globalization,* Hoad shows that during the recital where Joe Golder performs "Sometimes I Feel Like a Motherless Child," Egbo's earlier homophobic reaction is transformed into reflective self-affiliation. In the scene, Egbo watches Golder sing an iconic African American hymn and, at this moment according to Hoad, "It would appear that finally, in Egbo's eyes, Golder is baptized into blackness" (47). Golder's performance compels Egbo to think of his own identity and reflect on loneliness and alienation. He recognizes the interpreters as bicultural and fundamentally homeless, very much like Golder. Through Egbo's meditation, the novel suggests that he and his friends are, like Golder, adrift in a world of identitarian simplifications. From this reading, Hoad draws a worthwhile conclusion: "Artistic production, understood as a powerful affiliative force, in the mode of shared feeling across geographic and historical difference, can begin the work of social reproduction in the face of the crisis in generation experienced by all characters in the novel. A generative and forgiving *Black Atlantic* cosmopolitanism that can preserve internal differentiation and keep the harsher tonalities of satire emerges as *The Interpreters*' significant contribution to rethinking the designations of both 'Africa' and 'homosexuality'" (47). Half a century after the novel appeared, we do well to emphasize its coarticulation of the inside (the interpreters' rebellion) with the outside—that is, Golder's singularity beyond received significations of race and sex. To Hoad's reading I would add that Egbo's self-affiliation with Golder on the basis of race risks occluding specificities of sexuality and homophobia. This point is especially pertinent because the novel associates Egbo directly with virility and biological regeneration. Egbo's recognition of Golder's existential demand does advance us beyond retrograde inwardness, but he elides his own heteronormative outsider-ness with Golder's disruptive specificity. Exceeding Egbo's meditation, what the novel yields is richer. Golder's positioning within the interpreters' black-Atlantic cosmopolitanism emerges as immanent critique: the marginalized, traumatic outside that exposes the limits of their avant-gardism.

Where Sekoni's death in an automobile accident implicitly evokes Ogun as sign of the creative-destructive potentiality, Egbo's sexual conquest makes the evocation more explicitly. Sex with the young undergraduate is rendered as a kind of blood ritual that is at once destructive and creative. It is fascinating, therefore, that the first time Egbo sees Kola's rendition of the figure of Ogun, his interlocutor is Joe Golder the outsider. Egbo protests to Golder that Kola's portrayal of the archetype is "an uninspired distortion, that is what is wrong with it." Egbo is referring to the mythological narrative of Ogun that Soyinka has explored in other writings. In the myth, Ogun—god of war and metallurgy, patron of hunters and earthy lover of wine—is persuaded by the people of Ire to lead them into battle. Even though he would much prefer to remain solitary and unheralded, he finally relents and agrees to their need for leadership. But tragically on one occasion, he drinks too much palm wine before going to war. Drunk on wine and blinded by the blood of slain enemies, Ogun turns on his own people, slaughtering friend and foe alike. What Egbo rejects in Kola's rendition is that it focuses solely on Ogun's moment of blind carnage and detaches it as metaphor of sacrificial violence. This choice fails to reveal the complexity of the archetype. It is this complexity that Egbo considers more "accurate" as representation of Ogun. As he puts it, "He [Kola] has taken one single myth, Ogun at his drunkennest, losing his sense of recognition and slaughtering his own men in battle; and he has frozen him at the height of carnage. . . . It is his selectiveness I quarrel with. Even the moment of Ogun's belated awareness would have been . . . at least, that does contain poetic possibilities. This blood-spattered fiend is merely melodramatic. And then there is Ogun of the forge, Ogun as the primal artisan . . . but he leaves all that to record me as this bestial gore-blinded thug!" (233).

Now, Kola had anticipated complaints from his models about the accuracy of his portrayals: "Suppose you all took to complaining that I've made something of you which you aren't . . . I mean, the whole point is that you are substituting" (226). And in a sense, Golder is correct to defend the artist by reminding Egbo, "Well, surely you must concede him the right to select" (233). Egbo's outburst derives from a false assumption that the novel invites us to question. He wrongly assumes a rigid qualitative distance between frenzied warlord and "primal artisan." However, the very fact that Ogun's weapon of war can be turned on enemies and friends alike suggests the complexity of the archetype, that is to say, Ogun's unsettling ambiguity. Conversely, the side of Ogun that is master of the forge contains its own ambiguity: the artisan can fashion an implement of farming as well as of war.

For Soyinka, then, there is always the copresence of destructive and creative possibilities in human experience. But then, what might be creative in the destructiveness of colonial intrusion? And why does *The Interpreters* represent the Nigerian as well as foreign intellectuals and tourists who people the world of the novel as tragic failures rather than heroic champions of the anticolonial sentiment? *Aké* might appear not to be concerned with these questions as such, because the memoir's ostensible concern is the coming of age of its protagonist from the late-1930s to the immediate post–World War II years. *Aké* thickens the discursive terrain on which *The Interpreters* locates itself and, in doing so, puts us squarely in the presence of mid-nineteenth-century missionary discourse. If S. A. Crowther's missionary ethnography proceeded as epistemic violence in the sense that postcolonial theory has given the term, Soyinka nuances the very idea of epistemic violence by bringing it down to earth—historically and nonpolemically. In so doing, he alerts us to the dialectical possibility immanent to every discursive or historical phenomenon. I want to develop this point a bit more by focusing on two possible lines of narrative tension in the text.

At one level, *Aké* is about individual consciousness. At the novel's end, we see young Wole as he leaves the comfort of his protective Christian middle-class home for the first time. Likewise, the text narrates his entrance into the world of formal Western schooling, the onset of electrification in Abeokuta town (or the neighborhood of Aké, where Wole's family resides), and the muted impact of World War II on everyday life and consciousness in the town. The novel's opening paragraph hints at the fact that the world in which young Wole will come to some measure of self-awareness is a complex hybridization of traditional Yoruba norms and Western Christian modernity: "The sprawling, undulating terrain is all of Aké. More than mere loyalty to the parsonage gave birth to a puzzle, and a resentment, that God should choose to look down on his own pious station, the parsonage compound, from the profane heights of Itoko" (1). Being the area where the Anglican mission is sited, Aké represents the new Christian dispensation, while Itoko references the pagan traditional society. According to what he is being taught at school, the parsonage (Aké) is on higher moral ground than Itoko, the pagan quarter. By all avenues of reasoning available to the young boy, then, Aké should literally be on higher ground because it is of a higher moral and civilizational order. However, the topography of the town confounds this logic and confuses the young narrator: the pagan area called Itoko is on a hill, looking down on the "pious station" of Aké. Here, what is being deconstructed—in the guise of the child's naïve literalism—is the (Christian) logic of a hierarchy of cultures and systems of belief.

Yet, this contestation of missionary discourse of moral superiority is not accompanied by idealization of Yoruba tradition. In the course of the novel, the narrator's story of personal growth devolves into an account of two intertwined public developments: a powerful attack on tradition in the small town of Abeokuta and the emergence of a nationalist (as opposed to ethnic or religious) consciousness. This intertwined cluster of public developments constitutes the memoir's second line of narrative. Yoruba aristocratic tradition is challenged at the end of the novel, but the challenge and ultimate humiliation also serves to deal British colonial interests a blow. Likewise, Christianity and Western literacy emerge as socially disruptive, but they turn out, at the end of the novel, to be partially instrumental to the community's internal dialogue and capacity for self-interrogation and reconfiguration.

The first mission station of the Church Missionary Society was established at Aké, Abeokuta in western Nigeria in 1845. As we saw earlier in chapter 2, one of the missionaries involved in the establishment of the station is none other than Crowther, the first black bishop of the Anglican Church. In *Aké*, the young boy, in moments of childhood fantasy, imagines encountering the bishop's ghost on the grounds of the parsonage where the latter once lived and where his own father, nicknamed "Essay," is schoolmaster. By invoking Crowther at the beginning of his childhood memoir, Soyinka implicitly sets up a discursive genealogy that connects him with Crowther. The memoir thereby signals the irreducible connection between Christian missionary activity, formal colonial imposition, and the emergence of a Western-educated elite in Nigeria in the first half of the twentieth century. Soyinka positions these historical processes in terms of a dialectic of multiple determinations crowding in on the narrator's consciousness. The memoir constitutes an attempt to gather up the chaos of the dialectic into the reassuring order of intention and language.

We see this in the way Wole's story recedes into the background from chapter XII, as the memoir turns to the struggle against colonial taxation by the Abeokuta Women's Union (AWU), under the leadership of his aunt Beere, and mother, "Wild Christian." It is significant that the preceding chapter XI closes with language that describes the boy's confusing emotion of anxiety and exhilaration, following a promise to his father to be the "man of the family" by winning a scholarship to the elite Government College (*Aké*, 162). Here is the passage: "I went back to bed, fatigued, suffering a mild relapse of the fever. . . . The days regained definition and pattern. A sense of liberation, a deep psychic relief, a sense of lasting reprieve took over. Beyond a few times when I caught myself watching Essay with a baffled intensity, beyond the evidence of the photographs which had been framed and now hung on the walls, I accepted a sense of gratitude to an unseen Force for a deliverance from the suspected but unnamed Menace" (163). The language of menace and deliverance comes, of course, from the Christian vocabulary of the protagonist's parents. But in the overall design of the novel, "unseen Force" and "unnamed Menace" might be taken to imply futurity and its inevitable correlates: hope coupled with uncertainty. The future to which the novel points is the decolonization movement of the 1940s that led to the independence of many African countries in the 1960s. In *Aké*, the women's successful mobilization against taxation in 1947 heralds a more widespread nationalist mobilization against British colonialism. The mobilization is also directed against the traditional ruler of Abeokuta (the Aláké). In the novel, the traditional power of the king and his chiefs is conscripted, thanks to the policy of (Lugard's) indirect rule and "native administration," to serve colonial interests. The novel thereby dramatizes a dimension of black Africa's colonial experience that Africanist historians have demonstrated: that British colonialism often turned opportunistically to traditional African structures to justify colonial impositions. The description of the spatial orchestration of the palace suggests the symbolic and material power that the king and his chiefs (the Ògbóni) wield: "There is a public frontage at the palace of the Alake; it consists of a broad field which is almost square and runs the entire length of the palace. The field acts as a kind of buffer between the palace walls and the public street" (202). And as the following passage suggests, the seat of indigenous aristocratic power mutates into "Native Administration," and thrives as a world of relative privilege within an oppressive colonial condition: "To reach their own enclave, the *ògbóni* had to pass through the central elephant-topped archway, then turn left into the private path which led into their sector. The central driveway led directly into the palace complex, through a passageway under the long, two-storey building which formed the outer line of the palace structures. This building housed the offices and council rooms of the Native Administration, presided over by the Alake. And at the inner wall of that building, emerging into the tunnel beneath it into a courtyard, *the outer world stopped*" (204, my emphases). The women's mobilization is therefore shown to be as much against unchecked traditional norms, as it is against colonial taxation. The colonial apparatus emerges as foreign imposition that is able to operate, at least in part, because of the collaboration of elements of indigenous structures of privilege. As we may expect, resistance as it emerges in the novel is not a simple Manichean one, where the colonized confronts a stable and unitary colonial apparatus.

In Soyinka's rendering, the demonstrations against colonial taxation make possible a new collective self-understanding, one that emerges only as the struggle gathers momentum:

> And yet more and more caravans arrived. As yet another group was welcomed, Mama Igbore [one of the AWU leaders] shook her head and said, "It is as if the heavens themselves have opened up, as if the graveyards have opened and all the dead and forgotten peoples of other worlds are pouring to join us here."
>
> From a swiftly shifting point in the various groupings, a voice would rise in song, but now it was all rapture and plain festivity. The outwardly religious songs—inspired by the *orisa*, by Allah, or Christ—were begun by the adherents of the particular religion but were taken up by everyone irrespective of their leanings and chanted into the night. (217)

Sectional divisions are transcended here, as the energized collective—comprising women of different generations, social station, and religious persuasions—sing an ecumenical song together, coalescing at the moment of activism into a *politically* defined subject position. This datable, political subject position is thus depicted as neither simply identitarian nor poetically ahistorical; rather, it emerges from an acquired consciousness of possibility. It is also not unitary: it is characterized by what Ernesto Laclau would call the crisscrossing of multiple markers of selfhood (gender, age, religion, social station). *Aké* endorses the productivity of the uprising with the birth of a new baby by one of the demonstrators (216–17).

In their biography of Funmilayo Ransome-Kuti (the character named Beere in the novel), historians Cheryl Johnson-Odim and Nina Emma Mba have provided a detailed account of the antitaxation struggle. According to them, "Ransome-Kuti and the organization she led, the Abeokuta Women's Union (AWU), are credited with being the primary force behind the abdication of the traditional ruler of the Egba, Alake (King) Ademola II, in January 1949" (63). With this historical background in mind, it is legitimate to argue that the novel subordinates the women's uprising to a personal narrative of masculine self-actualization and incipient cultural nationalism.[12] In their otherwise different discussions of the novel, James Gibbs and Molara Ogundipe-Leslie have both argued that Soyinka's account of the uprising is not historically accurate in its details. Among the details they question is Soyinka's subordination of the women's organization to the male oversight of Daodu and Essay and, for Ogundipe-Leslie, his chronology of events. It will take us too far afield to enter here into a discussion of the novel's merits or demerits in terms of historical felicity. More immediately relevant for my purposes is that *Aké* undoes the boundary between, on one hand, the text's avowed status as memoir and autobiography and, on the other hand, its status as work of the imagination, act of will and site of desire. Precisely because *Aké*'s (or any text's) representation of the historical past is necessarily mediated by the representer's biases, one of the significant lessons the text has to offer is to be found in the cultural and political work it is designed to do in the present of its writing.

It is on this question—namely, the text's ideological work, rather than its documentary accuracy relative to the past it claims to recall—that we have to circle back to the interrelated issues of nation and identity. In *Aké*, the interior life and perspectives of the hero narrator is the cognitive ground from which the collective national aspiration is elaborated. Indeed, the narrator claims the right to embody, interpret, and disseminate the national experience in language. The figuration is drenched in utopic desire, as if, by the zestful cadence of his evocation of the uprising, and the overall lyricism of the novel itself, the novelist seeks to call into being a new, collective identity: "Mats arrived on the heads of the women. There began a transformation, not only of the physical terrain, but of the shapes and motions of the gathering. Fires were lit; for the first time, water and food were thought upon. The younger women were rounded up and assigned to different chores" (217). This desired collective identity (or more accurately, *identification*) sublates class, ethnicity, or gender, and instead delivers an alternative that is at once national and racial continental. But even as the novel replicates some of the problems associated with the rhetoric of cultural nationalism, it also exposes the limitations and self-importance of the postcolonial elite. One illustration of this critique can be seen in the anxiety expressed by Wole's grandfather about the destructively competitive world the boy is being groomed to enter (140–43). And from the child's perspective, some of the values and priorities of Essay, Dawodu, and their friends confound basic common sense. *Aké* ends on a note of cynicism, conjoined with helpless surrender: "It was time to commence the mental shifts for admittance to yet another irrational world of adults and their discipline" (230). In this way, despite its admiring identification with the native middle class—the interpreters, so to speak—whose ranks Wole is primed to join, the novel performs an implicit autocritique of that class. It is this autocritique that is fleshed out, as we have seen, in *The Interpreters*.

Clearly, both *Aké* and *The Interpreters* detail familiar scenarios of modernist yearning made urgent by the alienation and intensity, to evoke the cliché, of artists as young men. They should therefore remind us of the conventional Western European narrative of the rise of the bourgeois subject, the narrative that lies powerfully at the heart of classic accounts of nationalism, the rise of the novel and, indeed, capitalism itself. But it would be reductive to account for Soyinka's narrative project and substantive passion in the familiar, overarching terms of Western intellectual history. It is worthwhile, rather, to try to see what might be historically specific in Soyinka's representation of "indigenous" (Yoruba) tradition, as well as the emergent elite who—hubristically, we would be justified in saying—undertook the task of nation building. In Soyinka, the gesture toward nation and race, figured as coextensions of ethnicity, is unintelligible except as one consequence of the contradictions of nineteenth-century colonial imposition. From this perspective, Soyinka reveals an affiliation with the rhetoric of cultural nationalism as one would encounter it in other geopolitical contexts. Nevertheless, his elaboration makes nationalism in sub-Saharan Africa more than a version—mere epiphenomenon—of modernity and its vicissitudes as textualized in European discourses since at least the late eighteenth century.

To approach a rich elaboration of the cultural nationalism of writers like Soyinka, then, theory's critique of essentialism (and celebration of its antitheses) requires cautious specification. Despite what their own authorial claims might suggest, the nationalism of Soyinka and his generation is neither coherently nationalist nor coherently nativist. Dan Izevbaye succinctly captures this point when he writes that, based on the evidence of Soyinka's (1975) *Death and the King's Horseman*, "the language of this text had its beginnings in nothing—that point of contact between both languages [i.e., English and Yoruba] and, growing into a marginal discourse, was forced into resistance by its marginalization. It soon developed into a language that, by its accomplishment, has been generating its own discursive power as a new center of attention and the language of a new community" (168). Izevbaye does not specify the discursive and institutional developments he has in mind in his formulation that, having emerged from "its beginnings in nothing," African writing in the European languages "was forced into resistance by its marginalization." One cannot of course generalize about the study of African literatures either on the continent itself or in the European or North American contexts. But the relatively recent emergence of the literature (by and large a product of the mid-twentieth century) and the conditions of possibility of that emergence—namely, the negritude movement, black Atlanticist internationalism and self-assertion, and the related ferment of decolonization—all point to political and cultural struggle as an overarching subtext of the literature. In this sense, whether construed as an event in the realm of culture, a political-ideological current, or, later still, as part of an ongoing academic adventure, African literature is a product of the margins of hegemonic Western humanistic discourses. This discursive marginalization obtains just as much in academic contexts on the continent itself where, thanks to the ideology of "development," quantitative social sciences continue to hold pride of place. What we encounter in Soyinka's and Achebe's creative works is a polyvalent oscillation between multiple markers of identity and subject position: ethnicity, nationality, and, for want of a better term, "African-ness." By this term I mean their consciousness of themselves, and the reading world's consciousness of them, as something called "Africans," whose writing is informed by and in turn reproduces that consciousness. Specifically, and to take three of the most recognized African writers as our examples, Soyinka writes as someone of Yoruba ethnicity, Achebe of Igbo ethnicity, and Ngugi of Gikuyu ethnicity. But the ethnic specificity does double duty as metonym for, as the case may be, Nigeria or Kenya, in particular, and Africa in general. The rhetoric of cultural nationalism as we encounter it in these writers is thus inevitably transnational, by which I mean continental and racialized.

It is important to stress that this racialization does not necessarily translate into enabling or emancipatory perspectives, but neither is it inherently marked, a priori, by the metaphysics of blood and origins—the retrograde inwardnesses that continue to poison our world. The rhetorical form we might rightly designate as cultural nationalism often emerges in African literature with a specific dialectical inflection. Necessarily set in motion and tension by multiple axes of identity, it appears simultaneously as ethnic (Yoruba, Igbo, Ewe), national (Nigerian, Kenyan, Zimbabwean), as well as racial or continental (black and African). Frantz Fanon's essay on intellectuals and national culture, delivered in Rome in 1959 at the Second Congress of Black Writers and Artists, diagnoses this point clearly. Fanon distinguished "national consciousness" from "nationalism" and saw in the former a dialectical relationship between the self and other selves, so to speak. For Fanon, "Self-awareness does not mean closing the door on communication. Philosophy teaches us on the contrary that it is its guarantee. National consciousness, which is not nationalism, is alone capable of giving us an international dimension. This question of national consciousness and national culture takes on a special dimension in Africa. The birth of national consciousness in Africa strictly correlates with an African consciousness" (*The Wretched of the Earth*, 179). In this way, the dialectical interplay of identitarian categories generates both "national consciousness" as well as what Fanon, in the language of his time, called the possibility of an "international dimension."

With hindsight, of course, we should say that Fanon was rather optimistic in terms of the emancipatory role he set for intellectuals under colonial circumstances. But he was correct in identifying the tense relay between ethnicity, nation, and race and arguing for their compatibility with—indeed their necessity for—a genuinely cosmopolitan dispensation. In line with Fanon's insight, Soyinka's rhetoric moves back and forth—or is caught between—tribe/ethnicity, nationality, and race. This is occasioned by a conjunction of intellectual and concrete political desire, a historic interpellation that constitutes the writers into ambivalent defenders of traditional (read pagan) worldview, who also seek, as elite patriots, to envision secular, modern societies. In the final analysis, this utopic desire places them in the social-structural location once occupied by well-intentioned native missionaries such as Freeman and Crowther without, of course, the Christian missionary baggage. In this way, these writers make visible the contradictions, but also the possibilities, of the social and intellectual ferment that ensued in black Africa with nineteenth-century Christian missionary intrusion, formal colonialism, and twentieth-century decolonization.

My concern thus far has been to tease out, first, what *Aké* and *The Interpreters* can tell us about the contradictory interplay of race, nation, and ethnicity in an African context like Nigeria. Second, I have suggested that one consequence of this interplay is to make Soyinka's generation of African writers at once nationalist and internationalist in Fanon's sense. Against the grain of their overt claims, their rhetoric is caught between both impulses. This constitutive tension suggests a discursive texture that complicates the binarism that much of contemporary theory tends to set up between the national and the transnational. Current literary and cultural theory has gone a significant distance in equipping us to approach the discursive violence of blustery colonialists and native mimic men with sharper deconstructive nuance. But theory's achievement, precisely because it proceeds as philosophical engagements with colonial/postcolonial discourses across a range of genres, cannot exhaust the sites of critique available to us at this moment in time. In the context of ongoing explorations of the agency of the formerly colonized, Soyinka—himself seduced by the novelistic will to truth—offers a perspective that equips criticism to sidestep, on the one hand, the pieties of nationalism and, on the other hand, overarching theorizations of transnationalism and cosmopolitanism—theorizations that take the Western historical trajectory as modular but implicit referent.

In *Aké* and *The Interpreters*, "nation" in the African context appears, not as indexical reference but as antinomy, desire, and utopia. Nation, in other words, appears muddied by historical sedimentation—mired in contending tropes of ethnicity, African-ness, or blackness. Soyinka dramatizes for us that the labels *tribe*, *nation*, and *race* do not grasp African communities and desires in their contradictory historical specificity. Rather, they have more to do with the process of "worlding" (in Gayatri Spivak's sense) through which African realities were named from about the mid-nineteenth century. But notwithstanding their constructed-ness, they have by now acquired a subjective density for the human beings who recognize themselves in it and through it. This, as theories of ideology and subjectivity have taught us, is how individuals and collectives recognize the world in which they act, for better or worse. As we have seen, in recalling his childhood as imaginative literature, Soyinka tells a story of collective struggle where preconstituted identities are exploded at the moment of struggle, even as the explosion promises a new collective self-identification, contingent and multiply layered. In this enchanted and triumphant evocation of a moment of anticolonial struggle, *Aké* betrays its utopic yearning for the future of Nigeria in particular and Africa in general. It is as though through the sheer labor of representing a small African town in terms of utopian political transfiguration, the novelist seeks to will a desired intersubjectivity into being.

Understood in these terms, Soyinka's utopic yearning does not take its ethical substance from the certitudes of autarchic nationalism, still less the prosaics of the managerial ethos satirized in *The Interpreters*. To clarify what I mean by the ethical substance that drives Soyinka's work, we can draw on Theodor Adorno's aphorism on what critical thought, "responsibly practised" in the midst of daunting social challenges, might look like. In *Minima Moralia*, Adorno writes:

> The only philosophy which can be responsibly practised in face of despair is the attempt to contemplate all things as they would present themselves from the standpoint of redemption. Knowledge has no light but that shed on the world by redemption: all else is reconstruction, mere technique. Perspectives must be fashioned that displace and estrange the world, reveal it to be, with its rifts and crevices, as indigent and distorted as it will appear one day in the messianic light. To gain such perspectives without velleity or violence, entirely from felt contact with its objects—this alone is the task of thought. (247)

Adorno is writing of dialectical thought, but the idea that knowledge is critical precisely to the extent that it estranges the world in order to imagine a different reality—posed, necessarily, as potentiality—captures an important aspect of literature's promise. In keeping with what Adorno says of dialectical thinking, Soyinka's literary writing promises a conceptual reach that draws on the imaginative register proper to literary representation. But the historical context that feeds and vexes the representation gives it a specific ideational node. This ideational node complicates the distinctions and hierarchy that our disciplinary practices tend to set up between theory, criticism, and good old "literature."

The issue of globalism in literary studies has lately become central to the way we imagine the future of humanistic scholarship. One consequence of this is that discussions of nationalism often operate around a procedural consensus, over and beyond important distinctions to be made between critics. We could have a historicizing account that seeks out the resistance that third world nationalisms offer hegemonic Western discourses or a rejection of nationalism and identity talk altogether. In the latter case, the rejection is often mounted in the name of cosmopolitanism and transnationalism. By extension, the difference between these two modes of representing or analyzing postcolonial cultures gets posed, paradoxically, in terms of a structure of binaries: for instance, realism to, say, modernism and postmodernism, or nationalism to transnationalism and cosmopolitanism. An example of this sort of framing is Kwame Anthony Appiah's deservedly influential book *In My Father's House*, as well as his more recent *The Ethics of Identity*. It should by now be clear that I agree with the critical and ethical impulse driving Appiah's argument in favor of an open-ended, expansive, and relational understanding of identity. Yet, the terms within which he delimits and explores his concerns are ultimately constraining, insofar as he remains within a problematic that posits cosmopolitanism as the antithesis (laden with positivity) of a rival moral position (call it nativism, essentialism, or nationalism) that thereby acquires meaning only as negativity.[13] The significance of Achebe or Soyinka for globalism in literary studies is that their oeuvre exceeds any Eurocentric emplotment of global history. Their contributions demonstrate why theory and inherited critical categories do not, by their own lights alone, exhaust what creative literature might have to offer. Another way of saying this is to say that fictional narrative often, necessarily, tells us more than the criticism that seeks to explicate it or the theories that claim to speak for it. In order for current literary and cultural criticism to learn from an Achebe or a Soyinka, then, theory cannot aspire to the status of a universal that does violence to the particular in order to subsume it. This would be a false universalism, one that only closes off proper attention to the historicity of what we think, feel, and do, as well as the concepts with which we try to understand those thoughts, feelings, and doings. Thus construed, the resignifications of Africa that we have been sketching can usefully inflect how we conceptualize and teach issues of identity, nationalism, and cosmopolitanism in the moment of globalization.

Thinking with Change

Let me now turn to the issue of social change and its intercalation with rhetorics of crisis and sacrifice. In the preceding chapters, we came upon some ways in which African writers from Crowther and Freeman to C.L. R. James, Richard

Wright, and Peter Abrahams depict African realities in terms of the pressures and costs of sacrifice. In this chapter, we have also seen some ways in which Soyinka and Achebe deploy the motif of sacrifice in their evocations of black Africa's experience of colonial modernity. In *Arrow of God*, Obika's death is figured as sacrifice, but the mask that Edogo carves to celebrate the coming-of-age of his generation turns out to represent not the plenitude of a social group but a historical moment in the life of the society—in other words, the moment that coincides with the defection of Umuaro and defeat of Ezeulu. In *Interpreters*, Kola's painting memorializes on canvas something of the vicissitudes and contradictions of the novel's main characters. Egbo's protest is to be understood as interpretive interlocution, occasioned and enabled by Kola's craft. As act of interpretation, Egbo's protest challenges any pretension to mimetic finality that Kola the artist may want to claim. Whether Egbo is right and Kola wrong is irrelevant here; what is relevant is that through the debate over "The Pantheon," Soyinka's novel demystifies artistic representation in order to recode its value. Kola's work emerges as one interpretation among, at the least, one other possibility. As one interpretation among other possibilities, it necessarily foregrounds some dimension, thereby deemphasizing and marginalizing others.

Whether we approach the question through the conceit of Edogo's Agaba mask or through Kola's "The Pantheon" and Egbo's dissent, Achebe and Soyinka offer a related perspective on social change and the burden of representation. I want to elaborate this claim a bit more by means of Rey Chow's critique of Giorgio Agamben regarding sacrificial logic and the challenges of metaphysics and representation. In her provocative essay titled "Sacrifice, Mimesis, and the Theorizing of Victimhood," Chow takes issue with Agamben's transhistorical dismissal of sacrificial discourse in *Homo Sacer: Sovereign Power and Bare Life*. Agamben's theory of "bare life" insists on the ethical demand of the body as pure presence and physicality, beyond the inscriptions of law, culture, and narrative. In Chow's reading, Agamben's poststructuralist suspicion of power and its cultural narratives leads him to reject the lure of representational adequacy or any metaphysics rooted in sacrificial logic. Chow suggests that cultural criticism will benefit from grasping the motif of sacrifice as being intimately linked to the problem of representation itself. For her, the connection between the artistic-literary and the ethical-political might be thought of in terms of the logic of sacrifice insofar as the mimetic act does not encapsulate the object represented in its plenitude but necessarily leaves something out.[14] Drawing on René Girard, Chow contests Agamben's antirepresentational or what she calls antimimetic stance. She diverges from Agamben's ultimately secular dismissal of the discourse of sacrifice because his theory purports to apply to all social formations, from European antiquity to postmodernity. For her, although Agamben's reflections are significantly informed by the destruction of innocent lives that the twentieth-century witnessed—emblematized by Nazism and the concentration camp—his overgeneralized critique of sacrificial logic, added to his suspicion of power and its representations, is too grandly wrought to be incisive when we seek to make sense of conjunctural inflections, of past or present specificities. By contrast, Chow suggests that it is helpful to pay attention to who is deploying the notion of sacrifice, when and to what end.

Whether at the macro-level of politics or the micro-level of individual self-accountings, the issue of sacrificial logic is relevant to how we understand the past and how that past relates to present and future. This is where issues of representation and culture have to enter the conversation. For Chow, mimesis need not be grasped in terms of reflection, duplication, or re-presentation of a stable and self-evident referent. She reformulates the concept in a way that pushes it toward ritual—in other words, toward politics and culture. Following this line of thinking, what remains after any logic or politics of sacrifice is culture: art as representation and narrative recall. She writes,

> the mimetic-as-representation, even when it takes the positivistic form of appearing as/like something else, should be described more precisely as the accessible portion of a certain foregone *transaction*, a transaction, moreover, during which something was for one reason or another lost, given up, or surrendered—in other words, sacrificed. Rather than being a static replication or re-presentation of a preexisting plenitude, mimesis, one may argue, is the sign that *remains*—in the form of a literal being-there, an externalization and an exhibition—in the aftermath of a process of sacrifice, whether or not the sacrifice has been witnessed or apprehended as such. (137)

Much like Agamben's study that her discussion engages, Chow's argument ranges widely and reconstellates seemingly disparate theoretical idioms and conceptual categories. My interest here is specifically in the connection she establishes between sacrifice as religious idea or political rhetoric, and sacrifice as a logic that also manifests in literary representation. Such a connection emerges strikingly and recurrently in many well-known texts of African literature, as my analysis so far of Achebe and Soyinka sought to demonstrate. For my purposes, two conclusions can be drawn from Chow's argument. The first is that literature, as a narrative idiom in the domain of culture, might be understood as what remains after historical event. Literary utterances are necessarily occasioned by and testimonies to events in history, events that may rightly or wrongly be interpreted by participants or concerned parties in terms of the logic of sacrifice. The second is that literature is not a simple reflection of the historical event but what remains after the event itself. To reduce the literary to unmediated reflection is to reanimate the historical event in the realm of aesthetics, thereby risking a repetition of the original event's misrecognitions. To do this, at the level of artistic representation, is to risk merely refreshing a wound instead of working to heal it.

Taken together, the example of Achebe and Soyinka supports this insight: in them, literary representation becomes the textual trace—the cultural remnant—that witnesses to social change. Of course, change often comes with the accompaniment of violence. The aspect of violence that is as disturbing as its concrete devastations is that it often gets rationalized or interpreted in terms of sacrificial logic (consensual or otherwise). The texts we have been considering dramatize this relay with its ambivalences. Both writers make available to us the literary text as a mimetic act: in Chow's words, "the (visibly or sensorially available) substitute that follows, that bears the effects of (an invisible or illegible) sacrifice" (137). The texts of Achebe and Soyinka also dramatize why violence (colonial or postcolonial) can neither usefully nor ethically be theorized as abstract intransitive category; why sacrificial thinking is ultimately an impoverishing way of responding to change and futurity. Rather, violence is properly posed in local and transitive terms (who does what to whom and why). But this transitive approach will specifically not be in the service of a politics of blame, for this is the underlying logic of retribution or restitution, that is to say, the logic of sacrifice (i.e., of the self or the abjected other).

It is on this last point that the terrain of literature meets up with that of society and practical politics. Fear of difference often leads to attempts to eradicate it, at which point the threatening other becomes a target of aggression. Relating to the past, understanding the present, or working toward the future are all challenges that come with uncertainty and risk. Such challenges can be approached in many different ways. One is to understand the challenges in terms of crisis and radical fear of the unknown. This type of response brings forth in the subject a fear of externality itself, construed either as the future or the phenomenological other. It necessarily invites from the subject the obligation of embattlement and heroism: muscular, transitive, righteous. By contrast, another type of response approaches present realities and the unknown future in terms of contingency and opportunity. In this second type of response, the future is not a figure of looming monstrosity but of beckoning chance. Approached in this way, the present challenge invites nothing more or less than engagement: engagement nurtured by reflection and responsibility; action directed at the other, which is therefore action directed at the self. As a proverb in the Yoruba language has it, for every finger to point outward at the other, the remaining four have to point inward at the self. In this sense, the position I am arguing for rejects the thinking that constructs any present challenge as crisis demanding aggressive sacrifice—either self-sacrifice or sacrifice of the imagined other. Such a mode of thinking might profitably be replaced with one that approaches a present challenge as moment to recall the formidable insight that time is motion and change.

Testifying to the convergence of the aesthetic and the political, Achebe returns, in *Anthills of the Savannah*, to a rewriting of *Things Fall Apart* and, in doing so, elaborates a sustained meditation on the postcolonial state as well as the promise and limits of literary representation. For his part, Soyinka's first novel had enumerated a self-reflexive account of the vicissitudes of the postindependence generation of African intellectuals, only to return to a similar concern under the guise of autobiography. In this sense, the linear emplotment of European literary history (i.e., in terms of realism, modernism, and postmodernism) cannot equip us adequately to appreciate what the best of African literature has to offer on the level of transnational address and culture critique. We cannot of course predict what the future direction of the institutional category we call African literature will be. As I write, a new generation of African writers is addressing concerns that depart from the cultural nationalism of the mid-twentieth century. In regard to Nigeria alone, I think of Chris Abani, Chimamanda Adichie, Teju Cole, Helon Habila, Taiye Selasi, and Chika Unigwe. Born in Nigeria or with filial connection there, these are writers whose "Africa" is neither Achebe's nor Soyinka's. Where these younger voices, from all over Africa and in diaspora, will take the institutional category of African literature remains in progress. But it is the task of criticism to keep pace with the literature: to move, in other words, as the future moves. And it is the task of cultural theory, driven by conceptual and substantive investments in globalism and intercultural dialogue, to be attentive to the African specificity this chapter has explored. This is not an argument for reinventions of difference. It is an argument for particularity that defamiliarizes the signifier Africa—and, hence, African literature—in order to delink it from Eurocentric emplotment. It is there, in the particular, that we stand to encounter the universal, understood as datable event and ideational possibility.

To conclude, then: in the foregoing discussion, I have tried to show two things. The first is that Achebe and Soyinka are best read in ways that avoid linear categorizations, especially when the formal categories come with epistemological and political associations—for example, realist narration with essentialist constructions of wholeness, or modernism/postmodernism with decenterings of wholeness. I have suggested that it is a sign of the steady memory of Achebe's craft that the "postnationalist" or modernist critique of the postcolonial elite in *Anthills*, published in 1987, had been foreshadowed in his realist novels from the 1960s. As though traveling in the opposite direction, Soyinka's earlier *Interpreters*, from 1965, presents itself as a self-consciously modernist text, only to give way to the traditional bourgeois realism of *Aké*, published more than a decade later. What this suggests is that literary historical categories can take us some way in the analysis of African novels. However, they cannot take us all the way and may sometimes impede us from getting reasonably far. Second, my reading unpacks in their work the problematic of cultural nationalism where tribe-nation-race are yoked together in a metonymic relay and thereby misrecognized. Writing in *Aesthetic Theory*, Adorno offers a characteristic maxim that identifies what the proper relationship between universality and particularity should look like. He writes in defense of the particularity of artistic forms in their relationship to social critique. But his claim regarding the interplay of particularity and universality can speak as much to creative literature as to literary and cultural theory. According to Adorno:

> Today it is already evident that immanent analysis, which was once a weapon of artistic experience against philistinism, is being misused as a slogan to hold social reflection at a distance from an absolutized art. Without social reflection, however, the artwork is not to be understood in relation to that of which it constitutes one element, nor is it to be deciphered in terms of its own content. The blindness of the artwork is not only a corrective of the nature-dominating universal, it is also its correlative; as always the blind and the empty belong together in their abstractness. No particular in the artwork is legitimate without also becoming universal through its particularization. (180)

For Adorno, universality, or what I would in this context call theoretical generality, lives up to the naming precisely to the extent that its inner particularization, the historicity immanent to it, drives it forth. To be sure, I do not accept Adorno's Eurocentric conception of what exactly qualifies as art. As many commentators have shown, his insistence on immanence and the autonomy of art is a measure of his debt to Kant and Hegel. His materialist dissent from both thinkers thereby operates around a thoroughgoing cliché, namely, the eighteenth-century Eurocentric conception of art. And yet, traditional notions of art and literature are no easier to discard than are such notions as "man" and the "human." If poststructuralist theory has taught us persistently to put these metaphysical concepts under erasure, Achebe and Soyinka equip us to unpack the idea of Africa, textualized amid figures of tribe, nation, and race. Both writers deploy the cliché of "literature," with its full ideological baggage, because it empowers them to resignify and reposition another cliché, that which we call Africa. Looked at this way, African creative literature participates in a task of resignification that positions the continent, not as mere particularity that ratifies, or does not ratify, a theoretical generality that precedes and organizes it, but as itself the occasion for thinking generality in the thickness of its human—which is to say, its social-political—particularity.

Notes

1. For a by-now classic account of the African conversion understood in these terms, see Mudimbe, *The Invention of Africa*.

2. Achebe, *Arrow of God*, rev. ed. All quotations from the text will be taken from this second edition.

3. Neil ten Kortenaar develops an excellent reading of the theme of literacy in *Arrow of God* (as well as in Soyinka's *Isara: A Voyage around Essay*) in *Postcolonial Literature and the Impact of Literacy*. See Kortenaar, 22–62 and 63–106.

4. See Wren, *Achebe's World*, 164. I am also grateful to Evelyn Oby Ugwu for suggesting further possible ways of translating the epithet.

5. See Achebe, "Chi in Igbo Cosmology," in *Morning Yet on Creation Day*.

6. In 2012, a year before his passing in March 2013, Achebe published *There Was a Country: A Personal History of Biafra*. Achebe's publication of a memoir about the Nigerian civil war clearly shows that the experience of the war came to play a deep role in his vision of collectivity and the individual's responsibility to past and future. The book generated a lot of controversy and will do so for a while longer, if only because the issues surrounding it—tribe-ethnicity, nationality, and violence—continue to bedevil Nigeria. In this sense, *There Was a Country*, together with the debate it generated, reconfirms my overarching argument about the complexities of identity and (identification) as much in Nigeria as everywhere else in the modern world. I agree with Biodun Jeyifo's summation, expressed in his posthumous tribute to Achebe: "In due time, Achebe's works will undergo passage into the regime of posthumous commentary and debate, free of both the positive and negative consequences of their imbrication in the towering presence and subjectivity of Achebe himself. The anger, the bitterness and the outrage caused in many quarters by some of the views and claims made in the book will stay with us for some time to come. But I personally see no portent at all in the fact that this last book was the most controversial among all of Achebe's writings." Jeyifo's tribute, "Chinua Achebe: His Wondrous Passages," was published in his weekly column for the Nigerian newspaper *The Nation* on May 26, 2013.

7. In *Arrow of God*, Idemili is referenced as an important deity in the traditional Umuaro community. But in the novel, the deity is male, competitive, and under the custodianship of a brash and boastful priest (Ezidemili). By contrast, Idemili is identified as female in *Anthills*, and it is precisely the femaleness that is stressed. In this way, Achebe rewrites the prior representation of Idemili that we are given in *Arrow of God*. For a feminist reading of Achebe's self-rewriting, see Stratton. For an ethnographic discussion of the deity Idemili, see Amadiume.

8. A number of critics have identified this aspect of Achebe's work. For example, with regard to *Things Fall Apart*, see Cobham, "Making Men and History: Achebe and the Politics of Revisionism"; and Irele, "The Crisis of Cultural Memory in Chinua Achebe's *Things Fall Apart*" in *The African Imagination*, 115–53.

9. As I indicated in chapter 2, Bishop Ajayi Crowther established the Niger Mission at Onitsha in 1857. Located on the banks of the River Niger, Onitsha is today a bustling urban center. See Crowther, *The Gospel on the Banks of the Niger*.

10. During the Nigerian civil war (1967–70), Soyinka was incarcerated for alleged dealings with Biafran secessionists. In 1994, he was charged with treason in absentia by the military government of the Nigerian dictator General Sani Abacha (1943–98). More recently, he was highly critical of the so-called "war on terror" launched by the George W. Bush administration. Soyinka's commitment to a secular democratic ethos has put him in opposition to various forms of doctrinaire religious sentiments from Christian as well as Islamic organizations in Nigeria such as the evangelical "born again" Christians or the Boko Haram movement. See Jeyifo, *Wole Soyinka*.

11. See Soyinka, *Collected Plays 1* and *Idanre and Other Poems*.

12. See Gibbs and Ogundipe-Leslie. For a historical study of political organization and activism by women in southern Nigeria in the first half of the twentieth century, see Mba. For accounts of the Abeokuta Women's Union in particular, see Byfield and Johnson-Odim. In "Is

This Guerilla Warfare?" Ruth Lindeborg discusses the class location and gendered underpinning of Soyinka's nationalist investment in *Aké*. In her book *The Nation Writ Small*, Susan Z. Andrade uses the "Igbo Women's War" launched by market women of southeastern Nigeria in 1929 to propose a literary-historical account of African women's writing. She argues for an approach to Africanist feminist historiography and literary criticism that does not elide social distinctions between (literate) middle-class African women and poor "subaltern" women. My reading of *Aké* suggests that Soyinka's nationalism is neither coherent nor consistent. The bourgeois nationalism operating at one level of the text is complicated by the simultaneous dimensions of ethnicity and raced internationalism. In this way, the national is crisscrossed by the ethnic, even as it expands into the continental and transnational. This polyvalence, constitutive of the text's nationalist investment, offers a corrective to the tendency, in much of current theory and criticism, to cast nationalism in simple opposition to transnationalism and cosmopolitanism.

13. See Appiah, *In My Father's House*, esp. 137–57. See also his elaboration of cosmopolitanism as the ethical disposition most adequate to the world in which we presently live: *The Ethics of Identity*.

14. Rey Chow's essay originally appeared in *Representations* 95 (2006): 131–49. Page references for my quotations are drawn from this publication. The essay also appears with some expansion in Chow's *Entanglements, or Transmedial Thinking about Capture*, 81–105.

Epilogue: Gaps

In this book, I have been interested in a handful of writers of African descent. I have sought to elicit what the writings have to tell us if the immediate purpose of our listening has less to do with chiding imperialism for its failings and everything to do with understanding the past in order to imagine a possible future. This book would have accomplished a crucial part of its purposes if it does no more than point the path to fresh apprehensions of Africa-in-language, for students of diverse racial backgrounds and economic circumstances. From the moment of the discourse of abolition and legitimate commerce to the end of the twentieth century, African self-writing has participated in the representational dimensions of a social ferment that is global. The story of contemporary Africa cannot be comprehensively understood unless its immanent relationship to global modernity is taken as a paradigmatic threshold, and unless that immanence is grasped as the exogenous dimension of a human drama that was simultaneously endogenous in sources and consequences. In drawing now toward a set of conclusions, I would like to underscore some key themes set out in the preceding chapters.

In the last two decades, many excellent works have addressed Anglophone postcolonial writings, construed either in the temporal sense of a long twentieth-century durée or within the optic of literary globalism. Chapter 1 set out to engage this development in literary studies from the perspective of African literature. I have approached African literature as a problematic, not mere cultural capital or old-fashioned "literary tradition." As I approach it, African letters from the mid-nineteenth century unfolds as a problematic amid the familiar modernist splintering of subjectivity but does so from the situated particularity of black people. In this sense, modern African literature emerges within a problematic that encompasses black Atlanticism: that is to say, the presentness of our shared past of New World slavery.

My reasons for taking this approach should by now be clear. As we saw in chapter 1, Édouard Glissant's understanding of detour returns us to the point of imbrication, not point of "origin." Where the former denotes antagonisms, social intensities, and flux, the latter falls back on an image of collective selves at home in reassuring stabilities, even if not at peace therein. It is the seduction of the image of self-reconciled selves that needs to be exploded, so that modern

African literature can be seen in its full reach and grasp: as detour, at once local and global. Representations of national or racial belonging are not hardwired to emancipatory politics—that is, politics understood in terms of representation or practical action. It is the deployment of these representations, the ways they are put to work in different domains, that will disclose their productiveness or otherwise. And it is in our commitment to challenging their excesses that the test of our work—as scholars, teachers, and citizens—resides. Just as literature opens up multiple possible perspectives, thereby seducing the reader to inhabit or assess them, so do the inducements of competing ideologies in the political sphere. We are thus interpellated to think, act or choose not to act, in relation to these inducements. I have been arguing that moving beyond Eurocentric circumscriptions of "literature" equips us to approach African writing with due attention to its particular lessons for literary studies in the age of globalism.

Chapters 2 through 4 approached the three missionary moments as distinct iterations of a related problematic. While each is not discrete, I have not approached their interrelationship in terms of a causal link or historicist genealogy. For me, the point is not to establish how and why the nineteenth-century moment *generates* the twentieth-century moment as a historical reconstruction might frame the matter. Rather, my purpose has been to explore the ways in which each iteration, each moment, contains lessons internal to it and recoverable within it. In the manner of Theodor Adorno's monad in relation to an aesthetic object, each moment and iteration unfolds as a force field, doing so from within an enclosed interiority—that is to say, torsions of human will expressed in language. It is these torsions or, from the opposite perspective, these lessons that I have sought to elaborate. In this way, each of the texts—ranging from Crowther, Freeman, James, and Wright, to Abrahams, Achebe, and Soyinka—constitutes one instance within a black-Atlantic force field. Uneven in space and inconstant in time, this force field is not inconsequential, unless we make it so in our amnesia. Likewise, the point is not to impose a spurious uniformity on these utterances. The meek resilience of Crowther reads very differently from the haunting intensity of Richard Wright or the brash elegance of Wole Soyinka, to take these examples randomly. Nonetheless, articulating a shared epistemological ground holds significant lessons for us in the age of globalism. From each of the iterations analyzed, I sought to tease out ways in which they dramatize or imply possibilities that if not realized in our time, may or may not be realized in a future to come.

How do we position a figure like Crowther and the recaptives, moved from one vessel to another in the Atlantic and subject to legal redress that they couldn't have understood? How do we position a figure like Peter Abrahams, born of an Ethiopian father and a so-called colored South African mother and raised in segregated South Africa? How might one draw insights from these liminal figures in ways that allow us to complicate the established protocols of talking about the Achebes and Soyinkas of modern African literature? How might these writers in turn inflect literary globalism such that they are not belated repetitions of European literary realisms or modernisms? My investigations in the preceding pages were prompted by these questions. As we have seen, Crowther writes as a black subject ordained to guide the advance of European interests into the interior of West Africa. But it is paradoxically in this role that he and others like him inscribe one iteration of what later becomes the discourse of decolonization. The social location of the Yoruba (or is it Creole-Yoruba?) Crowther and the biracial English (or is it Ghanaian?) Freeman compels them to perpetuate colonialist ideology while also reconfiguring it. And at the concrete political level, they contributed to the exploitative advance of Western modernity into black Africa, even as they set the discursive and institutional foundations of the decolonizing movements of the twentieth century. In this sense, the story of Crowther, Freeman, and the black whitemen does not end with them: contemporary Africa is still living the story.

This is where the role of creative literature in the cultural-nationalism of the twentieth century becomes pertinent. Contemporary African writers are implicated in a dynamic that is similar to that of the black whitemen. The most influential African writers reflect on it in their fiction, even as they play it out. The enunciatory space is more complicated, and the identity on which the contemporary writers insist is no longer a Christian one. But the need to speak *of* and *for* a collective identity, from within an enunciatory space that is exterior to that identity, remains intact. To be sure, contemporary African writers do not claim a position of moral or cultural exteriority like the native missionary and catechist. Yet, I have been arguing that in order to be positioned to speak, the spokesperson has, at the moment of speech, to be supplementary to the group for whom he claims to be spokesperson. One cannot be observer and observed in the same motion and moment. At the moment of representation, the writer is an observer, a lonesome cognitive subject in the ethnographic act of observation. On this reasoning, the African writer-as-represcnter operates in a space that has to be conceptually disentangled from the space of the represented and the representation. Chapter 4 developed this claim by means of the work of Chinua Achebe and Wole Soyinka. But it is possible to show that African writers such as Ngugi wa Thiong'o, Ayi Kwei Armah, Nuruddin Farah, Dambudzo Marechera, Mariama Bâ, and Ama Ata Aidoo all meditate on the representational dynamic in their works, even if only implicitly.

I have also been arguing that Africa's experience of modernization (as social organization), and modernity (as literature and self-narration) is a journey without a telos. It has points of imbrication and entanglements ("Relation," in Glissant's terminology) but no point of arrival. Understood this way, a good way to appreciate the legacies and limits of African letters is in the mode of the "future anterior." My concern has been to take up one challenge that the archive of African self-writing imposes on us as the twenty-first century gathers pace. At this point in African and global history, we are the readers of the future that the earlier generations sought to interpellate. We thus keep faith with them by working toward the formation of that subject-to-come, who are our students and readers on the ground. In our information age, our students have to process a wide variety of representational modes and sources of knowledge. These range from academic discourses to visual media, to belletristic and popular modes. In the rest of this epilogue, then, I want to consider a couple of telling representations of Africa as a way of rounding up the concerns of this book.

I draw my first example from an article that appeared in the *New York Times Magazine* of January 29, 2006, adorning the cover under the caption "The Post-Colonial Missionary." Authored by best-selling American journalist and nonfiction writer Daniel Bergner, the article is titled "The Call." In it, Bergner tells the story of Rick and Carrie Maples and their daughters Meghan and Stephanie, an American family living in Kenya among the Samburu people. The Mapleses left their comfortable middle-class life in California to pursue missionary work among the Samburu people. Prior to receiving "the call" to convert the Samburu, Rick worked as salesman for a combustion engine marketing company, and Carrie was a pediatric nurse. We are told that the couple faced the normal challenges of middle-class American life, but moving to Africa as missionaries restored to them an inner serenity and sense of purpose. The article incorporates all the tropes we might expect, of the dedicated missionary whose heroism resides in a combination of Christian self-abnegation and unshakable commitment. Daniel Bergner is careful to note that unlike what used to be the case in the nineteenth-century wave of Christian evangelism in Africa when diasporic blacks were heavily involved, "probably fewer than 450 of the American missionaries in Africa [in 2006] are African-American" (74). Given the history of racism and colonial paternalism in situations of religious conversion, Rick and Carrie Maples are aware of the moral ambiguities of missionary work. As such, they rightly insist that they did not "want to be the great white missionaries bringing the great savior to the black man" (74). Judging by the Mapleses' humility and evident self-awareness, then, we are not dealing here with colonial condescension misconstrued as spiritual pastoralism. We are far away, that is, from a nineteenth-century story of Christian missionary perseverance.

I have had the experience of discussing this material with undergraduate students in my American university setting. Students have generally tended to reject what they see as paternalism in the Mapleses' account of their sacrifices. Only very occasionally have I had a student speak up in support of religious missionary work in Africa. One such student comes from a family that had done some missionary work in an African country. According to him, the Mapleses' understanding of themselves and what they are doing should not be so easily written off as stereotypical white arrogance. Better to be that sort of mushy liberal than a war-mongering imperialist; better a humanitarian volunteer moved by religious conviction than an unscrupulous captain of global finance. Yet even on this occasion, the student spoke with a hesitation that verged on embarrassment. It is never helpful to generalize about how students might react to a social issue or piece of writing. But it is fair to say that regardless of race, gender, or economic background, the undergraduate students I have interacted with tend to focus on and question what they see as missionary condescension in the article.

Without minimizing my students' insight and conviction, I want to suggest that the students who spoke in support of what the Mapleses represent have a crucial point. As I mentioned earlier, Rick and Carrie explicitly reject colonial condescension, too. And yet, there are moments in the article that could have come from the colonial period. The article closes by recalling a climb up the Nyiru mountain by a group that included the author and Rick Maples. Getting high up, they experience the awe that such a landmark would bring forth in any culture or belief system. Bergner conscripts the affective power of the terrain, making of it a ground for the Christian missionary's communion with God. Reporting Rick Maples's reaction to the scenery, Bergner writes: "Rick stood gazing toward the farthest ridge, the farthest peak. He stood at a precipice, and with his brush of grey hair and narrowed blue eyes he looked almost as fierce and unstoppable as the wind. I could hear, in my mind, a question he asked as we talked a few days earlier: 'is there such a thing as truth with a capital T?'" (75). At this point by the article's end, the report devolves into a drama of interiority, a dialogue between two main subjects: writer and missionary protagonist. Samburu culture and the people who live it recede into the background, and the topic of discussion becomes nothing less than the nature of truth itself. Bergner records for us Rick Maples's old question ("Is there such a thing as truth with a capital T?") and proceeds to answer it: "For him, the answer was plain. Now he said that every week he wanted to make long climbs like this, to learn the paths and pastures and peaks, to know the herders' routes and the cliffside dwellings, to know Nyiru itself. He didn't want his mission limited to the manyattas in the valley. He would bring the Truth up into the mountain" (75). Through the alliterative cadence of this closing paragraph, the journalist captures the solemn mood of the occasion up on the mountain. But the risk here is that the "manyattas in the valley" and the hamlets on the highland may be reduced to mere setting for Christian self-representation and spiritual fulfillment.

All of this is familiar and should not be a big deal, especially compared to the sorts of things state powers do under the radar or in full view of the global village. This is where I believe my tentative student was correct. It is better to have missionary organizations and nongovernmental organizations (NGOs) around than land mines and toxic waste. Moreover, such reports as the Mapleses sojourn among the Samburu would no longer be written if general readers, the audience of Sunday newspapers, find them as uninteresting as many of my students seem to do. With only minor tweaks in its register of idealist humanism, the article could just as well have focused on the sacrifices of an NGO worker or member of a transnational humanitarian agency. On a cursory reading, in each of these scenarios the narrative frame that constructs Western beneficence in helping Africa to overcome poverty, stifling customs (arranged marriages, excision, etc.) would remain intact. The humanity of the Samburu is pointedly emphasized, but the villagers are mainly recipients of the missionaries' or the aid volunteers' commitment. Ultimately, then, the issue this raises is one of seeking to move beyond cursory, conventional, readings.

How might we engage Bergner's article to elicit a fresh perspective on such issues as cultural encounter, individual commitments, and social change? "The Call" appeared along with images by accomplished photographer Jackie Nickerson. On the cover of the *New York Times Magazine* issue that published the article is a photograph of Rick Maples and a young man identified as Samburu warrior. Another photograph captioned "The Preacher" gives us a young man identified as Richard Losieku Lesamaja. The caption adds that Lesamaja is "a Samburu Christian and the Mapleses' best religious connection to the locals. He dreams of Bible school in Nairobi" (44). While preaching, it is not possible for Lesamaja to read directly from the Bible because it is yet to be translated into the Samburu language. The only way he is able to read biblical passages for his potential converts is therefore to translate, "as he read," from the Masai text into the Samburu language (46). Lesamaja offers a potentially different angle of entry into Bergner's article. Lesamaja is a mimic man, the dutiful African convert whose earnest Christian sentiments make him a sidekick to the white missionaries. What would the story look like if we moved Lesamaja the mimic man to the heart of our critical attentions? What might we learn if the native warriors are positioned in the background, and Lesamaja's dreams—of Bible school and higher education for himself—are given more philosophical and analytical space in their contradictory and tantalizing possibilities?

I belabor Bergner's article to illustrate where literary studies and humanities scholarship can serve to recast popular and academic knowledges about Africa. Lesamaja represents the aspect of Africa that often gets sidelined—not quite denied, simply marginalized—so that the continent and its cultures can remain within the realm of the known, instead of the contradictory and contestatory. By contrast, the various sites of violence and suffering show Africa as a nonmonolithic category in coeval time: crisscrossed by unstable social alignments, marked by fault lines of ethnicity, sexuality, race, and economic status.

In the figure of Lesamaja, Bergner's article gives us a glimpse of the latter-day native informant, the mimic man who follows the white missionary around seeking to convert "his people." To take the figure of the mimic man seriously is to grasp it as a powerful conceptual handle on Africa's postcoloniality. As we saw in the example of the black whitemen of chapter 2, the mimic man is not a poetic figure of resistance to colonial oppression. What the mimic man represents is the dynamic whereby social subjects struggle to formulate a vision of themselves and accomplish something—humble and delimited though this may be—within daunting structural constrains.

I know nothing about Lesamaja other than the information contained in Bergner's article. And yet, his story has always been fascinating to me ever since I read the article. Through Jackie Nickerson's photograph, combined with his story that Bergner provides for us, we perceive in Lesamaja a figure that is emblematic of a sizable proportion of modern Africa. He represents multiple subject positions, poised between languages: Masai, Samburu, and English. But he is also poised between cultures and classes: the traditional society to which he addresses his efforts, the signs of Western modernity (his American employers), and his own class, which is eighth-grade education (46). In a context of factional difference based on religious faith, his Christianity would put him in yet another subject position, distinct from fellow Kenyans who self-identify as Muslims or animists. So class, ethnicity, religion, language, and race are markers of Lesamaja's complex subject positioning. Neither the native informant nor the warriors and proverb-quoting elders of African literature should be inflated, through the logic of metonymy, to be fully representative of African realities. Reading Lesamaja in this way opens a path to engaging our students about the human reality we call Africa. His story discloses a twenty-first-century iteration of an older social dynamic. Like others of his social status, he provides us with a narrative frame wherein the continent is not simply a receiver of foreign aid, but a place where human beings live in the shadow of a past and the dream, however misty, of a future. If this sounds like a platitude, it is one I am delighted to repeat. For this book is designed to push back against a costlier platitude: the tendency to position the signifier Africa as always-already known and Africa's modernity as epiphenomenal to Western European priorities.

I want now to turn to three literary examples. The first comes from Caryl Phillips's *Crossing the River*. In the two decades since it appeared, Phillips's *Crossing the River* has become the black diasporic novel par excellence. Of the black diasporic writers of his generation, Phillips has consistently turned to Africa in exploring black experiences in the global age. *Crossing the River* frames its exploration of blacks in the Western hemisphere with the voice of an African father who sold his children into slavery and is reduced to living with the guilt. Meanwhile, the children suffer the humiliations of racism, yet struggle to remake the world for all. And so the father, whose voice begins and closes the novel, chants: "On the far bank of the river, a drum continues to be beaten. A many-tongued chorus continues to swell. And I hope that amongst these survivors' voices I may occasionally hear those of my own children. My Nash. My Martha. My Travis. My daughter. Joyce. All. Hurt but determined. Only if they panic will they break their wrists and ankles against Captain Hamilton's instruments. A guilty father. Always listening. There are no paths in water" (237).

For many readers, the voice of the African father who sold his children because his crops failed constructs Africa as mere dormant backdrop to historical processes happening elsewhere. In such a role, Africa functions as beginning, not coeval participant, in the experience of global modernity. To the extent that Africa is present in this scenario, it is as geriatric lament: passive and distant. However, I think this reading overlooks a casually sophisticated challenge that Phillips's text presents. As the passage just quoted indicates, the voice claims that his children include the ones he sold and "Joyce" (the Yorkshire white woman of the novel's fourth section), as well as "All" (237). To what or whom does this "all" apply? By this enigmatic universalism, the text accomplishes a counterintuitive challenge. Phillips repeats a familiar cliché—of the African old man going on about drums—and in so doing, he dares us to *choose* what "all" would mean. Posed differently, the question that *Crossing the River* puts before us is this: can a cliché of Africa be desedimented and resignified as a particular experience of modernity that is nonetheless addressed to "all"?

Phillips also throws the challenge from a different direction, in the closing scene of the first section titled "The Pagan Coast." In this section, Nash Williams is an African American former slave who joins the American Colonization Society's experiment in Liberia. Once there, he abandons the coastal colony and settles inland; Nash "goes native" and cuts off communications with his former benefactor and sublimated lover-admirer, Edward. We will recall that in the section's last scene, we leave Edward as he sings to himself, in the company of Madison. Like Marlow in search of Kurtz, Madison had trekked inland to locate Nash, reaching him just before he passes away. At Edward's insistence, Madison leads him back to Nash's station, where the liberal benefactor confronts Nash's polygamous family—his new tribe, so to speak. Phillips writes:

> Edward looked across at his former slave, and hoped that this man might usher him towards some understanding of the disorder that lay hereabouts. But Madison had about his person an air of nonchalance. And then it struck Edward with a terrible force. He was alone. He had been abandoned. Madison would not even meet his eyes. "Madison?" His former slave ignored him. Recognizing the hopelessness of his predicament, Edward opened his mouth and drew deeply of the foul air. He decided that he would sing a hymn, in order that he might calm his beleaguered mind. The natives stared at him, and

watched as the white man's lips formed the words, but no sound was heard. Still, Edward continued to *sing* his hymn. The natives looked on and wondered what evil spirits had populated this poor man's soul and dragged him down to such a level of abasement. Their hearts began to swell with the pity that one feels for a fellow human being who had lost both his way and his sense of purpose. This strange old white man. Madison turned away. (69–70)

In this exquisite rendition, Phillips parodies the nineteenth-century trope of Africa's diseased air, "malaria." The poverty and "foul air" alienate Edward from the environment and its people. But the whiteman is also strange and debased to the natives, beyond their epistemic horizon except as demonic presence. The horizon of the natives' knowledge of themselves is evoked by default, and it presents itself as opaque—present but not elaborated. Even as the whiteman is unreadable and can only be pitied as a "fellow human being," the natives are themselves rendered as inscrutable to the novel's purview. In my analysis of the enigmatic "all" invoked at the end of the old man's chant, I suggested that the generalized pronoun is Phillips's challenge to contemporary readers. I want now to suggest that a promising way of reading the opacity of the natives in the closing moments of "The Pagan Coast" is to grasp it as a *gap*, and a dare. What novelist Phillips leaves to us is the possibility of reading for and beyond this gap; that is to say, "listening" for what the novel also suggests cannot be heard without the mediations of culture. In the silent natives of *Crossing the River*, we encounter in fiction the tribes of the nineteenth century, about whom Crowther and his fellow black whitemen wrote.

Like the nameless poor and displaced of contemporary Africa, the men, women, and children of Nash's station inhabit something like the structural category of the subaltern. If Phillips stops short of presuming to capture what natives in nineteenth-century Africa thought of Europeans mouthing strange sounds in prayer, a poetic performance titled "Odo masquerade" offers a speech act that may too easily be misconstrued as traditional Africa. However, a careful reading of the performance opens up interesting dimensions that may teach our students a thing or two, to supplement Phillips's vision. This particular poem is included in *The Heritage of African Poetry*, an anthology edited by the Nigerian novelist and literary critic Isidore Okpewho. In turn, the original source of the poem is the anthology titled *Poetic Heritage: Igbo Traditional Verse*, a collection of traditional oral chants and performances translated by Romanus Egudu and Donatus Nwoga. Students of African literature will know, of course, that the figure of the masquerader features prominently in the work of both Achebe and Soyinka.[1] As Okpewho suggests, the Odo masquerade poem, like all such verbal arts, is best appreciated if approached as performance, complete with music, movement, and audience participation. This particular Odo masquerade performer begins by calling for the full attention of his audience—an audience that, we may imagine, would be a noisy crowd of men, women, and children out for a good time on a fine afternoon: "May the congregation here listen/Listen/For it's the *Odo* that hears the market din" (58, l. 1–2). Added to the agitation and enthusiasm of the crowd is the fact that other masqueraders would be on the same field, doing their own thing and competing, willy-nilly, with one another. And so, the *odo* masquerade-poet proceeds to warn off other masqueraders presumably performing at the same time:

> I ask the creator-scatterer of locusts
> To please retreat a pace
> For almighty Odo son of Diuyoko is girded with cloth
> And is going in peace—
> If soldier-ants advance, one advances,
> If they retreat, one retreats;
> He who has a basket should bring it to the wilderness
> For the numberless locusts
> Are hovering in the wilderness (l. 19–27)

In his explanatory notes to the poem Okpewho explains the lines I quoted above thus: "This is apparently a threat to another masquerader (here titled creator-scatterer of locusts) performing on the occasion. The *odo* masquerade poet is moving in peace with his group, but like soldier-ants they have a great capacity for acting together in the face of challenge. The *odo* is warning that the bothersome locusts (signifying his rival's powers) should be cleared out of the way to make room for his own performance" (186). In this way, we come upon conflict—the meat of literature and, we might add, of history big and small. Our masquerader's chant encodes within itself a social drama, and thereby points beyond itself to potential conflict of wills. Any account of the performance as traditional speech thus needs to register that "traditional" speech here is modern speech, to the extent that in each is a social drama of hierarchy, desire, and contestation.

Traditional speech, if this is what we choose to call it, also plays out for us the problem of hubris. Our oral poet shows robust self-esteem, even arrogance. The final lines of the poem run thus:

> I am a gong:
> The gong is inspired
> And it begins to talk:
> I am the gong with a melodious voice,
> The crowd is thick here,
> The white ants are fluttering
> They are in clusters;

> My *uturu*-voice
> Is singing in the *Odo* fashion;
> I've come, I've come, I've come,
> Son of the Almighty *Odo*:
> The copyist cannot pick up
> All that flows from my voice, what I am singing,
> I, the *Uturu*. (l. 47–60)

Uturu is the name of a kind of bird, and the Odo masquerader's mask/costume is presumably crafted in the form of the bird.[2] The insistence on the quality and singularity of his performance ("*odo* fashion"), the repeated assertion of his sheer presence (I've come, I've come, I've come), all point to the masquerader's pride and sense of mastery. It is, however, the closing triplet that consummates the performance and challenges us as readers trained in the culture of print. When he says that the copyist cannot keep up with him, the performer implies that the pace would be too much for the pen but also that his metaphysic exceeds the copyist's epistemic framework.

The reversal is perhaps meant to work like the final couplet of a conventional Shakespearean sonnet, where the logic of the preceding lines is overhauled and the reader is left stranded as a condition of his pleasure. The final line "I, the uturu" stations the masquerader directly in front of the copyist's gaze, thereby asking to be captured in the full stride of his hubris. But precisely in such capture, he turns things around: you can record my words only as that which exceeds your recording. And yet, we have access to the performance thanks to the craft of literacy and the Western literary training of the editors and translators, Romanus Egudu and Donatus Nwoga. The Odo chant evokes traditional Africa, but its transmission is enabled by modernity's technical resources, as well as the translators and annotators trained in European institutions of knowledge production.

All of this is interesting, and our students would benefit from catching the masquerader's rhetorical gimmick and its conditions of possibility. But there is more to be learned from the Odo masquerader's closing flourish. It is a performative contradiction in the sense that Jürgen Habermas articulated in his critique of Adorno's and Horkheimer's skepticism, in *Dialectic of Englightenment*, toward technocratic reason. Followers of the poststructuralist debates of the 1980s will recall Habermas's (*Philosophical Discourse*, 127) definition of the performative contradiction: "the embarrassment of a critique that attacks the presuppositions of its own validity." Clearly, our Odo performer is caught in one such contradiction. The performer challenges the copyist's ability to keep pace but with the knowledge that the resistance is itself to be captured. For the panegyric boast to work, the copyist has to be able to do what the boast claims is impossible.

However, contradictions would be embarrassing only if our anxiety is to stabilize or reconstruct a preconstituted foundation. On my reading, Phillips and the Odo masquerade are inviting us to glimpse contradiction without embarrassment, to listen without the guarantee of clear voicing. Where Phillips dramatizes the insight that any representation of pagans has to stop short before the opaque interiority of long-departed African natives, the Odo masquerader performs his verbal dexterity, in the manner of the traditional panegyric, by taunting the machinery of print literacy.

The examples of Phillips and the Odo performer offer two different faces of the signifier we recognize as Africa. In the first, African natives are alienating and inscrutable to the nineteenth-century Western sensibility. In the second, the quasi-religious figure of a masquerader praises himself as doubly enigmatic: he could go in peace or yet be as aggressive as soldier-ants. He is also proud of his gifts as raconteur: so proud that he insists on the inadequacy of writing, disingenuously inviting the transcriber to record the limit of his own craft. In different ways, then, *Crossing the River* and the Odo chant are iterations of what I have been calling the black-Atlantic detour. Whether through the flamboyant language of poetic virtuosity or that of ethnographic reticence, Phillips and the Odo masquerader offer a kind of knowledge that literary language can yield to supplement academic discourses of quantifiable value. What we should take away from these two examples is that Africa is text and desire. As such, in addition to whatever else it has been, Africa is also a product of intellectual labor and acts of language. It is precisely because of this that its unfolding realities can be resignified and differently pitched. Both the traditional African speech and Caryl Phillips's speech devolve around something we have learned to call Africa. But neither captures anything like the "real" Africa, nor should they. Representations of Africa are most productively approached, not as transparent reflectors of a singular materiality, but as emanations of desire that might nonetheless illuminate aspects of our shared predicament in the global age.

The final word belongs to the novel *Butterfly Burning* by Yvonne Vera (1998). Vera's novel is set in Zimbabwe in the 1940s, between two events of mass struggle in the former British colony: the insurrection of the late 1890s and that of the latter half of the twentieth century, known respectively as the first and second Chimurenga. Phillips's *Crossing the River* moves through the moment of westward migration in United States' history and concludes with World War II in England. Vera's novel is about the immediate postwar era. Through poetic prose, *Butterfly Burning* fictionalizes the deprivations and desires of the late 1940s from the perspective of black subjects in segregated Zimbabwe. In this way, from her vantage point in the 1990s when *Butterfly Burning* appeared, Vera returns to the mid-twentieth century in order to reimagine its human drama and historicity. The novel concerns the frustrated hopes of its protagonist Phephelaphi and her betrayal by loved ones. But though pushed to tragic self-immolation, Phephelaphi is not just a victim of social forces and human machinations. Vera will not evacuate the African raced and sexed subject of agency and interiority.

In this, Phephelaphi's deeply ambiguous story becomes a microcosm of the narrative of massive urban migration, a narrative that unobtrusively provides the novel with historical context. Referring to "the people" spreading out like a mob upon a train station, Vera writes:

> They curse and blame the trains, then cling even more to the city. The people have come from everywhere, and absorb and learn not only each other's secrets but each other's enigmatic languages. Accent rubs against accent, word upon word, dialect upon dialect, till the restless sound clears like smoke, the collision of words, tones, rhythms, and meanings more present than the trains beating past. They laugh when meaning collapses under the weight of words, when word shuffles against word, but they know something precious has been discovered when a new sound is freed, and soothes the gaps between them. (52–53)

This example provides a way of thinking about change at the dual level of social-political structure and collective identification. It also gives us a glimpse of the individual element in every collective event. In Vera's rendition, that category "the people"—much abused by nationalist ideologues—exists only as an agglomeration of individualities and inner lives: Fumbatha, Deliwe, Getrude, Zandile, and of course, Phephelaphi. Vera's representation of an emergent sense of collectivity, forged as contingent articulation in the face of immediate aspirations, could as well be addressed to developments and uprisings we've seen in recent times, for better and for worse. As sites of suffering continue to demand our attention across Africa, we do well to recall the creativity of the human beings we call "the people," even as we anatomize global relations of power and inequality. The people's durability, fragile and intransigent, is an image that should characterize modern Africa in dialogic interplay with rhetorics of crisis and lack. By looking at different iterations of missionary moments in the modern textualization of Africa, this book has charted one such little narrative. As Vera's lyrical narrator urges, meaning may "collapse under the weight of words" or "when word shuffles against word." Nonetheless, something fresh may yet emerge from the weight of words and abrasion of sounds. The crowd at the station, Vera reminds us, "know[s] something precious has been discovered when a new sound is freed, and soothes the gaps between them" (53). In our present conjuncture, postcolonial literary studies could do worse than listen for such sounds. Whether we listen or not, the sounds will in any case continue to pulse against the odds, in the varied codes where meanings persist.

Notes

1. I took up one such use in chapter 4, in the course of my discussion of Edogo's *Agaba* mask from *Arrow of God*. For fuller elaboration on the mask motif in Achebe and Soyinka, see George, *Relocating Agency*. See also my essay "Literary Africa."

2. Isidore Okpewho arrives at this persuasive conclusion on the basis of lines that turn on bird imagery, or suggest the Odo's appearance as a bird. See Okpewho, 185–86.

Bibliography

Abrahams, Peter. *A Wreath for Udomo*. New York: Knopf, 1956.
———. *The Coyaba Chronicles: Reflections on the Black Experience in the Twentieth Century*. Kingston: Ian Randle, 2000.
Abrams, M. H. *Doing Things with Texts: Essays in Criticism and Critical Theory*. Edited by Michael Fischer. New York: Norton, 1991.
Achebe, Chinua. "An Image of Africa: Racism in Conrad's *Heart of Darkness*." In *Hopes and Impediments: Selected Essays*, 1–20. New York: Doubleday, 1989.
———. *Anthills of the Savannah*. New York: Doubleday, 1987.
———. *Arrow of God*. London: Heinemann, 1964.
———. *Arrow of God*, rev. ed. New York: Doubleday, 1989.
———. *Morning Yet on Creation Day*. New York: Doubleday, 1975.
———. *Things Fall Apart*. London: Heinemann, 1965.
Adeeko, Adeleke. "Writing Africa under the Shadow of Slavery: Quaque, Wheatley, and Crowther." *Research in African Literatures* 40, no. 4 (2009): 1–24.
Adorno, Theodor. *Aesthetic Theory*. Translated by Robert Hullot-Kentor. Minneapolis: University of Minnesota Press, 1997.
———. *Minima Moralia. Reflections from Damaged Life*. Translated by E. F. N. Jephcott. London: Verso, 1974.
African Forum: A Quarterly Journal of African Affairs 1, no. 1 (1965).
Agamben, Giorgio. *Homo Sacer: Sovereign Power and Bare Life*. Translated by Daniel Heller-Roazen. Stanford, CA: Stanford University Press, 1998.
Ajayi, J. F. A. *A Patriot to the Core: Samuel Ajayi Crowther*. Ibadan, Nigeria: Spectrum Books, 2001.
———. "Bishop Crowther: An Assessment." *Odu* 4 (1970): 3–17.
———. *Christian Missions in Nigeria 1841–1891: The Making of a New Élite*. Evanston, IL: Northwestern University Press, 1969.
———. "Samuel Ajayi Crowther of Oyo." In *Africa Remembered: Narratives by West Africans from the Era of the Slave Trade*, edited by Philip D. Curtin, 289–98. Madison: University of Wisconsin Press, 1967.
Amadiume, Ifi. *Male Daughters, Female Husbands*. London: Zed Books, 1987.
Andrade, Susan Z. *The Nation Writ Small. African Fictions and Feminisms, 1958–1988*. Durham, NC: Duke University Press, 2011.
Appiah, Kwame Anthony. *In My Father's House: Essays in the Philosophy of Culture*. Oxford: Oxford University Press, 1992.
———. *The Ethics of Identity*. Princeton, NJ: Princeton University Press, 2005.
Apter, Emily. *The Translation Zone: A New Comparative Literature*. Princeton, NJ: Princeton University Press, 2006.
Arac, Jonathan. "Anglo-Globalism?" *New Left Review* 16 (2002): 35–45.
———. *Critical Genealogies: Historical Situations for Postmodern Literary Studies*. New York: Columbia University Press, 1987.

Armah, Ayi Kwei. *The Beautiful Ones Are Not Yet Born*. Boston: Houghton Mifflin, 1968.
Aryee, Seth Aryeetey. "The Bible and the Crown: Thomas Birch Freeman's Synthesis of Christianity and Social Reform in Ghana (1838–1890)." PhD diss., Drew University, 1993.
Attwell, David. *Rewriting Modernity. Studies in Black South African Literary History*. Scottsville, South Africa: University of KwaZulu-Natal Press, 2005.
Ayandele, E. A. *The Missionary Impact on Modern Nigeria 1842–1914*. New York: Humanities Press, 1967.
Azikiwe, Nnamdi. *My Odyssey: An Autobiography*. New York: Praeger, 1970.
Bâ, Mariama. *So Long a Letter*. Translated by Modupe Bode-Thomas. Oxford: Heinemann, 1981.
Badiou, Alain. *Ethics: An Essay on the Understanding of Evil*. Translated by Peter Hallward. London: Verso, 2001.
———. *Saint Paul: The Foundation of Universalism*. Translated by Ray Brassier. Stanford, CA: Stanford University Press, 2003.
———. *The Century*. Translated by Alberto Toscano. Cambridge, UK: Polity, 2007.
Bakhtin, M. M. *The Dialogic Imagination: Four Essays*. Edited by Michael Holquist and translated by Caryl Emerson and Michael Holquist. Austin: University of Texas Press, 1981.
Barber, Karin, ed. *Africa's Hidden Histories: Everyday Literacy and Making the Self*. Bloomington: Indiana University Press, 2006.
Baucom, Ian. *Specters of the Atlantic: Finance Capital, Slavery, and the Philosophy of History*. Durham: Duke University Press, 2005.
Benjamin, Walter. "Theses on the Philosophy of History." *Illuminations*. Edited by Hannah Arendt and translated by Harry Zohn. New York: Schocken Books, 1969. 253–64.
Bergner, Daniel. "The Call." *New York Times Magazine*, January 29, 2006.
Bhabha, Homi K. *The Location of Culture*. London: Routledge, 1994.
Birtwhistle, Allen. *Thomas Birch Freeman: West African Pioneer*. London: Cargate, 1950.
Blair, Sara. "Nation Time: Richard Wright, *Black Power*, and Photographic Modernism." In *The Oxford Handbook of Global Modernisms*, edited by Mark Wollaeger and Matt Eatough, 129–48. New York: Oxford University Press, 2012.
Bowen, J. T. 1857. *Adventures and Missionary Labors*. New York: Negro University Press, 1969.
Boym, Svetlana, *The Future of Nostalgia*. New York: Basic Books, 2001.
Brennan, Timothy. *At Home in the World: Cosmopolitanism Now*. Cambridge, MA: Harvard University Press, 1997.
———. "Cosmo Theory." *South Atlantic Quarterly* 100, no. 3 (2001): 659–91.
Byfield, Judith. "Dress and Politics in Post-World War II Abeokuta (Western Nigeria)." In *Fashioning Africa: Power and the Politics of Dress*, edited by Jean Allman, 31–49. Bloomington: Indiana University Press, 2004.
Carby, Hazel V. *Race Men*. Cambridge, MA: Harvard University Press, 1998.
Carretta, Vincent, and Ty M. Reese, eds. *The Life and Letters of Philip Quaque, the First African Anglican Missionary*. Athens: University of Georgia Press, 2010.
Carter, Jeffrey, ed. *Understanding Religious Sacrifice: A Reader*. London: Continuum, 2003.
Casanova, Pascale. *The World Republic of Letters*. Translated by M. B. Debevoise. Cambridge, MA: Harvard University Press, 2004.
Chakrabarty, Dipesh. "Postcolonial Studies and the Challenge of Climate Change." *New Literary History* 43, no. 1 (2012): 1–18.

———. *Provincializing Europe. Postcolonial Thought and Historical Difference.* Princeton, NJ: Princeton University Press, 2000.
Chiwengo, Ngwarsungu. "Exile, Knowledge, and Self: Home in Peter Abrahams's Work." *The South Atlantic Quarterly* 98, no. 1/2 (1999): 163–75.
Chow, Rey. *Entanglements, or Transmedial Thinking about Capture.* Durham, NC: Duke University Press, 2012.
———. "Sacrifice, Mimesis, and the Theorizing of Victimhood (A Speculative Essay)." *Representations* 94 (2006): 131–49.
Chrisman, Laura. *Postcolonial Contraventions. Cultural Readings of Race, Imperialism, and Transnationalism.* Manchester: Manchester University Press, 2003.
Clifford, James. "Diasporas." *Cultural Anthropology* 9, no. 3 (1994): 302–38.
Cobham, Rhonda. "Making Men and History: Achebe and the Politics of Revisionism." In *Approaches to Teaching Achebe's* Things Fall Apart, edited by Bernth Lindfors, 91–100. New York: Modern Language Association, 1991.
Comaroff, Jean, and John L. Comaroff. "Ethnicity." In *New South African Keywords*, edited by Nick Shepherd and Steven Robins, 79–90. Athens: Ohio University Press, 2008.
———. *Of Revelation and Revolution: Christianity, Colonialism, and Consciousness in South Africa. Volume One.* Chicago: University of Chicago Press, 1991.
Connolly, William E. *Why I Am Not a Secularist.* Minneapolis: University of Minnesota Press, 1999.
Cooper, Frederick. "The Rise, Fall, and Rise of Colonial Studies, 1951–2001." In *Colonialism in Question: Theory, Knowledge, History,* 35–55. Berkeley: University of California Press, 2005.
Corngold, Stanley. "Error in Paul de Man." In *The Yale Critics: Deconstruction in America,* edited by Jonathan Arac, Wlad Godzich, and Martin Wallace, 90–108. Minneapolis: University of Minnesota Press, 1983.
Couzens, Tim. "Introduction." In *Mhudi* by Sol T. Plaatje, edited by Stephen Gray, 1–20. Oxford: Heinemann, 1978.
———. *The New African: A Study of the Life and Work of H. I. E. Dhlomo.* Johannesburg: Ravan, 1985.
Crowther, S. A. *A Vocabulary of the Yoruba Language, Compiled by the Rev. Samuel Crowther.* London: Seeleys, 1852.
———. *Experiences with Heathens and Mohammedans in West Africa.* London, 1892.
———. *Journal of an Expedition Up the Niger and Tshadda Rivers.* 1855. London: Frank Cass, 1970.
———. *Journals of the Rev. James Frederick Schön and Mr Samuel Crowther.* 1842. London: Frank Cass, 1970.
———. Original Papers CA 2 031. 1844–1857. MS. CMS Archive. University of Birmingham, UK.
———. Original Papers CA 3 04. 1857–1880. MS. CMS Archive. University of Birmingham, UK.
———. *The Gospel on the Banks of the Niger: Journals and Notices of the Native Missionaries Accompanying the Niger Expedition of 1857–59.* 1859. London: Dawsons, 1968.
———. "The River Niger." Paper Read before the Royal Geographical Society, June 11, 1877. London, 1877.

———. "The Narrative of Samuel Ajayi Crowther." In *Africa Remembered: Narratives by West Africans from the Era of the Slave Trade*, edited by Philip D. Curtin, 298–316. Madison: University of Wisconsin Press, 1967.
Curtin, Philip D., ed. *Africa Remembered: Narratives by West Africans from the Era of the Slave Trade*. Madison: University of Wisconsin Press, 1967.
———. *The Image of Africa Volume 2: British Ideas and Action, 1780–1850*. Madison: University of Wisconsin Press, 1964.
Damrosch, David. *What Is World Literature?* Princeton, NJ: Princeton University Press, 2003.
de Kock, Leon. *Civilising Barbarians: Missionary Narrative and African Textual Response in Nineteenth-Century South Africa*. Johannesburg: University of the Witwaterstrand Press, 1996.
Delany, Martin R., and Robert Campbell. *Search for a Place. Black Separatism and Africa, 1860*. Ann Arbor: University of Michigan Press, 1969.
De Man, Paul. "Criticism and Crisis." In *Blindness and Insight: Essays in the Rhetoric of Contemporary Criticism*, 3–19. Minneapolis: University of Minnesota Press, 1983.
———. *The Resistance to Theory*. Minneapolis: University of Minnesota Press, 1986.
Desai, Gaurav. *Commerce with the Universe: Africa, India, and the Afrasian Imagination*. New York: Columbia University Press, 2013.
Diagne, Souleymane Bachir. "Keeping Africanity Open." *Public Culture* 14, no. 3 (2002): 621–23.
Diawara, Manthia. *In Search of Africa*. Cambridge, MA: Harvard University Press, 1998.
Dimock, Wai Chee. *Through Other Continents: American Literature across Deep Time*. Princeton, NJ: Princeton University Press, 2006.
Dirlik, Arif. *The Postcolonial Aura: Third World Criticism in the Age of Global Capitalism*. Boulder, CO: Westview, 1997.
Dunn, Hopeton S. "An Interview with Peter Abrahams: Custodian and Conscience of the Pan-African Movement." *Critical Arts* 25, no. 4 (2011): 500–13. doi: 10.1080/02560046.2011.639959.
Echeruo, M. J. C. *Victorian Lagos: Aspects of Nineteenth Century Lagos Life*. London: Macmillan, 1977.
"Editor's Column: The End of Postcolonial Theory? A Roundtable with Sunil Agnani, Fernando Coronil, Gaurav Desai, Mamadou Diouf, Simon Gikandi, Susie Tharu, and Jennifer Wenzel." *PMLA* 122, no. 3 (2007): 1–32.
Edwards, Brent Hayes. *The Practice of Diaspora*. Cambridge, MA: Harvard University Press, 2003.
Egudu, Romanus, and Donatus Nwoga, eds. *Igbo Traditional Verse*. London: Heinemann, 1973.
Ekeh, Peter P. "Social Anthropology and Two Contrasting Uses of Tribalism in Africa." *Comparative Studies in Society and History* 32, no. 4 (1990): 660–700.
Elliott, Jane, and Derek Attridge, eds. *Theory after "Theory."* London: Routledge, 2011.
Fabian, Johannes. *Time and the Other: How Anthropology Makes Its Object*. New York: Columbia University Press, 1983.
Fabre, Michel. *The Unfinished Quest of Richard Wright*, 2nd ed. Translated by Isabel Barzun. Urbana: University of Illinois Press, 1993.

Fanon, Frantz. *Black Skin, White Masks.* Translated by Richard Philcox. New York: Grove, 2008. Originally published as *Peau noire masques blancs* (Paris: Éditions du Seuil, 1952).
———. *The Wretched of the Earth.* Translated by Richard Philcox. New York: Grove, 2004.
Farah, Nuruddin. *Maps.* New York: Penguin, 1986.
Farred, Grant, ed. *Rethinking C. L. R. James.* Cambridge, MA: Blackwell, 1996.
Ferguson, James. *Global Shadows: Africa in the Neoliberal World Order.* Durham: Duke University Press, 2006.
Field, Roger. "Peter Abrahams." In *Encyclopedia of African Literature*, edited by Simon Gikandi, 4–6. London: Routledge, 2003.
Foucault, Michel. *The Archaeology of Knowledge and the Discourse on Language.* Translated by A. M. Sheridan Smith. New York: Pantheon, 1972.
Freeman, Thomas Birch. *Journal of Various Visits to the Kingdoms of Ashanti, Aku, and Dahomey in Western Africa.* 1844. London: Frank Cass, 1968.
———. *Missionary Enterprise No Fiction: A Tale Founded on Facts.* London, 1871.
Fyfe, Christopher. *A History of Sierra Leone.* London: Oxford University Press, 1962.
Gandhi, Leela. "The Pauper's Gift: Postcolonial Theory and the New Democratic Dispensation." *Public Culture* 23, no. 1 (2011): 27–38.
Gates, Henry Louis Jr. *Tradition and the Black Atlantic.* New York: BasicCivitas, 2010.
George, Olakunle. "Literary Africa." In *Africa in the World, the World in Africa*, edited by Biodun Jeyifo, 29–49. Trenton, NJ: Africa World Press, 2011.
———. "Postcolonial Reverberations." *Comparative Studies of South Asia, Africa and the Middle East* 36, no. 1 (2016): 195–203.
———. *Relocating Agency: Modernity and African Letters.* Albany: State University of New York Press, 2003.
Gibbs, James. "The Past Addressing the Present and Other Shaping Influences on Wole Soyinka's Autobiographical Writing." In *Multiculturalism and Hybridity in African Literatures*, edited by Hal Wylie and Bernth Lindfors, 235–47. Trenton, NJ: Africa World Press, 2000.
Gikandi, Simon. "Globalization and the Claims of Postcoloniality." *The South Atlantic Quarterly* 100, no. 3 (2001): 627–58.
———. "Introduction." In *Uganda's Katikiro in England* by Ham Mukasa, 3–33. Manchester: Manchester University Press, 1998.
———. *Maps of Englishness: Writing Identity in the Culture of Colonialism.* New York: Columbia University Press, 1996.
———. "The Embarrassment of Victorianism: Colonial Subjects and the Lure of Englishness." In *Victorian Afterlife*, edited by John Kucich and Dianne F. Sadoff, 157–85. Minneapolis: University of Minnesota Press, 2000.
Gilroy, Paul. *The Black Atlantic: Modernity and Double Consciousness.* Cambridge, MA: Harvard University Press, 1993.
Glissant, Édouard. *Caribbean Discourse: Selected Essays.* Translated by J. Michael Dash. Charlottesville: University of Virginia Press, 1989. Originally published as *Le Discours Antillais* (Paris: Éditions du Seuil, 1981).
Gollock, G. A. *Lives of Eminent Africans.* New York: Negro University Press, 1969.
———. *Sons of Africa.* New York: Friendship, 1928.

Gollmer, Charles. *Charles A. Gollmer: His Life and Missionary Labours in West Africa, by His Eldest Son*. London, 1889.
Goyal, Yogita. *Romance, Diaspora, and Black Atlantic Literature*. New York: Cambridge University Press, 2010.
Graff, Gerald. *Beyond the Culture Wars: How Teaching the Conflicts Can Revitalize American Education*. New York: Norton, 1992.
Guillory, John. *Cultural Capital: The Problem of Literary Canon Formation*. Chicago: University of Chicago Press, 1993.
Habermas, Jürgen. *The Philosophical Discourse of Modernity: Twelve Lectures*. Translated by Frederick Lawrence. Cambridge, MA: MIT Press, 1987.
Hall, Stuart. "Cultural Identity and Diaspora." In *Contemporary Postcolonial Theory: A Reader*, edited by Padmini Mongia, 110–21. New York: Arnold, 1996.
——. "When Was 'the Post-Colonial'? Thinking at the Limit." In *The Post-Colonial Question*, edited by Ian Chambers and Lidia Curti, 242–60. London: Verso, 1996.
Hardt, Michael, and Antonio Negri. *Empire*. Cambridge, MA: Harvard University Press, 2000.
Harris, Wilson. "The Frontier on which *Heart of Darkness* Stands." *Research in African Literatures* 12, no. 1(1981): 86–93.
Hastings, A. C. G. *The Voyage of the Dayspring. Being the Journal of the late Sir John Hawley Glover, R.N., G.C.M.G., Together with Some Account of the Expedition up the Niger River in 1857*. London: The Bodley Head, 1926.
Hegel, G. W. H. *Lectures on the Philosophy of World History: Introduction*. Translated by H. B. Nisbet. Cambridge: Cambridge University Press, 1975.
Henry, Paget. *Caliban's Reason: Introducing Afro-Caribbean Philosophy*. New York: Routledge, 2000.
Herskovits, Jean. *A Preface to Modern Nigeria: The "Sierra Leonians" in Yoruba 1830–1890*. Madison: University of Wisconsin Press, 1965.
Hirson, Baruch. "Communalism and Socialism in Africa: The Misdirection of C. L. R. James." *Searchlight South Africa* 1, no. 4 (1990): 64–73.
Hitchcock, Peter. "The Genre of Postcoloniality." *New Literary History* 34, no. 2 (2003): 299–330.
——. *The Long Space: Transnationalism and Postcolonial Form*. Stanford, CA: Stanford University Press, 2010.
Hoad, Neville. *African Intimacies: Race, Homosexuality, and Globalization*. Minneapolis: University of Minnesota Press, 2007.
Hobsbawm, Eric. *The Age of Extremes: A History of the World, 1914–1991*. New York: Vintage, 1996.
Hofmeyr, Isabel. *Gandhi's Printing Press: Experiments in Slow Reading*. Cambridge, MA: Harvard University Press, 2013.
——. "Reading Debating/Debating Reading: The Case of the Lovedale Literary Society, or Why Mandela Quotes Shakespeare." In *Africa's Hidden Histories: Everyday Literacy and Making the Self*, edited by Karin Barber, 258–77. Bloomington: Indiana University Press, 2006.
Houtondji, Paulin J. *The Struggle for Meaning: Reflections on Philosophy, Culture, and Democracy*. Translated by John Conteh-Morgan. Athens: Ohio University Press, 2002.

Irele, Abiola F. "Ezeulu as World Historical Figure: Preliminary Notes on Chinua Achebe's *Arrow of God*." In *The Responsible Critic*, edited by Isidore Diala, 97–111. Trenton, NJ: African World Press, 2006.

———. *The African Experience in Literature and Ideology*. Bloomington: Indiana University Press, 1981.

———. *The African Imagination: Literature in Africa and the Black Diaspora*. Oxford: Oxford University Press, 2001.

Izevbaye, Dan. "Elesin's Homecoming: The Translation of the King's Horseman." *Research in African Literatures* 28, no. 2 (1997): 154–70.

Jaji, Tsitsi Ella. *Africa in Stereo: Modernism, Music, and Pan-African Solidarity*. Oxford: Oxford University Press, 2014.

James, C. L. R. *Nkrumah and the Ghana Revolution*. London: Allison & Busby, 1977.

———. "Notes on *Hamlet*." In *The C. L. R. James Reader*, edited by Anna Grimshaw, 243–46. Oxford: Blackwell, 1992.

———. *The Black Jacobins: Toussaint L'Ouverture and the San Domingo Revolution*, 2nd rev. ed. New York: Vintage, 1989.

Jameson, Fredric. *The Political Unconscious: Narrative as a Socially Symbolic Act*. Ithaca, NY: Cornell University Press, 1981.

JanMohamed, Abdul. "Richard Wright as a Specular Border Intellectual: The Politics of Identification in *Black Power*." In *Beyond Dichotomies*, edited by Elisabeth Mudimbe-Boyi, 231–50. Albany: State University of New York Press, 2002.

Jenkins, Paul, ed. *The Recovery of the West African Past: African Pastors and History in the Nineteenth Century*. Basel, Switzerland: Basler Afrika Bibliographien, 1998.

Jeyifo, Biodun. "Chinua Achebe: His Wondrous Passages." *The Nation*, May 26, 2013.

———. *Wole Soyinka: Politics, Poetics, Postcolonialism*. Cambridge: Cambridge University Press, 2004.

Johnson, Samuel Rev. *The History of the Yorubas*. 1921. Lagos: C. M. S. Bookshop, 1957.

Johnson-Odim, Cheryl, and Nina Emma Mba. *For Women and the Nation: Funmilayo Ransome-Kuti of Nigeria*. Urbana: University of Illinois Press, 1997.

Jones, Donna V. *The Racial Discourses of Life Philosophy: Négritude, Vitalism, and Modernity*. New York: Columbia University Press, 2010.

July, Robert W. *The Origins of Modern African Thought*. London: Faber & Faber, 1968.

Keen, Rosemary. "Editorial Introduction." In *Church Missionary Society Archive Section IV: Parts 1–7*, 7–48. Marlborough, UK: Adam Matthew Publications, 1999.

Kessler, Michel J. "Review Essay." *Religion and Literature* 37, no. 3 (2005): 109–15.

Kesteloot, Lilyan. *Black Writers in French: A Literary History of Negritude*. 1974. Translated by Ellen Conroy Kennedy. Washington, DC: Howard University Press, 1991.

Kitching, Gavin. "Why I Gave Up African Studies." *African Studies Review and Newsletter* XXII, no. 1 (2000): 21–26.

Knapp, Steven. *Literary Interest: The Limits of Anti-Formalism*. Cambridge, MA: Harvard University Press, 1993.

Knapp, Steven, and Walter Benn Michaels. "Against Theory." In *Against Theory: Literary Studies and the New Pragmatism*, edited by W. J. T. Mitchell, 11–30. Chicago: University of Chicago Press, 1985.

Korang, Kwaku Larbi. *Writing Ghana, Imagining Africa. Nation and African Modernity*. Rochester, NY: Rochester University Press, 2004.

Kortenaar, Neil ten. *Postcolonial Literature and the Impact of Literacy: Reading and Writing in African and Caribbean Fiction*. New York: Cambridge University Press, 2011.
Koselleck, Reinhart. "Crisis." Translated by Michaela W. Richter. *Journal of the History of Ideas* 67, no. 2 (2006): 357–400.
LaCapra, Dominick. "Fascism and the Sacred: Sites of Inquiry after (or along with) Trauma." In *The Future of Trauma Theory: Contemporary Literary and Cultural Criticism*, edited by Gert Buelens, Sam Durrant, and Robert Eaglestone, 23–43. London: Routledge, 2014.
Laclau, Ernesto. *Emancipation(s)*. London: Verso, 1996.
Laclau, Ernesto, and Chantal Mouffe. *Hegemony and Socialist Strategy*. London: Verso, 1985.
Langley, J. Ayo. *Ideologies of Liberation in Black Africa 1856–1970*. London: Rex Collings, 1979.
Laotan, A. B. *The Torch Bearers, or the Old Brazilian Colony in Lagos*. Lagos: Ife-Olu Printing, 1943.
Lawrance, Benjamin N., Emily Lynn Osborn, and Richard L. Roberts, eds. *Intermediaries, Interpreters, and Clerks: African Employees in the Making of Colonial Africa*. Madison: University of Wisconsin Press, 2006.
Lazarus, Neil. *Nationalism and Cultural Practice in the Postcolonial World*. Cambridge: Cambridge University Press, 1999.
Lindeborg, Ruth H. "Is This Guerilla Warfare? The Nature and Strategies of the Political Subject in Soyinka's *Ake*." *Research in African Literatures* 21, no. 4 (1990): 55–69.
Lindsay, L. A. "To Return to the Bosom of Their Fatherland: Brazilian Immigrants in Nineteenth Century Lagos." *Slavery and Abolition* 15, no. 1(1994): 22–50.
Loiello, John Peter. "Samuel Ajayi Crowther, the Church Missionary Society, and the Niger Mission, 1857–1891." PhD diss., School of Oriental and African Studies, University of London, 1980.
Lugard, Lord. *The Dual Mandate in British Tropical Africa*. London: Frank Cass, (1922) 1965.
Macaulay, Herbert. "The Romantic Story of the Life of a Little Yoruba Boy Named Adjai." *Nigeria Magazine* 24 (1946): 169–79.
Mamdani, Mahmood. *Citizen and Subject: Contemporary Africa and the Legacy of Late Colonialism*. Princeton, NJ: Princeton University Press, 1996.
Mann, Kristin. *Marrying Well: Marriage, Status, and Social Change among the Educated Elite in Colonial Lagos*. New York: Cambridge University Press, 1985.
———. *Slavery and the Birth of an African City: Lagos, 1760–1900*. Bloomington: Indiana University Press, 2007.
Marable, Manning. *African and Caribbean Politics: From Kwame Nkrumah to the Grenada Revolution*. London: Verso, 1987.
Matory, Lorand J. *Black Atlantic Religion*. Princeton, NJ: Princeton University Press, 2005.
Mazrui, Ali. "Nkrumah: The Leninist Czar." *Transition* 26 (1966): 9–17.
Mba, Nina Emma. *Nigerian Women Mobilized: Women's Political Activity in Southern Nigeria, 1900–1965*. Berkeley Research Series 48, University of California, 1982.
Mbembe, Achille. "African Modes of Self-Writing." Translated by Steven Rendall. *Public Culture* 14, no. 1 (2002): 239–73.

———. "Necropolitics." Translated by Libby Meintjes. *Public Culture* 15, no. 1 (2003): 11–40.
———. "Provincializing France?" Translated by Janet Roitman. *Public Culture* 23, no. 1 (2011): 85–119.
Miller, Christopher L. *Nationalists and Nomads*. Chicago: University of Chicago Press, 1998.
———. *The French Atlantic Triangle: Literature and Culture of the Slave Trade*. Durham, NC: Duke University Press, 2008.
Miller, Hillis J. "Conrad: Should We Read *Heart of Darkness*?" In *Others*, 104–36. Princeton, NJ: Princeton University Press, 2001.
Mitchell, W. J. T., ed. *Against Theory: Literary Studies and the New Pragmatism*. Chicago: University of Chicago Press, 1985.
Mokoena, Hlonipha. *Magema Fuze: The Making of a Kholwa Intellectual*. Scottsville, South Africa: University of KwaZulu-Natal Press, 2011.
Moretti, Franco. "Conjectures on World Literature." *New Left Review* 1 (2000): 54–68.
———. *Distant Reading*. London: Verso, 2013.
———. *Graphs, Maps, Trees: Abstract Models for a Literary Theory*. London: Verso, 2005.
Mudimbe, V. Y. *The Idea of Africa*. Bloomington: Indiana University Press, 1994.
———. *The Invention of Africa: Gnosis, Philosophy, and the Order of Knowledge*. Bloomington: Indiana University Press, 1988.
Murphy, Laura. "Obstacles in the Way of Love: The Enslavement of Intimacy in Samuel Crowther and Ama Ata Aidoo." *Research in African Literatures* 40, no. 4 (2009): 47–64.
Musson, Margaret. *Aggrey of Achimota*. London: United Society for Christian Literature, 1944.
Nägele, Rainer. "The Scene of the Other: Theodor W. Adorno's Negative Dialectic in the Context of Poststructuralism." In *Postmodernism and Politics*, edited by Jonathan Arac, 91–111. Minneapolis: University of Minnesota Press, 1986.
Newell, Stephanie. "Local Cosmopolitans in Colonial West Africa." *Journal of Commonwealth Literature* 46, no. 1 (2011): 103–17.
Nielsen, Aldon Lynn. *C. L. R. James: A Critical Introduction*. Jackson: University Press of Mississippi, 1997.
Niven, Rex. *Nine Great Africans*. London: Bell, 1964.
Nkrumah, Kwame. *Ghana: The Autobiography of Kwame Nkrumah*. New York: International Publishers, 1971.
Obiechina, Emmanuel. *Culture, Tradition, and Society in the West African Novel*. Cambridge: Cambridge University Press, 1975.
Ogundipe-Leslie, Molara. *Re-Creating Ourselves: African Women and Critical Transformations*. Trenton, NJ: Africa World Press, 1994.
Ogungbesan, Kolawole. *The Writing of Peter Abrahams*. New York: Africana Publishers, 1979.
Okpewho, Isidore, ed. *The Heritage of African Poetry*. Harlow, UK: Longman, 1985.
Olaniyan, Tejumola. "Thinking Afro-Futures: A Preamble to an Epistemic History." *South Atlantic Quarterly* 108, no. 3 (2009): 449–57.
Olinto, Antonio. *The Water House*. Translated by Dorothy Heapy. New York: Carroll & Graff, 1970.

Page, Jesse. *The Black Bishop.* 1908. Westport, CT: Greenwood, 1979.
Park, Mungo. *Travels in the Interior Districts of Africa.* 1799. Durham, NC: Duke University Press, 2000.
Peel, J. D. Y. *Religious Encounter and the Making of the Yoruba.* Bloomington: Indiana University Press, 2000.
Perham, Margery. *Ten Africans.* London: Faber & Faber, 1936.
Peterson, Derek R. *Creative Writing: Translation, Bookkeeping, and the Work of Imagination in Colonial Kenya.* Portsmouth, NH: Heinemann, 2004.
Phillips, Caryl. *Crossing the River.* New York: Vintage, 1993.
Postel, Danny. "Out of Africa: A Pioneer of African Studies Explains Why He Left the Field, and Provokes a Firestorm of Debate within It." *The Chronicle of Higher Education*, March 28, 2003. http://chronicle.com/prm/weekly/v49/i29/29a01601.htm.
Pratt, Mary Louise. *Imperial Eyes: Travel Writing and Transculturation.* London: Routledge, 1992.
Presence Africaine 8–10 (June–November 1956). Special issue on the First International Conference of Negro Writers and Artists.
Radhakrishnan, R. *History, the Human, and the World Between.* Durham, NC: Duke University Press, 2008.
Rathbone, Richard. "Peter Abrahams's *A Wreath for Udomo.*" In *African Novels in the Classroom*, edited by Margaret Jean Hay, 11–24. Boulder, CO: Lynne Rienner, 2000.
Robbins, Bruce. *Feeling Global: Internationalism in Distress.* New York: New York University Press, 1999.
Rogers, J. A. *World's Great Men of Color* London: Macmillan, 1946.
Rooney, David. *Kwame Nkrumah: The Political Kingdom in the Third World.* New York: St. Martin's, 1988.
San Juan, Epifanio Jr., *Beyond Postcolonial Theory.* New York: St. Martin's, 1998.
Said, Edward W. *Culture and Imperialism.* New York: Knopf, 1993.
Sakai, Naoki. *Translation and Subjectivity.* Minneapolis: University of Minnesota Press, 1997.
Sanneh, Lamin. *Abolitionists Abroad: American Blacks and the Making of Modern West Africa.* Cambridge, MA: Harvard University Press, 2001.
Sarvan, C. P. "Racism and the Heart of Darkness." *The International Fiction Review* 7, no. 1 (1980): 6–10.
Sartre, Jean-Paul. "Black Orpheus." In *"What Is Literature?" and Other Essays*, 291–330. Cambridge, MA: Harvard University Press, 1988.
Schön, James Frederick. *Journals of the Rev. James Frederick Schön and Mr Samuel Crowther*, 1–254.
Scott, David. *Conscripts of Modernity: The Tragedy of Colonial Enlightenment.* Durham, NC: Duke University Press, 2004.
Shanker, S. *Textual Traffic: Colonialism, Modernity, and the Economy of the Text.* Albany: State University of New York Press, 2001.
Shepperson, George, and St. Clare Drake. "The Fifth Pan-African Conference, 1945 and the All African People's Congress, 1958." *Contributions in Black Studies* 8 (1986): 35–66.

Slemon, Stephen. "The Scramble for Post-Colonialism." In *De-Scribing Empire: Post-Colonialism and Textuality*, edited by Chris Tiffin and Alan Lawson, 15–32. London: Routledge, 1994.
Soyinka, Wole. *Aké. The Years of Childhood*. New York: Vintage, 1989.
———. *Collected Plays 1*. Oxford: Oxford University Press, 1973.
———. *Death and the King's Horseman*. New York: Hill & Wang, 1987.
———. *Idanre and Other Poems*. London: Eyre Methuen, 1967.
———. *The Interpreters*. London: André Deutsch, 1996.
Spillers, Hortense. "Moving On Down the Line: Variations on the African-American Sermon." In *The Bounds of Race*, edited by Dominick LaCapra, 39–71. Ithaca, NY: Cornell University Press, 1991.
Spivak, Gayatri Chakravorty. *A Critique of Postcolonial Reason: Toward a History of the Vanishing Present*. Cambridge, MA: Harvard University Press, 1999.
———. *Death of a Discipline*. New York: Columbia University Press, 2003.
Stratton, Florence. *Contemporary African Literature and the Politics of Gender*. London: Routledge, 1994.
Surin, Kenneth. "'The Future Anterior': C. L. R. James and Going *Beyond a Boundary*." In *Rethinking C. L. R. James*, edited by Grant Farred, 187–204. Cambridge, MA: Blackwell, 1996.
Taiwo, Olufemi. *How Colonialism Preempted Modernity in Africa*. Bloomington: Indiana University Press, 2010.
"Theories and Methodologies: What Was African American Literature?" *PMLA* 128, no. 2 (2013): 386–408.
Thiong'o, Ngugi wa. *A Grain of Wheat*. New York: Penguin, 2012.
———. *Petals of Blood*. New York: Penguin, 2002.
Tissières, Hélène Colette. *Transmigrational Writings between the Maghreb and Sub-Saharan Africa: Literature, Orality, Visual Arts*. Translated by Marjolijn de Jager. Charlottesville: University of Virginia Press, 2012.
Tölölyan, Khachig. "The Contemporary Discourse of Diaspora Studies." *Comparative Studies of South Asia, Africa, and the Middle East* 27, no. 3 (2007): 647–55.
Torgovnick, Marianna. *Gone Primitive: Savage Intellects, Modern Lives*. Chicago: University of Chicago Press, 1990.
Townsend, Henry. *Memoir of the Rev. Henry Townsend, Late C. M. S. Missionary, Abeokuta, West Africa*. London, 1887.
Tucker, Sarah. *Abbeokuta; Or Sunrise Within the Tropics*. New York: Robert Carter and Brothers, 1855.
Vera, Yvonne. *Butterfly Burning*. New York: Farrar, Straus and Giroux, 1998.
Walker, Deaville F. *Thomas Birch Freeman: The Son of an African*. London: Student Christian Movement, 1929.
Warren, Kenneth W. *What Was African American Literature?* Cambridge, MA: Harvard University Press, 2011.
Willan, Brian. *Sol Plaatje: South African Nationalist, 1876–1932*. Berkeley: University of California Press, 1984.
Williams, Raymond. *Marxism and Literature*. Oxford: Oxford University Press, 1977.
Worcester, Kent. *C. L. R. James: A Political Biography*. Albany: State University of New York Press, 1996.

Wren, Robert M. *Achebe's World*. Boulder, CO: Lynne Rienner, 1980.
Wright, Richard. *Black Power: A Record of Reactions in a Land of Pathos*. New York: Harper, 1954.
———. *Pagan Spain*. 1957. New York: HarperPerennial, 1995.
———. *The Color Curtain: A Report on the Bandung Conference*. 1956. Jackson: University Press of Mississippi, 1994.
Young, Robert J. C. "Postcolonial Remains." *New Literary History* 43, no. 1 (2012): 19–42.
Zachernuk, Philip S. *Colonial Subjects: An African Intelligentsia and Atlantic Ideas*. Charlottesville: University of Virginia Press, 2000.

Index

Abrahams, Peter: depiction of "traditional" Africa, 135; idea of artistic/authorial agency, 137–38; identity and racial kinship in, 133–35; realism and allegory in, 132, 141; rhetoric of sacrifice in, 135–38
Abrams, M. H., 29
Achebe, Chinua: nationality and ethnicity in, 156–58, 172, 175; on the archive, 64, 71, 139–41, 150, 160–61; rhetoric of sacrifice in, 151–52, 154–55, 177–80; realism and modernism in, 140, 159–62; translation in, 147, 153, 158
Adeleke, Adeeko, 104n5
Adorno, Theodor, 52, 174, 180, 184
Aesthetic autonomy, 45–46
Agamben, Giorgio, 30, 42, 64, 176–77
Aggrey, J. E. Kwegyir, 67, 98, 99–102
Ajayi, J. F. A., 69, 70, 81, 88, 95, 97, 105n12
Amadiume, Ifi, 181n7
Anderson, Benedict, 118
Andrade, Susan Z., 181–82n12
Appiah, Kwame Anthony, 8, 33, 158, 175
Apter, Emily, 60n3
Arab Spring, 2–3
Armah, Ayi Kwei, 109
Arac, Jonathan: on "arts of diaspora," 42–44
Aryee, Seth Aryeetey, 105n18
Attridge, Derek, 26
Attwell, David, 68–69
Auerbach, Erich, 41, 43
Ayandele, E. A., 70, 88
Azikiwe, Nnamdi, 49, 101–102

Bâ, Mariama, 146
Badiou, Alain, 3, 30, 64, 113; on negritude, 32–35
Bakhtin, M. M., 44, 45, 46, 61n13, 65, 66
Barber, Karin, 18n4, 104n8
Benjamin, Walter, 53
Bergner, Daniel, 186–89
Bhabha, Homi K, 28, 158–59
Bielby, M. R., 122
Birtwhistle, Allen, 97
Blair, Sara, 118–19
Blyden, Edward Wilmot, 8, 99
Boko Haram, 2–3, 116

Bowen, Thomas Rev., 98
Boym, Svetlana, 134
Brennan, Timothy, 60–61n8, 142n4
Byfield, Judith, 181n12

Campbell, Robert, 104n7
Carretta, Vincent, 78
Carter, Jeffrey, 19n8
Carby, Hazel, 88
Casanova, Pascale, 60n3
Chakrabarty, Dipesh, 86
Chow, Rey, 176–78
Chrisman, Laura, 52
Clifford, James, 51
Cobham, Rhonda, 181n8
Comarof, Jean (and John L. Comaroff), 7
Conrad, Joseph: 71, 190–91; controversy regarding *Heart of Darkness*, 139–41
Connolly, William E., 86
Couzens, Tim, 105n19
Crisis: idea of, 9–11, 28, 103
Crowther, S. A.: attitude to religion of Islam, 89; on "nation" and "race," 83–87; on Philip Quaque and idea of native agency, 78–80; on translation, 81–83, 90–93; rhetoric of sacrifice in, 76–79, 103
Crowther, Dandeson, 89–94
Crummell, Alexander, 9
Curtin, Philip D., 77, 78

Damrosch, David, 42
Davis, John A., 48
De Kock, Leon, 68–69
Delany, Martin R., 104n7
De Man, Paul, 27, 28, 64
Desai, Gaurav, 18n4
Diagne, Souleymane Bachir, 7–9
Dimock, Wai Chee, 60n3
Diawara, Manthia, 126
Dickens, Charles, 71, 77, 78
Diop, Alioune, 48
Dirlik, Arif, 60–61n8
Drake, St Clare, 47
Du Bois, W. E. B., 47, 99

209

Echeruo, M. J. C., 36–41
Edwards, Brent Hayes, 50, 52
Egudu, Romanus, 191–94
Ekeh, Peter, 6–7
Elliott, Jane, 26

Fabian, Johannes, 155–56
Fabre, Michel, 120, 128
Fanon, Frantz, 34–35, 48–49, 111, 145–46, 172–73
Farah, Nuruddin, 15, 64
Fish, Stanley ("interpretive community"), 56
Foucault, Michel, 8, 11, 30, 66
Fraser, Alexander Garden Rev., 101
Freeman, Thomas Birch Rev., 67, 95–98, 105n18
Frere Town, 104n3
Fyfe, Christopher, 62

Gandhi, Leela, 60–61n8
Gates, Henry Louis Jr., 35, 41, 49, 120–21
Gibbs, James, 170
Gikandi, Simon, 38, 83
Gilroy, Paul, 47, 50, 52, 53, 158
Glissant, Édouard, 47, 51, 52, 139, 141, 183, 185
Glover, John Hawley, 84
Gollmer, Charles Rev., 69, 98, 105n11
Gollock, Georgina Anne, 99–100, 105n20
Goyal, Yogita, 142n8

Habermas, Jürgen, 52, 193
Hall, Stuart, 29, 56, 112, 139
Hardt, Michael, and Antonio Negri (*Empire*), 33, 34, 35, 113, 149–50
Harris, Wilson, 142n11
Hegel, G. W. H., 65–66
Henry, Paget, 142n4
Hinderer, David Rev., 71, 98, 104n6
Hirson, Baruch, 142n4
Hitchcock, Peter, 42, 44, 45
Hoad, Neville, 165–66
Hofmeyr, Isabel, 18n4, 104n8
Holquist, Michael, 61n13
Houndtondji, Paulin J., 33

Intermediaries, Interpreters, and Clerks: African Employees in the Making of Colonial Africa (edited by Benjamin N. Lawrance, Emily Lynn Osborn, and Richard L. Roberts), 104n8
Irele, Abiola F., 33, 181n8
Izevbaye, Dan, 171–72

James, C. L. R.: collectivity and identity in, 111–13; idealization and romanticization in, 110; in relation to sacrificial logic, 116–18; modernization in, 114–16; reader and future subject in, 58–60, 114–15, 117
Jameson, Fredric, 42, 64, 65, 165
JanMohamed, Abdul, 126, 128, 129
Jenkins, Paul (editor, *The Recovery of the West African Past: African Pastors and History in the Nineteenth Century*), 104n8
Jeyifo, Biodun, 181n6
Johnson-Odim, Cheryl, 170
July, Robert W., 62

Kane, Cheikh Hamidou, 13
Keen, Rosemary, 105n14
Kenyatta, Jomo, 48, 49, 117
Kessler, Michel J., 19n8
Kesteloot, Lilyan, 33
Kitching, Gavin, 10, 18n7
Knapp, Steven, 36–41
Korang, Kwaku Larbi, 115–16
Kortenaar, Neil ten, 181n3
Koselleck, Reinhart, 9–11
Kourouma Ahmadou, 13

Laclau, Ernesto, 54–57, 139, 169–70; and Chantal Mouffe, 112
LaCapra, Dominick, 19n8
Langley, Ayo J., 47
Lazarus, Neil, 44, 142n4
Logan, Rayford W., 49
Loiello, John Peter, 70, 88
Lugard, Lord, 87
Lukács, Georg, 65

Macaulay, Herbert, 99
Mamdani, Mahmood, 86–87, 146–47
Mann, Kristin, 19n9
Marable, Manning, 110–11
Matory, Lorand J., 104n1
Mazrui, Ali, 109
Mba, Nina Emma, 170
Mbembe, Achille, 7–9, 11, 30, 44
Miller, Christopher L., 33, 51
"Mimic man," 173, 188–89
Modernization, 6, 7, 50, 58, 59, 87, 107–108; 130–32, 138, 143–48
Mokoena, Hlonipha, 104n8
Moretti, Franco, 41, 42

Mudimbe, V. Y., 8, 9, 26, 60n5, 156
Murphy, Laura, 104n5
Musson, Margaret, 101

Newell, Stephanie, 18n4, 104n8
Nickerson, Jackie, 188–89
Nielsen, Aldon Lynn, 142n4
Nkrumah, Kwame, 48; photographs of, 119–120
Novelization effect, 44–46, 65–66, 77, 109, 121–122, 127–28, 141
Nwoga, Donatus, 191–94
Nyerere, Julius, 48–49

Obiechina, Emmanuel, 18n1
Occupy Nigeria (demonstrations), 2–3
Ogundipe-Leslie, Molara, 170
Okpewho, Isidore, 191–94
Olaniyan, Tejumola, 142n8
Olinto, Antonio (*The Water House*), 19n9

Padmore, George, 48, 108
Park, Mungo, 72, 84
Peel, J. D. Y., 67–69, 83, 89, 104n9
Peterson, Derek R., 104n1
Phillips, Caryl, 189–91
Plaatje, Solomon T., 106, 117
Postcoloniality, 23–26, 28–35, 60n7
Pratt, Mary Louise, 64, 142n8

Quaque, Philip, 78–79

Ransome-Kuti, Funmilayo, 170
Reader, and social identity, 40; idea of reader-on-the-ground, 26, 57–60, 186
Recaptives, 17, 19n9, 63, 66–67
Reese, Ty M., 78
Returnees. *See* Recaptives
Robbins, Bruce, 60n3

Sacrifice, idea of: in missionary discourse, 103; in African literature, 11–16, 175–78
Said, Edward W., 24, 30, 35, 43
Sakai, Naoki, 157
San Juan, Epifanio, 28, 142n4
Sanneh, Lamin, 62
Sartre, Jean-Paul, 33–35

Schön, James Frederick Rev., 69, 71, 78, 79
Scott, David, 142n4
Shepperson, George, 47
Slemon, Stephen, 60n8
Slessor, Mary, 98
Soga, Tiyo, 67, 68, 69
Soyinka, Wole: nationality and ethnicity in, 170–75; realism and modernism in, 162 63, 171–72; rhetoric of sacrifice in, 163–64, 177–78; sexuality in *The Interpreters*, 164–66; the ghost of Bishop Crowther in *Aké*, 167–68
Spillers, Hortense, 100
Spivak, Gayatri Chakravorty: 28, 35, 57–58, 186; on "worlding," 25, 60n4, 174
Surin, Kenneth, 58, 59

Taiwo, Olufemi, 104n5
Taylor, Christopher, 71
Thiong'o, Ngugi wa, 13, 14, 48, 64, 172
Tissières, Hélène Colette, 18n4
Tölölyan, Khachig, 61n16
Townsend, Henry Rev., 69, 71, 95, 98, 105n11

Venn, Henry (1796–1873), 64, 70, 79
Vera, Yvonne, 13, 194–95

Waddell, Hope Rev., 98
Walker, Deaville F., 95, 97
Warren, Kenneth W., 47, 52, 53–57, 61n18
Watt, Ian, 65
West, Cornel, 118
Willan, Brian, 142n6
Williams, Raymond, 50
Worcester, Kent, 110, 117
Wren, Robert M., 148, 154
Wright, Harrison M., 95, 98
Wright, Richard: 47, 49; idea of "hardness" and militarization in, 126; identity and racial kinship in, 122–24; interaction with modernism, 118–19, 127; rhetoric of sacrifice in, 127–130; science and rationality, 120–26

Young, Robert J. C., 60–61n8

Zachernuk, Philip S., 104n1

OLAKUNLE GEORGE is Associate Professor at Brown University. He is author of *Relocating Agency: Modernity and African Letters* and coeditor of Wiley-Blackwell's *The Encyclopedia of the Novel*.